MW01042490

CYA—*Change Your Attitude*
Creating Success One Thought at a Time

Tom Bay and
David Macpherson

MacBay Presentations
Newport Beach, California
Sylvania, Ohio

MacBay Presentations
304-1/2 Fernleaf Avenue
Corona Del Mar, California 92625
        and
7707 Westbourne Court
Sylvania, Ohio 43560

Library of Congress Catalog Card Number 97-94139
ISBN 0-9659497-0-2

For additional copies of *CYA—Change Your Attitude,*
contact Bookmasters at 1-800-247-6553 or
http://www.bookmasters.com/marktplc/00200.htm

With a great amount of pride, joy, and certainly humility I dedicate this set of written pages to my outstanding family.
Cathy, my very supportive and caring wife. She has always been there for me . . . sometimes pushing . . . sometimes pulling and always loving and understanding. (For me to remarry after twenty years plus of being single this woman had to be a goddess . . . She is!!)
David and Paul my two favorite sons. Since I only have two sons this makes me especially blessed. They have been with me through thick and thin and have become my idols. David and Paul are the personification of a commitment to excellence in all they have pursued in life . . . As sons . . . As friends and now husbands. I am proud.
Margie and Renée, my two favorite daughters-in-law, have given our family a wonderful gift of balance. Their outward beauty is a direct reflection of their inner spirituality and love.
Brian and Lauren, my grandchildren, give me constant reason to always have the right attitude.

I dedicate this book to my wife and my stepchildren.
I thank them for their understanding and, most of all, for their friendship, laughter, and love.
Nobody knows my attitudes toward almost everything better than my wife, Buck, and my stepchildren, Shelley, Tami, and Nick Taylor.
Nobody has put up with the writing of this book more then my family. Nobody has taught me more about the right attitudes for successful relationships than my family.
Nobody has loved me more than those four people. I really didn't practice the right attitudes until I was married for several years. My deepest apologies to all the folks, specially my friends and relatives, who were kind enough to tolerate my wrong attitudes, let's say up to 1990.
Each in her or his own way helped me to change my attitudes.
Change my mind. Get out of my comfort zones.
Help create new opinions, outlooks, perspectives, and viewpoints.
Thanks everybody, especially Buck, Shelley, Tammie, and Nick (and Winston)!

Contents

Preface

CYA—Change Your Attitude is a fast-paced reality check presenting fifteen right attitudes that can help you achieve success and happiness. Our approach is one that you learned when you were a child; we show and tell. After telling about each attitude and ways you can develop it, we show you people and organizations demonstrating that right attitude. *CYA* profiles the right attitudes of 130 people around the globe, thirty companies, six communities, and four social agencies. Although many examples are well-known names, most are ordinary people with extraordinary attitudes. Our message is simple: If these people changed their attitudes, you can change yours.

In addition to giving you living, breathing examples--97 percent are still breathing—*CYA* provides spaces to record reflections about your attitudes as well as suggestions for journaling topics. *CYA* concludes by describing a major attitude adjustment— living a 360-degree life in which no single facet of your life dominates the others. Stress, workaholism, and burnout can unbalance your life, so we list steps you can take to eliminate these wrong attitudes. *CYA—Change Your Attitude* is a book you'll refer back to whenever you need a lift or a laugh, whenever you are tempted to cover your anatomy instead of changing your attitude.

Acknowledgments

For forty-one years, Marvin and Lauretta Bay have been the cause of my right attitude; they adopted me at the age of four. God bless their souls.

David Macpherson, my partner, has shared his vision and original concept for *CYA*, as well as his loving friendship. I look forward to sharing many more accomplishments with you, David.

Hyrum and Gail Smith walk their talk daily and share their love with those around them. Hyrum, thank you for giving me the opportunity to teach in the same positive way you have.

Tracy Skousen, a former colleague at Franklin Quest, is the epitome of class, honesty, integrity, and commitment. Tracy, I hope to work with you again; you are a great teacher.

Luann Peterson, my assistant, manager, and close friend, always makes me look good. Luann has a special gift of getting things done without complaining. Thanks, Luann, for always tying up my loose ends.

Thanks also to Susie Broughton, Sandy Darlington, Steve Jones, Joe Smith, Lynne Partridge, Sydne Kalet, Rea Richey, Jerry Aull, Linda Eaton,

Helen Layton, Holland Meads, Ruth Hanchey, Lenny and Dottie Ralphs, Mark Petersen, and so many others. If I've missed anyone in this book, I'll fix it in the next one. I'm new to writing books, so I'll learn as I grow.

Mac and Jane Macpherson were my first heroes; I thank them and God for my life. Also, I thank Buck, Shelley, Tami, Nick and Winston for making my life so enjoyable; and J. J. Taylor for his continuing inspiration.

Tom Bay's assistance in writing our first, but not our last, book has been immeasurable. Tom, your concept of a 360-degree life really elevates *CYA* to a lifelong endeavor.

I thank Hyrum and Gail Smith who took a risk many years ago and began a business in their basement. Today their vision has evolved into Franklin Covey Co.

I also thank all the Franklin folks I have had the privilege of working with for the last nine years.

I thank Taylor and Jean Hartman for their friendship and for sharing the color code/character code system. Taylor has taught me how to be a better yellow personality by acquiring the desirable characteristics of other colors.

I am indebted to Don and Mary Haas, Dick Chiara, Jim Sautter, and Charlie Hauck for their contributions to our "You May Have a Bad Attitiude If" sections.

I appreciate Clare Wulker's creative suggestions, publishing advice, and crisp editing. Thanks to Clare's typesetting and interior design, Tom and I have a book.

I thank Jackie Everly for her encouragement and professional advice.

Thanks also to my editors and manuscript readers: my wife, Fr. Bob Yeager, Fr. Mike Billian, Jennifer Weiher-Madrigal, Joe Hessling, Julie Bihn, Nick Covill, Casey Weiher, Erin Widner, Karin Bihn, Ben Cedar, Brian Tong, Dana Harmon, and Tom Chizanowski.

While assembling my acknowledgments, I remembered my mentors, heroes, and those past and present who enjoyed having a good time and shared that attitude with me. Their right attitudes toward life have impressed me and sometimes even influenced me. I should have paid more attention to these people at the time, but then, I have a yellow personality and we yellows don't always pay attention. (See chapter 6 for an explanation of the color code.) Anyway, I appreciate their wonderful attitudes in action. I salute and admire each one. I also recommend that readers make a list of people whose attitudes toward life have helped them—it's a wonderful, enlightening experience.

Assessing Your Attitude

*What life means to us is determined not so much by what life brings
to us as by the attitude we bring to life; not so much by what happens
to us as by our reaction to what happens.* LEWIS L. DUNNINGTON

Attitudes collided big time on April Fool's Day in 1996. Cincinnati's
Riverfront Stadium had a noisy crowd of 53,000 when—a mere seven
pitches into the game—the unthinkable silenced the crowd. Umpire John
McSherry collapsed. After McSherry was taken to the hospital, the
umpires huddled with the Reds' team managers and owner; they decided to
continue the game, perhaps bowing to Reds'owner, Marge Schott.
Elsewhere, Reds and Expos players met; they insisted the game be
postponed until the following day. Reds' catcher Eddie Taubensee said,
"Life is precious. Everybody's shook up. If I go out there and the same thing
happened to me, I wouldn't expect [them] to just throw Joe (Oliver) out
there and go [on and] play. You just can't do that."

Montreal Expos manager Felipe Alou commented, "It's a family
thing. For almost everybody [in baseball], the family is baseball
people—the umpires, the media, the coaches, teammates. When somebody
goes through something like this, we're family."[1]

A few fans instantly booed the announcement that the game would
be postponed; one fan, however, couldn't let go of his disappointment and
later wrote to a Columbus sports columnist to complain:

I am absolutely irate, as are many others that attended
Cincinnati's opening day. Don't get me wrong, I'm sorry

that John McSherry died, but it was an outrage to cancel the game.

Baseball is attempting to win back fans, yet 50,000 people take a day off work to attend and they cancel the game. Would the game have been canceled if a fan died? I don't think so.

When somebody in my company dies, we don't close the business; we say our prayers and go about our jobs. Grow up, you pampered, spoiled babies.[2]

A clash of attitudes, indeed. We suggest to this writer that by postponing the opening game, baseball won back more fans than it would have by resuming play.

One player has been key to winning back fans because his attitude has captured fans' imagination. Cal Ripkin, Jr., reminded them why they come to watch wealthy men swat at a small ball with sticks of wood. Ripkin gave baseball a just-in-time attitude transfusion when he broke Lou Gehrig's record by playing in 2,130 consecutive games. As he circled the bases to a standing ovation, fans rejoiced with a humble man who was just doing his job—one that he obviously enjoyed. As Ripkin took that victory lap around the field, he stopped now and then to retrieve articles that fans had dropped over the wall in their excitement. He looked a bit teary-eyed. It was a triumph of right attitude! Later in the season, Ripkin maintained his right attitude while playing third base.

When Ripkin played in his 2,216th consecutive game, he broke the world record held by Sachio Kinugasa of Japan. Faced with another standing ovation, baseball's iron man tipped his cap and waved while making his way back to the dugout. As fireworks filled the sky, Ripkin came out of the dugout to shake hands with Kinugasa. He waved at the crowd and disappeared into the dugout. Why hide? In his words, "Unless you've been lucky enough to go through it, you can never understand the embarrassment all that attention causes." Ripkin explained how "It stops the flow of the game and the game of baseball is what everyone comes out to see." What refreshing humility!

Later Ripkin commented, "The celebration wasn't for me—it was a celebration of international baseball, of Japanese baseball. It was about two people who share a passion for the game. The celebration was breaking of the record, but I felt we shared that moment, that it was ours equally."

Now that we've set the stage with some right and wrong attitudes in the preceding baseball stories, we'll look at what makes up the wrong attitude. After that, we introduce the right attitude and explain how you can develop it. Chapters 2 through 6 discuss fifteen characteristics of a right attitude. The last chapter suggests ways to deal with stress and to achieve success, happiness, and a balanced 360-degree life.

THE WRONG ATTITUDE

The wrong attitude has these characteristics:

W	Worrying about things we can't control.
R	Rushing to judgment.
O	Overreacting.
N	Neglecting areas of control.
G	Giving up too soon.

A wrong attitude is any thinking that causes us to act in ways that hurt us or isolate us from others. We have attitudes about everything: ourselves, home, others, money, sex, jobs, schools, neighbors, neighborhoods, sports teams, intelligence, ethnic races, old or young people, fear, guilt, hurt feelings, unworthiness, and anger. We choose whether our attitudes will improve, who we are or hurt others. A wrong attitude results in stress for the person who holds it and for anyone within shouting distance. These people have wrong attitudes:

- Worriers are God wannabes who think they control the universe. No one taught them how to distinguish between the things they control (their lives) and those they cannot control (life on Neptune). Understanding that difference alone could reduce their worrying by at least three-quarters. With wrinkled brows and hunched shoulders, worriers have nothing to show for their wasted time and energy. Unfortunately, worrying makes them too tired to take care of the things they really can control.

- People who rush to judgment don't believe in hearing both sides; they prefer jumping to conclusions. Who needs facts, anyway? Once they have decided who is wrong, that's it, end of story. After all, just how many times do you expect them to make up their minds?

- Overreacters have short fuses; they impugn evil intent in the most benign situations. They demand revenge for every real or imagined slight. Overreacters are the most likely to actually follow through when they yell they are going to murder someone. While fueling tantrums, their anger splashes on guilty and innocent alike. Overreacters originated the phrase, *Ready, fire, aim*. Keep your distance.

- Neglecters are perpetual children who abdicate their responsibilities to families, friends, or employers. While blissfully ignoring major parts of their lives, neglecters become obsessed with one thing. Sometimes it's work. Sometimes it's the Internet. Sometimes it's sports or shopping. Sometimes it's drinking, gambling, or partying. Sometimes it's a hobby. Actually, anything that has no responsibilities attached will do.

- Those who give up too soon have resigned from life. Already dead but not buried, they feel empty and powerless; with what little strength they have left, they manage to spread negativity. Charter members of Depression 'R' Us, they kibbitz about life's unfairness and society's swift decent to hell. Everything is just as bad as they always thought it would be; and everyone else is getting worse every day.

For many of us, these characteristics of a wrong attitude are uncomfortably familiar for we have the seeds of each within ourselves. We can activate these wrong attitudes as easily as we do the right attitudes—fortunately, the choice is a personal one that is revokable. The ability to change is our birthright—all we have to do is accept it.

Wrong Attitudes in Action

- In February 1996, nine out of ten Americans believed incivility was a serious problem.A U.S. News/Bozell Worldwide poll found that more than 90 percent of those surveyed believed incivility contributed to violence. Eighty-five percent agreed that it divided the national community and eroded healthy values.[3] Eradicating incivility should keep all of us busy for some time.

- After receiving a faxed order, a businessman called the jewelry store that faxed the order. Lacking the name of a contact person, he asked for the owner. After identifying himself to the owner, he added, "How are you today?"
  The response was both loud and immediate, "I don't have time for small talk, what do you want?" Upon hearing the reason for the call, the owner said, "Well, you should have asked for the office manager." Then he handed the phone off saying, "Here, you should have answered this yoyo's call. I'm too busy." Well, the owner got that right—he should never answer a phone.

- Aggressive driving behavior, aka road rage, caused almost 27,600 of the nation's 41,907 fatalities in 1996. National Highway Traffic

Safety Administration chief Ricardo Martinez said aggressive drivers speed, tailgate, weave, pass on the right, run stop signs and lights, make hand and facial gestures, scream, honk, and flash their lights. Martinez said that these people "climb into the anonymity of an automobile and take out their frustrations on others at any time." After steadily declining, highway deaths have increased slightly for the last four years—that's much too much road rage.

• Although the Soup Nazi episode was one of "Seinfeld's" best comedies, such outrageous people are always funnier on TV than face-to-face. The Soup Nazi established rules for how people ordered his soup. One minor slip up, and no delicious soup with bread. If he simply did not like the way someone looked, no delicious soup and bread.

   In real life, dealing with people so compulsively protective of their turf is more frustrating than funny. From the stories we've heard, we know that every company has at least one Turf Nazi. For instance, a Stamp Nazi at a package mailing service answered a request for 100 postcard stamps like this: "I can't sell you that many. If I sell you all our postcard stamps, I won't have any for anyone else." This service provider's message: I'm in charge here and I don't want customers who may come in to buy stamps to think we're inefficient because we're out of stamps, so we won't sell them to you so we can sell them to others, unless of course, they want too many stamps in which case they're out of luck.

• And then there was the neophyte waiter who took drink orders at a table and promptly returned with the drinks. As James placed a glass before his last customer, she looked up in puzzlement. "That's not what I ordered," she said.

   Studying his order pad, the waiter read: "A strawberry daiquiri in a plain drinking glass with whipped cream on top." Pausing, James looked his customer in the eye, "That's *exactly* what you ordered," he crowed in triumph. "Oh, no," she replied, holding her ground and raising her voice.

   Fortunately for everyone concerned, the manager appeared to whisk the offending drink away, motion another waiter into action, and send James to tend a corner table. James confused his need to be right with his duty to fulfill a customer's desires.

The preceding examples document our belief that it is time for large-scale attitude make overs. Need more proof? What about talk radio, television talk shows, the political climate in Washington, strikes in various professional sports, pro-life and pro-choice hate-fests, and insurance companies' myopic emphasis on dealing with health problems instead of promoting healthy life choices? Greed has replaced responsibility, nastiness has kayoed humor, and obnoxiousness has buried graciousness. Even the Statue of Liberty has replaced her SEND ME YOUR TIRED, YOUR POOR sign with snarling pit bulls in blinking red neon.

There are, however, still signs of hope:

- The California Employment Development Department in Santa Ana recently received an envelope bulging with $2,500 in cash. The enclosed anonymous note addressed "To Whom It May Concern" read: "Several years ago I was layed [sic] off from my job and I collected unemployment for a little while. . . . Now, thank the Lord that I have the money to pay back the state."

- At a 1996 Ku Klux Klan rally in Ann Arbor, Michigan, things got violent when anti-Klan protesters saw a Confederate flag on a man's jacket and beat him to the ground.

    Keshia Thomas, a black eighteen-year-old, threw herself between the protesters and the KKK supporter. Later she explained, "Just because you beat somebody doesn't mean you are going to change his mind." What a brave voice of reason.

We believe people of different beliefs still can reason together once they learn to listen to each other (see chapter 3 for listening skills). We believe people have good instincts, that they can be civil—even gracious—when they realize how their attitudes affect others. All we need to do is CYA.

YOU MAY HAVE A WRONG ATTITUDE IF . . .

- Your Rottweiler hides under the bed when you come home.

- You have been downsized out of your car-pool.

- Your only degree is a BAA (bad ass attitude) with a major in whining.

- You sent your toll-free work number to your friends and relatives across the country but they never call.

- You think March 13 is a national holiday; that's Blame It On

Someone Else Day.

- Your idea of personal empowerment is denting someone's fender and leaving a note saying, "Hi, Sucker."
- You ran into Albert Belle who practically begged for your autograph.

THE RIGHT ATTITUDE

The RIGHT attitude has these characteristics:

R	Reality, risk-taking, and responsibility (chapter 2).
I	Imagination, innovation, and integrity (chapter 3).
G	Goals-oriented, graciousness, and greatness (chapter 4).
H	Habits, health, and humor (chapter 5).
T	Time, thinking, and trusting (chapter 6).

Sometimes a big, rather than right, attitude is enough to set the wheels in motion. It was 7:15 Sunday morning in Bellaire, Ohio, when cars began blocking the southbound lanes of Route 7. Slowly they forced a determined four-year-old on a twelve-inch bike with training wheels onto the berm; Ricky had been pedaling in the fast lane of a four-lane highway. Although his sense of direction was confused, his heart was in the right place. Ricky was going to see his grandma who lives north of Bellaire. When stopped, he was about a mile south of home. The chief of police commented: "That's a big attitude they have at that age. That kid had just pedaled his butt off." When do big attitudes begin to shrink? Must they?

Prior to the 1996 Olympics in Atlanta, the Olympic Torch Relay made its serpentine way through the United States. As was true of most small communities along the way, hundreds lined Marysville, Ohio, streets. Some of the biggest cheers came as Kevin McCoy received the torch. A couple of days later, McCoy graduated from high school where he had been active in the Fellowship of Christian Athletes and a manager for the football team. The eighteen-year-old was also a Drug Abuse Resistance Education role model. McCoy has spina bifida; because he needed both hands to move his wheelchair, the torch was hooked to his chair.

Defining Attitude

As Kevin and Ricky prove, attitude is everything! Attitude is the way you respond to life each day—all day. "It's all attitude. Attitude is the way you define and interpret your experiences. Your attitude is the sum total of your beliefs, assumptions, expectations, and values. It determines the meaning or significance you attach to events and your response to them," said author Adam Robinson.[4]

Attitude is why some people are so successful; they've gone through hardships and down times, yet their buoyant positive expectations keep returning them to the top of the water. Everything comes back to attitude. I (TB) call this the Rocky attitude. In the first *Rocky* movie, Sly Stallone never gave up; nor was he knocked out. He always got up off the mat before the bell rang. Bloodied and proud, Sly stood tall at the end of the fight. Life can bloody you, but get up off the mat before the bell rings and you're a winner. It takes a right attitude to stand tall at the end of each day's bout.

Wrong attitudes have caused many people to do poorly in their jobs or when making career changes. According to research by Robert Half International, seven out of every ten fired employees have attitude problems; these range from not getting along with others to refusing to follow instructions or being dishonest, negative, or unmotivated.[5]

Attitude is the way we look at the world through our expectations and beliefs about the world and ourselves. On average, we process 50,000 thoughts during one day. According to author Robert Cooper, research suggests every one of our thoughts affects each of our cells; this is why our attitudes affect our productivity. When our expectations are positive, we are helpful and generous toward others and exercise better judging, problem-solving, decision-making, and creative skills. When our expectations are negative, we have less ability to solve problems and make breakthroughs because we feel insecure and emotionally fragile.[6]

We need to learn how to process thoughts so we are thinking in a way that benefits our lives, not hinders them. Our attitudes dictate our actions until we drop; so, why not become a dictator and decide what you are going to do? For example, Adam Robinson points out that smart students have a different attitude than ordinary students. Smart students realize that they can teach themselves far better than any school possibly can. Because of this attitude, they approach schoolwork differently. They have different skills, goals, habits, priorities, and strategies because they see education differently.[7]

According to futurist Alvin Toffler, "The illiterate of the future are not those who cannot read or write, but those who cannot learn, unlearn, and relearn." No matter what formal educational level you've reached, additional education is in store for you—otherwise you risk becoming roadkill on the information superhighway. The real trick is to internalize the necessity of lifelong learning. The real challenge is doing this when you are very comfortable with the way things are going in your life. (We discuss lifelong learning further in chapter 2.) Check off all attitudes that describe you in the following list:

O Aggressive	O Gracious	O Positive
O Angry	O Guilty	O Proud
O Balanced	O Healthy	O Realist
O Belittling	O Hopeless	O Responsible
O Bigoted	O Humorous	O Risk taker
O Confident	O Imaginative	O Rusher
O Controlling	O Innovative	O Stressed out
O Coping	O Motivated	O Team player
O Defensive	O Negative	O Thinker
O Depressed	O Neglectful	O Understanding
O Goal oriented	O Overreactor	O Worrier

Your Attitude Makes a Visual Statement

Through the seasons, nature presents us with an infinite variety of attitudes from gloomy mist to glorious sunshine; its variety allows us to forecast the weather based on our understanding of nature. In a similar fashion, our own moods, whether gloomy or bright, always speak to those around us. This means your attitude is the statement you make even when you don't speak. When your attitude is too loud, no one can hear what you are saying. For instance, if you saw a woman with her hands on her hips talking to a man with his arms crossed over his chest, would you need to hear their conversation? Of course not. Even though your attitude is not always this obvious, it is always the cause of your effect on your world. As soon as an attitude begins forming in your brain, it begins showing as your entire body reflects it. By your walk, the way you carry your head and shoulders, and the expression on your face, you stimulate specific emotional responses in others. They can recognize your wrong attitude that warns them not to get close to you.

Anthropologist Ashley Montagu has noted that some people have psychosclerosis, a hardening of the attitudes; for years they have been warehousing old hates, expectations of failure, fears, remorse, guilt, loneliness, revenge, and so on. Over time, because of such factors as family, education, and social pressures, we select specific attitudes as our way to look at life. Thus, attitudes are the sum total of our expectations, beliefs, assumptions, and values. Our individualized focus on life allows all of our senses to become receptors. Picture your attitudes as a glass shield that covers your head and body; nothing gets to your eyes, ears, nose, or brain without passing through your attitude shield.

Think about how having something in front of you sometimes distorts your hearing. How much do your attitudes allow you to hear? Some attitudes cause selective hearing; you hear what you expect to hear. Sometimes having something in front of you distorts your sight. How much do your attitudes allow you to see? Some attitudes are like cataracts that distort other people and their actions; other attitudes are clear lens through which everything is in sharp focus. I (DM) know what I'm talking about—I've had cataract surgery.

Every so often we all need to perform an attitude check, to take off our attitude shields and evaluate the attitudes developed over a lifetime. When necessary, we must clean off some old attitudes and replace them with new attitudes—that's what this book is about. In the following box, list several attitudes you want to replace:

Altitude and Attitude

When you find an attitude particularly difficult to change, check your altitude; you may have restricted yourself to viewing life from the bottom of a rut, when your new attitude requires you to be on a mountain top. Develop an altitude of self-assurance of a good outcome. Even when you think you are in a bad situation, it may lead to something better.

John-Roger and Peter McWilliams point out the connection between attitude and altitude:

> Altitude is our viewing point, the perspective we have. The higher our viewing point, the more we can see. The more we can see, the more information we have, the better we can make a well-informed decision. . . . Attitude is the way we approach things—our point of view. Do you look at life as an adventure to be enjoyed or a problem to be solved? There are infinite possibilities for living in either

Adventureland or Problem City. The choice . . . is yours.

The connection between attitude and altitude is easy to see. If we have a good attitude, our altitude will lift, and if we have an elevated altitude, our attitude will rise. The reverse is also true. . . . Altitude is raised through meditation, contemplation, prayer, spiritual exercises, creativity, service—connecting directly in some way with the uplifting energy of life.

Attitude is lifted through inspiring lectures, reading, seminars, therapy, support groups, books, movies, TV shows—learning concepts and techniques that naturally lead to an enlightened approach.[8]

When Attitudes Are at Odds with Behavior

Sometimes attitudes and behavior aren't in harmony as they are supposed to be. When attitudes are pointing north and behavior is headed west, we must find a way to realign either the attitude or behavior and relieve the discomfort of what psychologists call *cognitive dissonance*. Say, for example, someone offers you a bribe to overlook faulty building construction. You want and deserve a new Jaguar (attitude) but cannot accept a bribe (behavior). You refuse the money to bring your attitude and behavior into harmony.

When you feel out of sync, ask yourself if any of the following situations are going on. In these three situations, attitude and behavior are not evenly balanced; however, you can live with such an attitude-behavior conflict when either one has more value for you:

1. *When the rewards make the conflict acceptable.* Suppose you were brought up to dislike green people. One day you make an anti-green remark and your friend takes offense because he is, after all, green. Being colorblind, you had no idea he was; you are shocked. If you had suspected he was green, you probably would not have become friends. Now you experience discomfort—your original attitude of disliking green people conflicts with your behavior of being his friend. At this point we would suggest CYA—the enjoyment you derive from your friendship with Kermit is greater than your dislike of a whole category of people.

2. *When the issues causing the conflict are not that important.* Stephen Hawking, the world's foremost physicist, is also the longest survivor of amyotrophic lateral sclerosis, or Lou Gehrig's disease. Hawking's movement is restricted to his left hand that operates a control panel. To communicate with others, he depends on a computer program's

synthesizer that has a decidedly American accent. As a native Briton and holder of Newton's chair at Cambridge, that computer voice must have been grating at first. Hawking has accepted the synthesizer's accent as a fact of life. And his life is too busy to allow petty dissatisfactions to interrupt.[9]

3. *When the external source of the conflict is not under your control.* Heather Whitestone lost most of her hearing due to a childhood virus. This physical disability did not stop her from becoming Miss Alabama or Miss America in 1995. Whitestone views negative thinking as more of a handicap than deafness.

Attitudes Affect Job Performance

A 1996 survey by Accutemps found that bosses are spending nine weeks a year resolving personality clashes (read attitude problems) between employees. Accutemps, a temporary staffing service, hired an independent researcher to ask 150 executives from America's largest companies only one question: What percentage of management time was wasted on resolving personality conflicts in their offices? The response was 18 percent which becomes more interesting when compared with 13 percent in 1991 and 9.2 percent in 1986. See, we're not making this up: Wrong attitudes obviously are escalating.

Accutemps Chairman Max Messmer suggested three reasons why the workplace has become more conflict-ridden: increased competition, the rapid pace of business, and company restructurings. Messmer encouraged managers to clearly delineate responsibilities and use a team approach in everyday projects. (See teams in chapter 6.) He also suggested that managers encourage co-workers to solve their own problems, being careful of not only what they say but also how they say it.[10]

Employees' attitudes are important to organizations because they affect job behavior. Managers focus on those employee attitudes that affect work performance, such as how satisfying an employee finds the job, how involved the employee is, and how committed the employee is to the organization. One indication of an employee's attitude is attendance; recently the U.S. Bureau of Labor Statistics reported that absenteeism has increased by 15 percent in the last five years. This translates to a cost of $110 to $150 per employee annually.

On the next page, take a minute to list five attitudes your work reflects, such as conscientiousness, boredom, or competency. Circle the numbers of any attitudes that need to be changed. (If you are not employed, list five attitudes you want your work to reflect):

1.
2.
3.
4.
5.

In a recent poll of CEOs, more than 80 percent admitted that they got where they are not by their aptitudes, but due to their attitudes. Not one of them finished in the top 2 percent of any class. They got where they are strictly on attitude. Because right attitudes are good business, managers try to shape their employees' attitudes through persuasion and modeling. Then, employees either become convinced of the attitude's worth or admire the attitude exhibited by others and adopt it. Still, managers sometimes ask workers to behave in a manner inconsistent with their attitudes. Here, employees can realign their attitudes and behaviors by noting that these behaviors are externally imposed, beyond their control, or rewarding enough to offset the discomfort.

Employees may be comfortable with incompatible or mismatched attitudes and behaviors in each of the preceding situations. However, these situations can affect organizations significantly. To illustrate the last situation, some otherwise honest employees don't hesitate to bring pens, markers, or paper home from work. A box of paper clips here, a few floppy disks there, a long-distance phone call to mom, or surfing the Internet for an hour are of minimal importance—until multiplied by 20, or 200, or 2,000 employees. Only a decade ago, security managers investigated missing supplies, cash, and merchandise; now they also monitor employees' theft of time, intellectual property, and on-line information.

Have you heard about the employee who trundled scrap materials home every night in a wheelbarrow? Finally, the guard asked what he was building with all the scraps. The employee answered, "Oh, them scraps ain't worth nothing. But, you know, I get a real good price for the wheelbarrows." Whether you think this story is funny probably depends on whether you are an employee or management. According to John W. Jones writing in *Security Management*, employee theft amounts to more than $100 billion in the United States annually. Ouch, it's definitely time to CYA.[11]

Attitudes in Action

Our attitudes reflect the favorable or unfavorable values that special objects, people, or events have for us. Our attitudes show what we expect of ourselves and out of life as well as revealing our basic values. Early in life, we imitate the attitudes of our parents, teachers, friends, and leaders. Entering adolescence, we latch onto the attitudes of those we admire, respect, or fear. In later life, some people continue the adolescent process; they adopt the behavior and attitudes of popular sports figures, entertainers, or cult heroes. Other adults—perhaps most—remain unswayed by fame and form their attitudes by considering the details of issues or events. They base their responses on their own personal values, desires, or fears. Think about those whose attitudes you adopted and list them in this box:

People whose attitudes I adopted:	

Fortunately, we never carve our attitudes in stone; we can mold and change them almost day to day. This is why advertisers aim their glitzy, appealing ads squarely at consumers' attitudes. For example, if you form a favorable attitude about a well-advertised athletic shoe, you probably will look for that brand while shopping.

Attitude is the way we respond to life each day—all day. It is the way the people of Oklahoma City responded when the Alfred P. Murrah Federal Building collapsed on April 19, 1995. That bombing killed 169 people, including 19 children, and injured more than 500. As a shocked nation watched, the people of Oklahoma City opened their hearts, homes, and pocketbooks to victims of the bombing and to rescue workers from around the country. Modeling care and concern, some residents combed through the building in search of survivors, while others tended to the injured. They baby-sat children, comforted survivors and their loved ones, cooked for the rescue workers, prayed, and remained amazingly gracious in the face of a relentless media barrage. Undefeated by the heart-wrenching scene, the people of Oklahoma City pulled together to help each other. In short, they made us proud of their right attitudes.

Without taking anything away from the generous people of Oklahoma City, we must mention that throughout this book we describe scores of people with right attitudes. Right attitudes are spawned not only in the midst of a major catastrophe but also in the day-to-day needs of people around us.

ATTITUDE CAUSES A RESULT

Charles Swindoll's definition of attitude says it all:

> The longer I live, the more I realize the impact of attitude on life.
> Attitude, to me is more than facts. It is more important than the
> past, than education, than money, than circumstances, than
> failures, than successes, than what other people think or say or do.
> It is more important than appearance, giftedness, or skill. It will
> make or break a company . . . a church . . . a home. The remarkable
> thing is we have a choice every day regarding the attitude we will
> embrace for that day. We cannot change our past. . . . We cannot
> change the inevitable. The only thing we can do is play on the one
> string we have, and that is our attitude . . . I am convinced that life
> is 10 percent what happens to me and 90 percent how I react to it.
> And so it is with you. . . . We are in charge of our attitudes."[12]

Successful people focus on results. They do not react to trivial
difficulties around them but keep focused on what they expect out of life.
This keeps the minutia from taking over; they are aware of it but do not
devote their entire time to immediate little problems. They look ahead to
achieving their goals next year, next month, next week.

I (TB) am an avid runner, but not always a happy runner. Sometimes
I sign up for a race weeks ahead without considering that the weather
could be bad, that it begins too early in the morning, or that there are no
refunds. After a particularly long week, during which I had been in
situations where I was not in control, I stumbled out of bed early one
Saturday. I was supposed to run the Coronado-San Diego Bridge.

As soon as I got to the starting point, I knew this was not going to be
an easy run for me. My negative self-talk began when I got there. Why was
I out there? It was too cold—the intelligent runners were still in bed. Then
gun went off and the crowd swelled forward. I started hyperventilating and
slowed down. I realized that I was talking myself down instead of thinking
about how I was enjoying this run.

At the base of the bridge, the theme from *Rocky* blared from huge
speakers. I really got into that and went flying—for at least 100 yards—
and then it hit me. I had given no thought to a bridge's construction; I might
as well have been running up a mountain. Watching the runners ahead of
me, my negative self-talk was going full blast. Three-quarters of the way
up, I came up even with Julie in a wheelchair. Noticing that she was
extremely focused on what she wanted, I immediately turned off my
negative self-talk. If Julie had lost her focus, she would have gone flying
back down the bridge at 50 mph. Julie's example gave me a blast of energy.

As I began to think about how this race was tougher than I thought it would be, I heard the strains of *Chariots of Fire* from the two huge speakers at the top of the bridge. The sun just happened to be coming up, and I thought yes, I can do this. Then Julie went flying by me. I finally caught up with her going into Balboa Park. After the race I introduced myself and told her how exciting she had made the race. Julie told me that while recovering from an auto accident she decided that the wheelchair would not be the result of her life. The chair was the result of the accident, but not of her life. That was a motivational speech for me.

HOW TO DEVELOP THE RIGHT ATTITUDES

We are the first to admit that changing attitudes is not brain surgery or rocket science. What it is, is come-in-out-of-the-rain horse sense, also known as stop-banging-your-head-against-the-wall common sense. As Stephen Covey has said, however, "What's common sense just isn't common practice."[13] So we are going to show you ways to develop the right attitude. We believe your life will be enriched by increasing your awareness that once you create new attitudes, your behavior changes to align with your desired new outlook.

Although your attitude determines to what extent you develop your potential, nothing happens until you mix attitude and action. If Walt Disney had only thought about making movies, there would be no Disneyland. If Mother Teresa had stayed in her convent, the Missionaries of Charity would not have 517 centers in 120 countries. Your first step is to decide which attitude you want to develop; for example, you may desire to be more affectionate to your children, or to be less critical. Write down the attitude you want to develop:

```




```

Steps two through eight involve goal setting, journaling, visualizing, making time, self-talking, affirming, and acting as if.

Goal Setting

Goal setting is essential to making a change. For example, when I want to drive to a distant city, I (DM) ask the AAA to create a map for my trip. To do that, I must give the AAA two basic pieces of information: where I am beginning my journey and where I want to end up. So, too, with goal setting; consider where you are and where you want to be.

By deciding on a specific attitude, you are establishing a place where you want to be. So begin by reviewing who you are right now and identify any problem feelings or thoughts. Then develop appropriate goals to change your attitude. (We say more about goal setting in chapter 4.)

Journaling

Journaling involves making notes about where you have been and where you are going. As you journal, you reinforce your determination to change; you also record for yourself how things have gone so far. Later, when you are working on a different facet of your overall attitude, you can review your earlier journal entries to learn what pitfalls to avoid. Reading about all the things you have overcome to change an attitude is also a real motivator to make other changes.

Journal in a notebook or on a floppy disk each day. On the first day, describe your goal, the reasons you want to change, and how you are going to change. Each day add examples of how you demonstrated your new attitude. If you slipped up, note that too; once you have listed the slip ups, concentrate on your successes. Slipping up is something we all do; remember you are aiming for improvement, not instant perfection.

Talking about slip ups, California child psychologist Dr. Darrell Burnett believes parents must be positive models for their kids. Try as they might, however, sometimes parents slip into negative modes. When they do, their kids are the first to remind them. Burnett cites this example in his booklet/audiotape *Raising Responsible Kids*: While driving home after work, he was looking forward to celebrating the newly completed dining room addition. Two hours of gridlocked traffic later, a testy Burnett got out of the car, entered the house and walked directly to the dining room. Instead of praising the finished product, he groused about a smudge on the new wallpaper. At that, his fourteen-year-old daughter, Jill, said as only teens can, "Hey, everybody, Dad's home! Let's all play Find the Flaw."

Throughout the book, we frequently suggest subjects for journaling as we do here:

CYA Journaling Exercise: Give three reasons you want to change your attitude, and five steps you are going to take to do so.

Visualizing

Visual images stimulate growth; that's why visualizing is key to changing your attitude. Stanford Research Institute found that "89 percent of what we learn is visual, 10 percent of what we learn is auditory, and 1 percent of what we learn is through other senses."[14] As the Torah states, what you can see is what you can be. Take for example, Hubert H. Humphrey. During a trip to Washington, D.C., when he was twenty-four, Humphrey wrote to his wife: "Honey, I can see how someday, if you and I just apply ourselves and make up our minds to work for bigger and better things, we can someday live here in Washington and probably be in government, politics, or service. ... Oh, gosh, I hope my dream comes true—I'm going to try anyhow."[15] Humphrey's dream came true; he was our 38th vice-president and served in the Senate for twenty-three years.

Visualizing involves choosing quiet times to relax during which you can imagine yourself demonstrating your new attitude. Make this a special personal time during which you relax your body and see a new you. Choose three specific times to visualize each day. Practice visualizing on waking and when retiring and at least one other time during the day.

Begin visualizing by deep breathing—take a deep breath, hold it for a count of five, and slowly release the breath to a count of five. Do this five times. Next, relax the muscles in your body starting with those in your feet. Say to yourself: "The muscles in my feet are relaxing, they are getting very heavy."

Continue in this fashion with your ankles, legs, thighs, hips, lower back, abdomen, stomach, chest, upper back, shoulders, arms, neck, head, and face.

After you are completely relaxed, visualize yourself doing something that illustrates your new attitude. For example, if you want to stop slouching and look more confident, see yourself standing tall and looking others in the eye as you interact with them. Enjoy this view; take pleasure in your new confident appearance. While visualizing, you may think of new opportunities or things you have not considered.

I (TB) find New Age music is great in helping me relax; each night I listen to fifteen minutes of music while visualizing great attitudes for the next day.

Making Time

Change requires a commitment of time—plan to spend at least twenty-one days working on a specific attitude characteristic. Also, resolve now to spend time on attitude changes throughout your life. If you are a gardener, you can understand the reason. Each year, despite your best efforts, weeds spring up in your flower beds and garden. You pull them, knowing that if you did not, next year they would multiply and crowd out the desirable plants. Removing new weeds makes room for the plants you want. Removing wrong attitudes on a regular basis makes room for the right attitudes to flourish. (We discuss making time to make changes further in chapter 7.)

Self-Talking

Author John Tschohl concisely explains why self-talk is so important: "You can't count on receiving enough compliments from others to sustain your ego and equip yourself, emotionally, to do good work. So, learn to compliment yourself." Easier said than done, we answer. Praising ourselves is difficult because we feel conceited; we suspect we are babying ourselves, and God forbid that we should do that.

Tschohl explains further, "It is essential to success that one praises oneself from time to time. Doing so is one of the very effective means of maintaining one's motivation. People need positive strokes to equip them to repeatedly do their best work."[16]

Unfortunately, we all have built-in negative self-talk tapes that need to be obliterated. Three techniques can help you: First, imagine how you would react if someone else said to you what you say to yourself. If your self-talk tapes say all you're good for is spending money, answer back with any number of other things you do adequately.

A second technique is to argue with yourself; don't accept any negative statements as facts. Separating fact from fable helps you see yourself more accurately. Defend yourself with the same gusto you would use to defend your best friend.[17]

Triathlete Jacqui Lewis suggests, "The way to combat negative thoughts is to listen to them and question their reality basis—then you can change the thought to a more realistic and less self-defeating one. Practicing positive thinking sounds really hokey, but it really does work."[18]

And third, don't take failure or rejection personally; instead, think about possible causes of your problems. When an associate doesn't greet you, does she hate you, or was she distracted by her pager going off? Concentrate on the least negative cause rather than the most negative cause.[19]

Because you can think of only one thing at a time, don't let negative thoughts begin; occupy your mind with positive self-talk. Imperfect creatures that we are, we sometimes take actions that lead us away from our goals—or we even forget that we have goals. At these times, we need to talk to ourselves. Say, for example, you have reverted back to slouching and mumbling—definitely not characteristics of the confident attitude you want to acquire. Reassure yourself that this is not a permanent problem; you can change because you want to change. Visualize yourself standing straight and speaking clearly.

Ask yourself what else you can do to appear confident. For instance, motivational speaker Brian Tracy suggests repeating the phrase, "I like myself!" whenever you need to reduce stress and calm yourself. Also, whenever you pass a mirror, say it five times and try not to smile.[20]

Affirming

My wife and I (TB) post our attitude affirmations on our bathroom mirrors. That way I face my right attitude each morning and evening. (An example: I am healthy, I am patient, I am successful.)

Affirmations can help keep your mind on track by not allowing any room for discouraging negative thoughts. Affirmations are especially helpful for people who habitually think the worst. The marvelous part of affirming is that your unconscious believes what you tell it and works to make that come true. Therefore, you do not have to believe what you say; you only need to really want it to become true. Whenever doubts occur, for example, you can create a confident attitude by affirming: I look confident because I am confident.

CYA Journaling Exercise: Based on your three reasons for changing your attitude, write three statements that affirm your new attitude.

Acting as If

Act like the person you want to be and that is what you become. Once you start doing something, such as standing tall, maintaining eye contact when you talk to people, and speaking distinctly with energy in your voice, motivation kicks in and helps you keep doing it. Acting as if may seem difficult the first time you do it; like anything else, the more you act as if, the better you become. Acting as if gets the chemistry moving in the right direction. Don't wait for motivation to tap you on the shoulder; fake it until you make it. Act first and motivation naturally follows to keep you going in your chosen direction.

Just as an organization's attitude is created by every member, a person's attitude reflects the sum total of the person. The choice is ours. As Ben Franklin said "although we cannot control what goes on in the world around us, we can always control what happens inside of us." More recently, critics proclaimed that Michael Crawford's 400th performance of *Phantom of the Opera* was as great as his first performance. We suspect Crawford did some faking during his reign as phantom.

This story of two brothers illustrates how effective acting as if can be. After two computer hackers were found guilty of stealing corporate secrets, the police chief had ST for secrets thief tattooed on their foreheads. Nicholas barely could hold up his head and walked about hunched over so no one would see his shame. He hitchhiked out of his hometown in Vermont. In each town he entered, however, people questioned the brand on his forehead. Nervous, pathetic, and burdened by his punishment, Nicholas fled to New York City, where he died a pauper.

His brother, Gregory, stayed in Vermont and donated his computer equipment to a local school. Determined to show the town that he had learned from his mistake, he became a truck gardener. Gradually he earned the friendship and respect of the townspeople. As an old man, Gregory was celebrated as the town's most honest citizen. One day while he was working in his fields, a stranger stopped to ask for directions. As he looked at Gregory's withered face, he asked about his forehead. "Oh, it was so long ago—I'm not sure any more," Gregory said. "But I think the letters ST mean saint." Acting as if makes all the difference.

As motivational speakers, we know the value of acting as if. Like everyone else, we have days when our flights are late or weeks when we have crammed ten presentations into five days. That tenth audience, however, doesn't know anything about our schedule; that audience deserves an enthusiastic speaker who becomes his material and speaks with energy and conviction. Magically, when we're finished and listening to the applause, we feel like walking billboards for CYA. Of course, if there is no applause, that's also due to our attitudes.

ATTITUDE DETERMINES REALITY

When we (DM) met in 1960, Gilbert Provencher had spent the last fourteen years of his life in a hospital bed. At fourteen, Gil broke his neck while diving into a swimming pond. Due to his permanent spinal cord injury, he was bedfast the rest of his life and required constant care. Gil's parents reassured him that they would care for him the rest of his life, but Gil had other plans and a can-do attitude.

Gil could move only his left shoulder and upper arm. Part of Gil's rehabilitation therapy was based on his love of art. His father created an arm brace so Gil could start drawing with charcoal; that led to water colors; the next step was oil painting.

While Gilbert was developing his artististic talent, he appeared on the television show, "Strike It Rich." Mrs. Gimble, of Gimble's Department Store, happened to see Gilbert on that show and was struck by his courage and his ability to paint. At seventeen, Gilbert the artist was discovered.

Subsequently, Gil and his family moved from New Hampshire to south Florida because the warmer climate was better for him. For a decade or so, Mrs. Gimble sponsored Gilbert Provencher's art show during the winter season in posh Palm Beach. During these years, Gil's artwork provided an income for his parents and himself. In 1965, Gil died at the age of thirty-three.

I feel fortunate to own one of Gil's oil paintings. Each time I look at that clown's head, I am reminded of Gilbert's determination to succeed. I am reminded of his family's love and the sacrifices his parents and his sister Sonia made. For all of them, family came first.

Because of his attitude, Gilbert's reality was not based on the immobility of a paraplegic, but on the mobility that allowed him to reveal love and good cheer in his paintings. Chapter 2 talks about how we can focus our reality as Gilbert did. It also discusses our responsibility for ourselves and others, and the need for taking risks.

ENDNOTES

1. "Players Didn't Want to Play Out of Respect for McSherry," *Columbus Dispatch*, April 2, 1996, p. 2F.
2. George Strode, "Even after Umpire Died," *Columbus Dispatch*, April 7, 1996, p. 4F.
3. J. Marks, "The American Uncivil Wars," *U.S. News & World Report*, April 12, 1996, pp. 66-72.
4. Adam Robinson, *What Smart Students Know* (New York: Crown Trade Paperbacks, 1993), p. 12.
5. John C. Maxwell, *Developing the Leader Within You* (Nashville, TN: Thomas Nelson Publishers, 1993), p. 98.
6. Robert K. Cooper, *The Performance Edge* (Boston: Houghton Mifflin Co., 1991), pp. 114–15.
7. Robinson, *What Smart Students Know*, p. 12.
8. John-Roger and Peter McWilliams, *You Can't Afford the Luxury of a Negative Thought* (Los Angeles: Prelude Press, 1991), pp. 487, 489.
9. Bruce Berger, "Dancing with Time," *American Way*, February 2, 1992, p. 40.
10. Lynn Steinberg, "Yakkers, Slackers Make Us Peevish at Work," *Seattle Post-Intelligencer*, June 19, 1996, p. 5H.
11. John W. Jones, "Ensuring an Ethical Environment,"*Security Management* , April 1996, p. 23.
12. Charles Swindoll, *Improving Your Serve* (Waco: Word, 1981).

13. "The 25 Most Influential People," *Time,* June 17, 1996, p. 30.
14. Maxwell, *Developing the Leader,* p. 140.
15. Ibid., p. 141.
16. John Tschohl, "Eliminating Self-Imposed Limitations," *The Selling Advantage,* July 29, 1996, p. 2.
17. "It's Your Best Weapon Against Depression,"*First,* December 18, 1995, p. 71.
18. John Hughes, "Athletes Who Truly Want to Win Work at Developing Their Mental Fitness," *The Orange County Register,* August 7, 1996, p. 1(Accent).
19."It's Your Best Weapon," p. 71.
20. Brian Tracy, *The Psychology of Achievement,* "Building a Self-Concept" (Chicago: Nightingale-Conant Corp., 1984). Sound cassette.

Relishing Reality with Its Responsibilities and Risks

A ship in port is safe, but that's not what ships are built for.
GRACE HOPPER

Reality is the totality of real people, things, and events in our lives—no room for fantasies here. Relishing reality means delighting in your reality—in your unique world that no one else shares. Delighting in traffic tie-ups, grouchy employers, or sadistic bill collectors? Yes, what choice do you have? Reality doesn't change but your attitude toward it can. Facing reality means claiming ownership of your life. Drifting through life is not an option; reality requires being totally honest about yourself and your life, as well as dealing with change, whether you like it or not. We aim to show that educator Roy Blitzer was exaggerating when he said, "The only person who likes change is a wet baby."[1]

As members of the human race, our reality is that we have responsibilities to ourselves and others. One of our chief responsibilities is to realize and develop our potentials; to do that, usually we must take risks. Striving for our personal best means taking ourselves seriously enough to never abdicate control to someone else or allow anything to take over by default. If this sounds too strenuous for you, CYA and keep reading.

YOU MAY HAVE A WRONG ATTITUDE IF . . .

- You claim—along with blues singer Muddy Waters—if it weren't for my bad attitude, I'd have no attitude at all!

- You always leave a smidgen in the coffee pot so someone else must brew more.

- Your bumper sticker growls HANG UP AND DRIVE!

- Your body honestly wants to work but your brain refuses to be retrained.

- You were asked to leave a sales presentation for resort condos.

- You treat risk as a four-letter word.

- You hosted a family reunion and no one came.

REALITY

In the twentieth century, the world has seen more change than at any other time in history. Up to about 1800, people figured their children and grandchildren would have lives similar to their own. Then someone accidentally hit fast forward.

At the beginning of this century, life expectancy was 47; today it is 76; in 2025, it will be 80. In 1900, the 45 United States had 76 million people; in 1990, the 50 states had 254 million people, and in 2025, there will be 323 million. Our shared reality is that our population growth has slowed and we are living longer.

When our country celebrated the arrival of the twentieth century, there were few cars and no motorized airplanes or talking movies; no air conditioning or frozen food; some people had electricity, but no electric washers or vacuum cleaners. Doctors could not treat illnesses with sulfa, insulin, penicillin, or psychoanalysis.

Throughout this century, inventions have been spewing forth like candy from a torn piñata: wonder drugs, television, computers, copiers, faxs, the Internet, compact discs, ATMs, and space exploration. The Berlin Wall is down and the cold war over. Today's jet planes are large enough to house a reenactment of the Wright brothers' historic 120-foot flight. Driven by our global economy, the environment is being depleted, jobs are changing, and communication is burgeoning. Our progress has been uneven—we've walked on the moon, but can't figure out how to stop terrorist bombings.

Sometimes reality seems overwhelming. How do we keep up with everything? What are we to do? Well, we can begin by realizing that many things, such as values, have not been lost; other institutions may have changed but are still recognizable, such as the family structure. Let's start with your reality.

CYA Journaling Exercise: Write about your reality; define each part of your reality and decide which parts you would like to change. Make sure these are parts you can change.

Look at each part of your reality and decide if it falls into what Stephen Covey calls your circle of concern (you can do nothing but worry) or into your circle of influence (a problem you can control). A third option is that this part of your reality is OK as is. Say, your relationship with your spouse is OK; you worry about your kids; and your dog is scratching constantly. Stop worrying about your kids; instead, concentrate on maintaining your loving relationship with them. Change your dog with a flea bath. This is a simplistic example, but you get the idea: appreciate the good in your reality, change what you can, and don't worry about the rest.

Reality or Future Babble?

Doomsayers believe that the rate of change is running a million times faster than our ability to adjust to new situations. We say to them CYA and stop exaggerating. We remember futurists twenty years ago claiming that no one would be writing checks in 1995 because everyone would be banking electronically; that phones would all have video screens; that instead of driving, people would be flying by using back-pack-powered engines. Well, change does not take place logically or as predicted. With a little effort you can learn to watch how things shake out without worrying.

When all the uncertainty in your reality makes you a little jittery, resolve to remain relatively free of anxiety by taking these three steps:

1. *Respond creatively to change.* All of us today are inundated with more news than we really can handle. Cameras seem to be poised in every corner of the globe, waiting to record whatever happens. This instant accessibility has turned some of us into news junkies who must know what's happening everywhere. One way to respond creatively to change is to decide how much news you really need to know. After you write that in the box on the next page, decide which of the media you want to inform you:

News I need to know:

Media:

Dan Brady, the central zone director for Nestlé Ice Cream Company, has responded creatively to change. Brady explained to me (DM) how the Internet helps him communicate with his staff and access information from his company. Brady commented about how much easier his children adapt to changes because they have grown up using computers.

2. *Integrate new elements into your life rather than relying on outdated habits.* Begin by reevaluating your habits to determine which ones are wasting your time or money. Have you ever watched dozens of little turtles in an aquarium at a discount store? Frantic to escape, they climb over each other trying to get out of a tight spot. Lots of action—no progress. Do any escape? No, they just keep climbing over others and getting climbed on in return. Some writers might be tempted to compare the turtles in that aquarium to our national government, but we aren't. Our message is he who steps on others and gets stepped on in return needs to change his habits. As General Motors has shown us with its Saturn Corporation, doing something the same way because you have always done it that way is no reason to continue when there's a better way. The Chinese philosopher Confucius put it another way, "Dumb man fall in same hole twice." Think about any outdated habits you may have and list them here:

Outdated habits:

3. *Focus on results when making decisions.* By focusing on results, you make responsible decisions. Say, your spouse wants to go to a Florida hotel with a pool, but you prefer a beachfront hotel. To focus on the result—making both you and your spouse happy—you would look for the best beach/pool facility on either coast of Florida. Describe a conflict you have and the desired result here:

Conflict and result:

Dealing with reality is one of the chief tenants of Buddhism, along with developing self-reliance and achieving personal improvement. Buddhism is based on ancient teachings that 12 million people find relevant in today's world. Luci DiCrescenzo's reality in Hallandale, Florida, included caring for her mother, who had Alzheimer's disease, for eight years. How did she keep calm and focused? DiCrescenzo commented: "In Buddhism, attitude is everything. It's about finding something good in a garbage pail." She added, "As life bumps you back and forth, Buddhism stabilizes you. You don't fall apart."

While watching his wife battle ovarian cancer for nine years, Stephen Bonnell of Coconut Grove, Florida, also found solace in Buddhism. Piper Bonnell died in 1995 at age 44. Bonnell commented: "Because of Piper's belief, she was able to fight strong and die in peace. It kept us in a very positive frame of mind. As tragic as it was, we were able to look at this in a positive light. We believed that any challenge is a stepping-stone to our own growth."[2] Beautiful attitudes.

Change

In *Confessions of a Street-Smart Manager,* David Mahoney recounted this story told by Mike Dorizas, a former professor of his. It says a lot about responding creatively to change:

> If you drop a frog into a pan of hot water, the frog would immediately react to the heat by jumping out of the pan. But, . . . if you carefully place the same frog in a pan of comfortably cold water, then slowly raise the temperature of the water a degree at a time, the frog will accept this change, perhaps without noticing it, and stay in the water until the heat kills it.[3]

(Don't try this at home, kids, especially with a brother or sister's frog.)

Like the frog, when we fail to notice small, slow changes taking place around us, we risk getting cooked. An example is the rigid mindset of U.S. automakers that kept making humongous gas guzzlers in the seventies, while foreign car makers provided a growing small-car market with gas sippers. Fortunately, U.S. car makers eventually felt the competitive water getting too hot and jumped before they croaked. In this section, we look at the characteristics of change as well as economic and educational changes that affect all of us.

Elwood Chapman advises considering change as an opportunity. Echoing Luci DiCrescenzo, he says the more you expect out of a new situation, the more you are apt to find. By moving into a lifestyle transition with a positive attitude, you have won half the battle before you start.[4]

When I [TB] studied merchandising at Chaffey Junior College in Alta Loma, California, Elwood Chapman was the chairman of the department. Even in the early sixties, his favorite saying was, "Your attitude is showing." I learned as much about attitudes from him as I did about merchandising. Today, Elwood Chapman is a well-known attitude guru.

Change Demands Change. Love, ego, survival, and variety—those are the four human needs that require each of us to make changes in our lives. We make changes because of our desire to be loved and to love. We make changes because of our desire for self-esteem. We make changes to protect or enrich our lives. We make changes to chase away boredom. Naturally, we think we should control all of these changes and determine exactly when they will take place. However, none of us has complete control over our lives—just over part of our lives.

By working within our individual areas of control, however, each of us can meet the challenge of change in our lives. Several years ago when we met Ruth Hanchey at a Franklin training conference, she was a divorced mother supporting herself and her daughter. Most of Ruth's corporate and public seminar presentations kept her in Florida. Realizing that education was important, she had started work on her Ph.D. Ruth's well-ordered life was comfortable, and she foresaw no changes.

One afternoon, after presenting a Franklin seminar, she talked with one of the participants from Orlando, Pat Williams. Subsequently, they talked over the phone and those talks led to dating. They found they shared many of the same attitudes: Love for learning, love of children, a passion for public presentation, and a need to and love of sharing. During one of their conversations, Pat asked Ruth, "Do you have any regrets?" Ruth replied that she regretted not having more children. "I can fix that," Pat said.

On April 5, 1997, Ruth Hanchey married Pat Williams. Ruth's daughter was there, as were Pat's five children from a previous marriage and his thirteen adopted children. Now, Ruth and Pat make presentations together and are planning a book. Ruth Williams continues her work with Franklin Covey Company. Pat Williams continues as senior executive vice-president of the Orlando Magic. Ruth and Pat believe in magic--the magic of CYA!

Whenever change enters your life, change your attitudes and perceptions; just as Pat Williams did, become a change manager. For instance, if you hear a rumor that your company is going to lay off employees, assume a calm, objective attitude. In today's marketplace, you probably already have your resume in order and can start asking around, giving little hints that you might be available. At work, start by finding out if the rumor is true. Your boss should know. Explain that if the company is downsizing, you'll need to plan your future. Ask about your options: can you transfer to another plant or division; how much severance pay will you receive; how long will you have health insurance? If you will be retained in a different position, you'll need to be flexible and responsible as the new position may require new skills such as using a computer.

Although most of us would rather work for a company that changes than for a stagnant firm, change in a business setting often causes fears about the economic, psychological, and social areas of our lives. As long as it is not our department that is transferred to Siberia, most of us accept changes gracefully. Instead of worrying about how to get along on less money, start planning how you can increase your salary. Instead of worrying that you cannot do a new job, start planning how you can learn the new facets of your job through retraining or having someone show you. Look for the benefits of the new position. Visualize yourself at your new job. Instead of worrying about not being accepted in your job, start planning to be friendly and open. Maintain a positive attitude that is always welcome during times of transition; be patient with the company and yourself.[5]

Current changes in demographics are forcing advertisers to change their focus. For forty years, corporations, marketers, and advertising firms have been aiming products at the 18- to 34-year-old market. Now the demographics reveal baby boomers are getting gray. Representing one-third of the population and one-half of the workforce, boomers are moving into their more affluent years. All these facts make them a force to be reckoned with. Smart advertisers are preparing for the aging of their markets by figuring out what boomers will need for the second half of their lives. Not-so-smart firms that ignore these boomer demographics are in for a tough time.

Major changes—loss of a job, a serious illness, loss of a loved one, a loved one with a debilitating disease—can torpedo your attitude if you do not take steps to keep afloat throughout the crisis. Again, start by realizing that this is a problem you can solve and then devise a plan of action to manage your change. (See chapter 7's discussion of a 360-degree life for more about handling major changes.)

The hard cold facts are that life changes, growth is optional, and only you can decide to grow with change. The happiness you get from life is equal to the attitude you have toward life. List two changes that have brought you happiness:

Happy changes:
1.
2.

Change Is Constant

Futurist John Naisbitt suggests that we must make uncertainty our friend. (Of course, that's probably easier when you're holding a crystal ball.) He believes that as our world becomes more global, we are becoming more individual. For example, more people are choosing to work at home. With a fax machine, modem, computer, and overnight delivery services, anyone can access the world from home. Naisbitt believes that the world will be dominated by person-to-person communication through electronic networks. He says that we are becoming a network of networks, and networks may eventually replace nations. In 1996, 50 million people used the Internet. By the year 2000, as many as 1 billion people will be using it.[6]

Having taken a look at the future, let's look at present and past teen attitudes because—like everything else—they've changed. In 1996, the Horatio Alger Association of Distinguished Americans commissioned a survey of teen attitudes; NFO Research, Inc., asked 938 teens what they wanted. Today's teens responded that they wanted successful careers and families; without families they knew they won't be satisfied. Kids in the 1980s wanted to make money; in the 1970s, they were challenging parents and authority.

The things teens fear also have changed. Today's teens worry about crime, violence, AIDS, drugs, and environmental problems. Kids in the 1980s worried about unemployment and inflation; in the 1970s they feared nuclear disaster and world war.[7]

When we were teens, the four-minute mile was sacrosanct. For hundreds of years, no athlete ever ran a mile faster than four-minutes. Experts pontificated about why humans could never break the four-minute mile: some argued our bone structure was all wrong, others said we lacked sufficient lung power. They all agreed that humans were not created to run faster. Then on May 6, 1954, Roger Bannister ran a mile in 3:58.00. Six weeks later another Brit, John Landy, broke Bannister's record by 2 seconds. Since then, hundreds of runners have broken the four-minute mile. The only thing that changed was the *expectation* that change was possible.

There are three kinds of people in the world: People who make changes happen, people who watch changes happen, and people who stand around saying, "Huh? What happened?"

• Dr. Albert Schweitzer made things happen. Abandoning promising careers as a musician, philosopher, and theologian, Schweitzer built a hospital in Lambarene, Gabon, in 1913. He and his wife devoted their lives to healing the sick, some of whom were lepers. Schweitzer funded the hospital by giving concerts, making recordings, writing books, giving lectures, and winning international prizes, such as the Nobel Peace Prize.

- Janelle Goetcheus is making things happen for the homeless who are ill in Washington, D.C. Goetcheus is a doctor who operates Christ House, a nonprofit ecumenical center where the homeless can recover from illnesses.

- A group of people who make things happen are those in the sandwich generation. Faced with parents who are becoming more dependent on them at the same time their own children still need care, sandwich generation members make daily lifestyle changes to accommodate the demands of both age groups. Somehow, most sandwich generationers also manage to hold down jobs. As a result, an increasing number of employers are providing counseling, senior care, child care, and flextime.

The other two kinds of people—watchers and unconscious—are at the mercy of change. To summarize, we quote Patricia Fripp, who suggests three ways to handle change:

1. Know that change of some kind is inevitable, and that it is often good and healthy.
2. Participate in change. Be eager to make a difference. Don't react from necessity. Act by thinking, planning, and taking action.
3. Believe strongly that you can make a difference. [8]

CYA Journaling Exercise: Explain why you would or would not stop all change if you could.

Global Economy Changes

While reflecting on our growing global economy, futurist John Naisbitt forecast that parts of that economy will get smaller and more efficient. He foresees huge companies breaking up into small companies and cites these statistics to prove his point: Currently, more than 50 percent of U.S. exports are created by companies with fewer than twenty employees. Some small companies are efficient enough to take a new product from idea to market in fewer than ninety days.

Naisbitt also noted that

- America's entrepreneurial economy is its real strength; small companies are responsible for 90 percent of our current economy while Fortune 500 companies account for only about 10 percent.

- In 1972, there were 170 countries and in 1996, 200 countries. By the year 2000, we may have 300 countries. Smaller countries and democracies are increasing. We are heading for a world of 1,000 countries.

- While the global economy is not spawning a collection of global business giants, we are developing a collection of local businesses with increased integration.[9]

Just as automobiles have facilitated suburban living, jets have promoted globalization. Air travel has made places more accessible and more similar. Rosabeth Moss Kanter uses this example: Her son has "gone on outings with peers in Rome, São Paulo, Manila, and Jakarta to experience the local culture. In each city he visited a local shopping mall, where the boys—all wearing Levi's—played video games and ate a McDonald's hamburger." [10]

Kanter notes that people everywhere want to buy the world's best products without leaving home. Consumers are not only demanding higher standards but also pushing for more choices by using their knowledge of products and their access to them. On an individual level, globalization brings with it anxiety and insecurity about the future. Understanding the characteristics of globalization—mobility, simultaneity, bypass, and pluralism—can help defuse this uncertainty.

Mobility. Money, people, and ideas are on the move. Investors can now complete electronic transactions that leave no paper trails. Recruiters choose professionals and managers from an international labor market. American companies report they recruit "locally for unskilled workers, nationally for higher-skill levels, and internationally at the highest levels."

On-line computer services and databases place specialized knowledge from any media at the world's fingertips. American universities are adding to the cross-fertilization of ideas by graduating Ph.D.'s from all over the world. Former University of Michigan President James J. Duderstandt saw a need for graduate schools to design interdisciplinary programs, develop programs required by industry, and encourage internships.[11]

Simultaneity. When manufacturers introduce new products today, their plans include the whole world instead of a single nation. How times have changed—it took twelve years for black and white televisions to become as popular in Japan and Europe as they were in the United States. It took the United States four years to catch up to Europe and Japan in VCR purchases. When CDs arrived, global market penetration evened out in a year!

Bypass. Companies are now able to create work-arounds to do business efficiently. For instance, by using alternatives and new technology, wireless cellular phone systems bypass land-wire systems. In similar fashion, using next-day package delivery services and fax machines bypasses government postal services. And, mail-order companies bypass stores by selling directly to consumers.

Pluralism. An article on the front page of the *Wall Street Journal*, July 5, 1991, illustrated pluralism: Companies in one city, one state, four countries, and two continents were involved in producing and selling one product: "Precision ice hockey equipment is designed in Sweden, financed in Canada, and assembled in Cleveland and Denmark for distribution in North America and Europe, respectively, out of alloys whose molecular structure was researched and patented in Delaware and fabricated in Japan."

Thanks to globalization, the ball is now in the consumers' court. In the bad old days when manufacturers ruled, all cars and phones were black. Today, mobility and alternatives give consumers more choices. One result of easily accessible product information is the emergence of world standards. ISO 9000 is the European process assurance standard, a de facto world minimum standard. The acceptance of the ISO 9000 standard reflects an attitude change that has taken years to evolve. Many countries also use our Malcolm Baldrige National Quality Award criteria to measure the quality of business practices.

In our globalized economy, companies alert to change have begun thinking like customers instead of producers:

- Customers buy services. Instead of producing machines that simply move information, firms are figuring out how to help customers manage that information. For example, today's computers are much more user-friendly than they were just five years ago.

- Customers want resources applied for their benefit; they don't care who owns them. As a result, most cars today contain parts made in various countries because this is the least expensive way to produce cars.

- Customers suffer from invisible mistakes. Now, farsighted managers worry more about invisible mistakes; these include failing to take risks or innovate. Merchandisers are especially prone to getting too comfortable with the status quo, as shown by the demise or merger of well-known chains, such as R.H. Macy, Allied Stores, and Associated Dry Goods.

- Customers think products should be created to meet their needs. After listening to consumers' needs, Ocean Spray became the first U.S. juice producer to use innovative paper packaging from Tetrapak of Sweden.

- Customers want their convenience to come first. Not too long ago, when called about turning on utilities, companies responded, "Oh, sometime on Friday, possibly in the morning, but you never know." Now many companies are turning on utilities during the evening at their customers' convenience.[12]

Treasury Secretary Robert Rubin summarized our economic position at Boston College's Conference on Prospects for a Global Economy: "You all know that we are now in a global economy and there can be no turning back. The Luddites couldn't stop the Industrial Age, and the isolationists cannot stop globalism." (The Luddites smashed labor-saving machinery in the textile industry early in the nineteenth century.)[13]

Walt Disney Company's financial statements are proof that it is part of a changing global economy. This multinational corporation has three profit centers: theme parks and resorts, filmed entertainment, and consumer products. In 1984, theme parks accounted for 75 percent of Disney's income and films, 1 percent. By 1993, theme parks had decreased to 43 percent and films increased to 36 percent.[14] In 1984, Disney's overseas revenues totaled $142 million, or 8.4 percent of total revenues. In 1994, Disney's overseas revenues—excluding Euro Disney—increased to $2.4 billion, or 23 percent of total revenues.[15] Currently, Disney has responded to global economic demands by reducing its annual film production from about 100 to 20. Although the size of Walt Disney Company exaggerates the amount of revenue shifts and sources, these figures illustrate how global markets change. All businesses today must monitor their revenue sources carefully.

Isolationists have been grumbling that the Keebler elves and the Pillsbury dough boy were kidnapped by the British. What's more, a Swiss company owns Carnation, a French company owns Mack Trucks, and a Japanese firm owns CBS Records. These are just a few of the largest companies held by foreign owners. Companies from the United Kingdom are the biggest investors in U.S. firms, followed by Japan, the Netherlands, Canada, and Germany.[16]

Stating that we are part of a global economy is one thing; facing a drastic change in the workplace caused by the resulting competition is quite another. Telephone operator Rose DiMaggio Trela learned this firsthand. She had been looking forward to celebrating her fiftieth anniversary as an operator in October of 1996. Then AT&T announced it would be closing that Peabody, Massachusetts, office a few weeks before her anniversary date.

When Trela began work, a single party line handled the calls for an entire neighborhood, and families gathered around during rare long-distance calls. (For you youngsters, a party line meant that your neighbors could listen in as long as they did not breathe or comment too loudly.) In 1946, Trela answered the phone: "AT&T, this is Rose, how may I help you?" In 1996, she used a number to identify herself to more than 650 callers a day. Trela was one of 40,000 AT&T employees being downsized due to increased automation and technology. Trela had hoped to keep working; she said, "I always loved operating. It was an honor to work for the phone company." Such a gracious attitude!

Losing a job is a change that has four phases:

1. Denial (This can't be; it isn't happening to me.)

2. Resistance (I am angry, depressed, and afraid.)

3. Exploration (How can I turn this negative happening around?)

4. Commitment (Things have to get better.)

In 1996 when Minnesota Mining and Manufacturing announced a plant in Ohio was closing in six to nine months, even the manager's reference to his "team that worked hard and well to respond to the incredible competition in the marketplace" didn't soften the blow. Ironically, in the past year the employees had suggested so many ways to do things better, cheaper, and faster that 3M had recognized them for their teamwork. Now 114 workers were losing their jobs. Some would transfer to Minnesota, a few would retire, and others would look for new jobs. Note how employees' reactions to 3M's closing mirror the four phases:

- We're all out there waking up during the middle of the night. We don't sleep well. We can't eat. Everything's all mixed up.

- The staff has kept us updated that we weren't really turning a profit here for   several years. I guess maybe I should have seen it coming, but really I didn't want to see that. Maybe I was just ignoring it more than anything.

- All I have [to pay off] now is my mortgage. When I started here in '84, I knew that any time those doors could close. I've done every job on that floor; I feel fortunate. I've chosen not to transfer out of state because of my family ties. But I have that opportunity. . . . I have a couple of opportunities to check into other [local] jobs.

- I hate the thought of picking up and moving halfway across the country with just me and my daughter. But I've got eight years invested in this company. I've got to keep that in mind.

- If I am given the opportunity [to relocate] no, I won't go. I'll take one of the options that they offer me and then try to find another job. It bothered me more after I lost my first job after 27 years. . . . This one bothers me [because] I enjoyed working here. This was a good corporation to work for. Maybe people don't see that with the plant shutting down, but I've been treated fairly. There's a very limited marketplace [for people over 50] I'm afraid.

- My wife and I are probably rare in that this is . . . a blessing in disguise. We'll be all right. I am going to go back to school and finish my degree. Maybe in three years the opportunity with 3M will be there. Who knows?[17]

Educational Change

A recent survey of 919 small businesses reflects the need for future workers to choose their high school classes with employability in mind. Arthur Andersen's Enterprise Group found 25 percent of the businesses were worried that a lack of skilled workers would restrict their growth. Currently, manufacturing has rebounded and absorbed the skilled and experienced workers who lost their jobs in the preceding downturn. Today's high school graduates who opt not to go to college often lack the math, communication, computer, and teamwork skills employers require. Students need to take charge of their lives, to set employability goals, and to acquire the skills to fulfill those goals. Otherwise, they will continue to be qualified only for entry-wage jobs and join the glut of service and fast-food workers, whose wages remain lower than in the manufacturing sector.

In 18 months, Lincoln Electric Company rejected more than 20,000 job applicants who did not possess even entry-level skills. This Euclid, Ohio, firm had 200 openings with hourly pay ranging from $8.39 to $20. Lincoln has the reputation of being a good place to work because it ties productivity and profitability together. In 1994, the average factory worker received $19,800 plus a bonus because the company did well, bringing the average total compensation up to $55,614.

Lincoln found that few of the applicants it screened could do high school trigonometry or read technical drawings. Most did not show any aptitude for learning how to operate computer-controlled machines to make welding equipment.

Lincoln has not laid off a worker for 100 years; during 1994-95 it has spent more on recruiting than in the previous ninety-eight years. The search for qualified workers continues; only factory workers with advanced math skills, good communication skills, and computer skills need apply.[18]

Lincoln's experience and Andersen's survey point up the fact that our high school graduates are not prepared for technical jobs; they wind up in retail and fast-food establishments by default rather than by choice. Today's job security no longer resides in the employer; it rests in employees who are employable enough to leave one job and get another. More than ever, today's job market requires planning for a future that will probably include retraining in later years. Employees also need to be alert to what is going on in their industries; investing in additional training is today's job insurance.

In light of America's participation in the global economy, schools should emphasize the study of languages. International marketing personnel find that learning a language improves cultural understanding and business relationships. Recruiters seek out people who speak a second language because it shows the attitude they are looking for: an openness to learn about another culture.

Ambitious students sometimes use their language skills to impress interviewers from prestigious colleges. But lately even knowledge of a second or third language doesn't always produce the desired effect. For instance, in answer to an interviewer's question, "What's so special about you?" a high school senior answered that she was studying Mandarin Chinese. She was a bit crestfallen when the interviewer replied, "Oh, half the population of Harvard speaks Chinese. What else?"[19]

As a nation, however, our students need more encouragement to study languages. People from other countries tell this joke about language skills: What do you call a person who speaks three or more languages? Multilingual. What do you call a person who speaks two languages? Bilingual. What do you call a person who speaks only one language? An American.

Although many large companies have paid all or part of some employees' tuition for relevant course work in the past, today many are taking the next step and requiring further education. Major companies are implementing training programs for employees to improve the quality and consistency of their service. Walt Disney Company, McDonald's, and Consolidated Edison Company are just a few of the firms requiring employees to attend training and education programs.

New York-based Con Edison uses internal telecommunications networks and satellites to send educational programs from its learning center in Queens or from universities to locations throughout its system. An example is an evening program with Rensselaer Polytechnic Institute in which participants can earn master's degrees. Con Edison also provides individualized training through interactive CD-ROMS and self-study computer labs.[20]

Making Changes

While change is swirling around you, why not use it to your advantage and make some changes of your own. The following items are an adaptation of Frederick Hudson, Ph.D.'s life maps that can help you determine your desires, passions, and goals. Write the answer to each of these items in the box that follows. If you are journaling, answer them in your journal where you can go into more detail.

• Change is a cycle that includes periods of stability and periods of movement. So, what are you doing now, standing still or moving? What change do you want or need to make? If you have become stuck—perhaps even taken root—list ways you can break free.

Standing still or moving?
Needed change:

• The six main passions or motivators in our lives are a sense of self, intimacy, achievement, a search for meaning, creativity and play, and compassion. List these motivators in the order they affect your life and explain their effect if you are journaling.

1	4
2	5
3	6

• Fears and bad attitudes can keep you from having the life you desire. List the things that are getting in your way and explain the steps you are going to take to overcome them.

Fears	Steps
1	
2	
3	

- To get where you are going, you will need certain life skills. List them and tell where and how you are going to acquire them.

Life skills:	

- To take charge of your future, you must dream (visualize) and plan. Hudson says, "The dream comes first. Reality chases after the dream, to make it happen." Write down your dream and plan for achieving it.[21]

My dream is	

RISK

The story is told of a man living near the Missouri River. A farmer like his father and grandfather, Claude staunchly believed that God would always take care of him. Life was good; Claude's crops flourished and his animals were healthy.

When the Missouri began rising, Claude thought to himself, God will take care of me. As water covered the first floor, Claude picked up his cat and moved up to the second floor. Watching things he barely recognized swirling past his house, Claude marveled at the river's power. The next day when neighbors rowed up to his bedroom window to take Claude to higher ground, he refused to leave as God would provide.

Water rose over the second story and Claude reluctantly moved into the attic. Volunteers yelled through a small attic window, pleading with him to get into their boat, yet Claude steadfastly refused. The following morning, water began seeping into the attic and Claude wearily moved onto the roof; certain that God would provide, he refused to climb into a neighbor's boat. As water covered the roof, Claude gingerly climbed up the chimney; exhausted by his ordeal, Claude fell asleep and was swept away by the rising water.

While a helicopter crew was recovering his body, Claude was asking St. Peter, "Why didn't God take care of me?" Peter answered, "Well, we sent three boats and a helicopter—what were you waiting for, the U.S. Marines?"

We are all a bunch of clods when it comes to risk taking; none of us is ready to make the leap of faith that proves we know what we are doing. Like Claude, we hope for divine intervention, forgetting that hasn't happened for just under 2,000 years. We doubt our own judgment; we love our safe comfort zones and hate uncertainty—we are human. Our doubts, however, come from lifetime experiences that often are not relevant; if your lemonade stand failed for three summers in a row when you were a child, that does not mean you cannot successfully run your own business today. Whenever you doubt your abilities, remember what playwright Neil Simon said: "If no one ever took risks, Michelangelo would have painted the Sistine floor."

The most important inventor in this century, Thomas Edison, took so many risks he had to write them down. Some of Edison's inventions include the printing telegraph, a modernized typewriter, a practical telephone, the first phonograph, the incandescent bulb for home use, the first power station, motion pictures, a storage battery, a cement mixer, a dictating machine, a mimeograph, and synthetic rubber from the goldenrod plant. Altogether, Edison patented 1,093 inventions.

While attempting to create rubber from the goldenrod plant, Edison conducted 10,000 experiments. We know that because he described each experiment in a notebook. About halfway through these experiments, Edison mentioned conducting 5,000 experiments to a reporter. Bemused, the reporter asked, "Do you mean that you have made 5,000 mistakes?"

"No, no," answered Edison, "we have successfully discovered 5,000 ways it does not work." Remember that answer the next time you are tempted to hit yourself upside the head and shout "Dummy, you made *another* mistake."

Risk is inherent in living; therefore, recognize risk and research it as an essential part of your success. Unless you work for a publicly traded company, you don't have to be right all the time to succeed; research shows that we accept risk when we think there's a fifty-fifty chance for success. Take a minute to figure out your lifetime risk-taking average. List your risks on the following page:

Successful risks:	Unsuccessful risks:

Your average is probably close to 50 percent—far superior to the batting averages of professional baseball players, whose goal is to hit safely one-third of the time. When their averages exceed .300, players receive millions of dollars for their efforts. Not a bad deal for standing at the plate and risking striking out. Like risk taking, being a .300 batter takes a lot of practice. Great baseball players know they will be hitless 65 to 70 percent of the time but they accept that risk as a necessary part of their lives.

A Calculated Leap of Faith

Risk requires us to make a calculated leap of faith. We say *calculated* because the amount of risk planning that we do can reduce the doubts that usually kick in when we consider taking a risk. The Wright brothers were risk-takers with day jobs as bicycle makers and afterhours dreams of flying. Orville and Wilbur were geniuses who hedged their risk by planning their strategy: First, they conducted tests with kites and gliders to learn how to control a plane's motion. Second, they developed a lightweight 12 to 16 horsepower engine and experimented with powered flight.

Finally, at Kitty Hawk, North Carolina, Orville flew their plane for 120 feet in 12 seconds on December 17, 1903. The brothers said it was probably the most emotional time of their lives. This telegram to their father reveals their feelings: "Success. Four flights Thursday morning. All against a twenty-one-mile wind. Started from level with engine power alone. Average speed through air thirty-one miles. Longest fifty-nine seconds. Inform press. Home Christmas." Because the Wright brothers planned their risk taking so well, the world changed dramatically. Write down the risks you would like to take in the future on the following page.

```
┌─────────────────────────────────────────────────────────┐
│ Future risks                                              │
│                                                           │
│                                                           │
│                                                           │
│                                                           │
│                                                           │
└─────────────────────────────────────────────────────────┘
```

Sometimes FEAR becomes an acronym for **F**inding **E**very **A**cceptable **R**eason not to do something. Before she retired, Mother Teresa was a risk taker who didn't look for every acceptable reason not to nurse the sick and dying. By the time she retired, Mother Teresa had opened more than 500 missions throughout the world, all funded by donations. At a children's mission in New Delhi's worst slum, 141 children ranged in age from newborns to about 10. That mission had a staff of 13 nuns and 56 young women who were helpers and nursemaids; its budget was less than $6,000 a month.

How many of us would choose to spend the rest of our lives as she did—even for a Nobel Peace Prize in 1979? Hunched over at eighty-six—only 4 feet, 10 inches tall—would we walk through the streets of India, collecting unwanted babies and looking for the sick and dying? My (DM) attitude is no, I wouldn't do this, but thank God somebody does it. Her attitude is no, not somebody—I am grateful to do this. For years Mother Teresa risked her own health and well-being to serve the children and the dying. When media members stuck microphones before her deeply lined face, her eyes twinkled as she risked international condemnation for the staunch moral values she proclaimed. While the politically correct risked their values, Mother Teresa took political risks.

Christine Brennan downplays the risk she took in choosing her career. Brennan is an international sports reporter for the *Washington Post,* a commentator for National Public Radio, and a guest on CNN and ESPN. She reminisced about her childhood: "I cannot stress how much my childhood of being a sports fan helped me. I never lacked for confidence. I'm six feet tall. I always kept up with other kids. I was beating boys up to a certain age." Despite the lack of female role models in the late 1970s, Brennan took a risk and turned her love of sports into her profession.

After interning at the *Toledo Blade,* Brennan went to the *Miami Herald,* where she covered the Miami Dolphins; part of her job was conducting postgame interviews in the locker room. Other than some "whoops and hollers," her first interview was uneventful. Since then she has interviewed players in roughly 600 men's locker rooms without any serious problems.

In 1985, when Brennan became the first woman to cover the Washington Redskins while working for the *Washington Post,* the local press made her the story. Fortunately, times have changed. Brennan estimates that today well over 1,000 women are covering sports.[22]

You Stumble Only if You Are Moving

Admittedly, some risks end in disaster. In the 1980s, the Coca-Cola Company enjoyed a larger market share than PepsiCo until the Pepsi Challenge. In that series of blind taste tests, people chose Pepsi consistently. When Coke lost its market share, management instructed Sergio Zyman to reverse its decline. Zyman knew that people taking part in the Pepsi Challenge were drinking room temperature Pepsi that was sweeter than Coke. So he produced a sweeter formula and called it New Coke. After less than three months, New Coke was replaced by old Coke, renamed Classic Coke. A year later Zyman left Coca-Cola and started an advertising business with this motto: "Think unconventionally, take risks." After seeking Zyman's advice recently, Coca-Cola CEO Roberto Goizueta admitted that "we became uncompetitive by not being tolerant of mistakes. You stumble only if you're moving." That last sentence has right attitude stamped all over it!

More Risk Takers. Ralph Burnet took a risk three decades ago when he joined a real estate firm to make money during the slow summer months at his ski shop. The next year he sold the ski shop and entered real estate full time.

Burnet took another risk when he began his own firm with $18,000 during the 1973 recession and oil embargo, and in an extremely tight mortgage lending market. To drum up business, Burnet borrowed $250,000 for a billboard campaign that launched his company.

Today Burnet Realty is the third largest real estate broker in the country; its 2,000 agents sell more than $6 billion worth of homes in southern Minnesota, western Wisconsin, and Chicago. Burnet Financial Group includes a mortgage lending firm, a title company, insurance company, and relocation division. Believing in corporate responsibility, the group donates 5 percent of its pretax income to charity.

Burnet's business philosophy includes taking risks. He says, "So many companies are [risk adverse] stifling the greatest gift their employees have—their creativity. We try new things here every month. And if we try ten of them and six work, I think that's great."

"And so what if you try something and don't like it?" Burnet adds. "Don't admonish yourself. In fact, pat yourself on the back for trying something new. You've grown. You sure don't want to be standing around with a walker someday saying, 'Gee, I didn't like what I was doing.' Because you don't get a second chance."[23]

When Iris Harrel asked a friend to teach her carpentry, she probably did not realize what a risk she was taking. After discovering her talent for woodworking, she took classes and applied for jobs in Texas. In the early '80s Harrel faced open discrimination; contractors refused to take a chance that subcontractors would not take a woman seriously. Harrel moved to California, opened her own remodeling business, and employs eighteen. Her advice to other risk-takers: Stick to your guns because little has changed.

Garage Risk Takers. Business books are rife with stories of entrepreneurs who started well-known businesses in their garages:

- Before the orchards in Santa Clara County were morphed into the Silicon Valley, William Hewlett and David Packard started out in a Palo Alto, California, garage. From their initial $538 investment in 1939, they built a company that provides quality high-tech products, computer products, electronic test equipment, medical electronic equipment, analytical instruments, and electronic components. Today, Hewlett-Packard Company is as well-known for its attitude of employee empowerment as for its products.

- In 1962 trumpeter Herb Alpert and Jerry Moss started A&M Records in Alpert's garage; they hoped to put out a great product, treat people fairly, and have fun. While Alpert and the Tijuana Brass were on the road promoting records, Moss was on the phone taking orders. In 1992 they sold the company to PolyGram for about $450 million. Alpert is especially proud of the three Christmas records A&M produced with proceeds totaling more than $43 million benefiting the International Special Olympics.

Sez Who? Sometimes, you can't listen to naysayers, you just have to take a risk. Despite the flunking grade Fred Smith received on his paper that described starting a next-day air express company, he took a risk. Although his college professor derided the very idea, Smith was sure he was on to something. During some very lean years, he persevered and proved himself a person of vision. In 1995 Federal Express revenues reached $9.4 billion; the firm had 119,000 workers in 210 countries.

Hyrum and Gail Smith began Franklin Quest Company in their basement in 1983. Franklin trains people to manage their time and provides Franklin Day Planners® that clients use to become better organized. In 1996, Franklin's profits totaled $450 million.

Remember, you have a fifty-fifty chance of success—the odds are even better if you plan well; take that risk. We discuss the SMART planning strategy in chapter 4.

CYA Journaling Exercise: Write about one of the risks you have taken, explaining why you were or were not successful.

RESPONSIBILITY

A sense of responsibility is the basic characteristic required to maintain the right attitude for success and excellence. Responsibility is nothing more than being able to respond to people, places, and things; it is respond ability.

Corporate Responsibility

While speaking about corporate responsibility, former Labor Secretary Robert Reich highlighted the growing gap between rich and poor in the United States. Since 1979, the earnings of richest fifth have increased by 25 percent; the poorest fifth has taken a 10 percent cut in earnings. Reich cited these reasons for the gap: differences in education and training, weak labor unions, and a low minimum wage (which has since increased). He also blamed the breakdown of a social compact that once made it unseemly for a company to prosper while its workers withered. Reich urged business leaders to treat employees like assets to be nurtured rather than expenses to be cut: "It is possible to maximize shareholder returns and also invest in the workforce. In fact, it may be the only way. What is the one unique source of competitive strength over the long term? It is your workers."[24]

As an example of corporate responsibility to employees, Con Edison has reduced its workforce by 20 percent over the past ten years without resorting to layoffs. The power company has moved people from phased-out positions to other areas where they were needed. By holding job fairs, Con Edison helps employees learn about open positions in other departments; interested employees can arrange interviews right there. More than 200 power plant employees have found jobs in new areas and obtained necessary retraining.[25]

Personal Responsibility

As an individual, you have many responsibilities—they are as common as brushing your teeth, as awesome as rearing your child, as instinctive as eating and drinking, and as creative as solving a problem. You are responsible for your own attitudes. When everything is going well, most of us can accept this responsibility. When things bottom out, however, we also become responsible for fighting off negativity, for not blaming others, for pulling ourselves together, and learning from experience. In other words, for getting over it. The following points summarize our responsibilities:

- It's not what happens to you that determines your success or failure, it's how you respond that counts.

- Things work out best for the people who make the best of the way things work out.

- How you perceive your world is the world you will live in. You can be a victim, volunteer, or victor.

- Unless you embrace and manage change, it will enslave you.

- Winners anticipate and respond to events effectively. Everybody else reacts according to their emotional mood at the time.

- Rights without responsibilities are called entitlements. Nothing in life comes without accountability. Like rings on a tree, we are the sum total of our actions.

- Our greatest limitations are those we place on ourselves.

- You make your own circumstances; circumstances don't make you.

- You are your own scriptwriter, and the play is never finished, no matter what your age, position, or place in life.[26]

One person who accepts personal responsibility is my (DM) barber, Dick Dietsch who has been cutting hair for almost 37 years. Dietsch embraces and relishes being responsible for his hair cutting art, his wife, his family, and his properties. He has a good time—especially when taking care of his customers. It wasn't always that way. When Dietsch first started cutting hair, he was afraid to talk to his customers. He finally decided it was his responsibility to make them feel at home.

Dietsch responds to people and situations responsibly. Whenever he doesn't know how to do something, he researches the best way. For instance, in 1991, he and his wife, Sue, remodeled their Devil's Lake, Michigan, cottage. Dietsch designed, speced, and contracted out any work they could not do. The Dietsches did about 95 percent themselves; it was the only responsible way. Dietsch responds the same way to his family and friends. (And he still charges only $9.00 for a responsible barber's haircut.)

To help yourself truly relish responsibility, fill in the responsibilities list in figure 1 on the following page. Write down the names of all the people (including yourself), jobs, and other personal or professional situations for which you have a responsibility. Remember that others can and do share some of the responsibility for various items on your list.

Next, fill in the simple time log on the right side of the list showing how much time you currently spend on your responsibilities. Finally, try not to be intimidated by the list; it helps to work on this list at various times. Fill it out now and in about six months, and every six months after that to increase your awareness of each responsibility.

Most of us run into responsible people every day without realizing it. For example, Mary was my (DM) waitress at the Talk of the Town restaurant in Marshall, Michigan. The first impression Mary makes is that she definitely knows what she is doing—that is, putting the customer first. Mary mentioned that even though she was scheduled to start work at 9 A.M. the next day, she scheduled herself for 7 A.M. because several of the waitresses would be on vacation. Tomorrow's job required more than a scheduled response from her. Many of us know to the second how long it will take to do something or drive somewhere, but we still hedge and give only a half-hearted response. Not Mary! Responsibility could be her middle name.

Three well-known responsible people are Dave Thomas, Heather Whitestone, and Jacques Cousteau—each assumed responsibility for a personal crusade.

R. David Thomas feels responsible for children without loving families. Thomas was born out of wedlock and adopted as an infant. In addition to founding Wendy's International, he started the Dave Thomas Foundation for Adoption to facilitate the adoption process.

Besides speaking to social and civic groups to encourage adoption, Thomas has testified before congressional committees to change laws such as the 1980 Family Reunification and Preservation Act. Thomas believes social agencies should emphasize placing children in loving homes rather than trying to reunite families that exist in name only—families where abuse and torture take place.

Figure 1 Responsibilities

	Hours per week

Former Miss America Heather Whitestone has a severe hearing impairment for which she has accepted responsibility. Even though she had to practice for six years to learn to pronounce her last name correctly, she didn't give up. During her frequent speeches, Whitestone stresses the importance of screening infants for possible hearing losses because the first year of life is most important in developing language skills. Whitestone's take-responsibility-for-yourself attitude is evident in her five-point approach to life: have a positive attitude, have a dream, be willing to work, face your problems, and have a support team.

Jacques Cousteau, who died in the summer of 1997, was a self-appointed guardian of the oceans and everything in them. Through Cousteau's films and television specials, people have become more aware of the oceans' importance. In addition to his efforts to slow the degradation of the oceans, Cousteau wasn't shy about speaking out when the French government resumed nuclear tests in the Pacific. That very day, Cousteau issued a protest in France, spoke to the world press for ten minutes, and wrote an article for the *New York Times* syndicate.

Presently divers cannot dive deeper than 1,800 feet; even so, Cousteau was still looking for a way; he thought there might be cures for diseases at lower levels. "We explore not for pleasure, but perhaps to save life. . . . At the very bottom of the ocean, life is blossoming." Only death at at age eighty-six could extinguish his responsible attitude.

CYA Journaling Exercise: Describe how someone you know has taken personal responsibility.

We love to take responsibility for our generosity, graciousness, kindness, or charity. We're not so ready to take responsibility for our anger; when we can tell ourselves, she makes me so mad, we obviously aren't responsible. Our mistakes also remain unclaimed—the devil made me do it. Keep in mind that no one—except maybe Mom and the tax collector—can make you do anything. When you make an angry response, you're allowing yourself to lose it. If you make a mistake, it was your choice.

When you become upset, choose a responsible response by following these steps suggested by Ron and Mary Hulnick:

1. Admit that you are upset. Nothing is funnier than a red-faced person shouting, "I'm not angry." Give yourself permission to feel upset.

2. Accept your feelings. Despite all the psycho babble, having feelings does not make you a wuss or a stereotyped woman.

3.   Take responsibility for your feelings. Any feelings floating around inside you are all yours. No one makes you feel that way—you choose those.

4.   Replace inner upset with inner loving. Anger can stem from a bruised ego; its OK to admit that you hurt, as long as you follow that admission with self-love.

5.   Make a constructive response. A caring, positive response can turn you from an angry individual to a responsible, confident mench.[27]

CYA Journaling Exercise: How do you express anger? How could this expression be improved?

GET OVER IT AND GET ON WITH LIFE

Tired of the same old, same old? Me (TB) too. In fact, I planned to write a book about using attitude ladders to get out of life's ruts until David and I decided to collaborate on this book. Our lives develop ruts when we do the same things the same way; some ruts are innocuous, such as driving the same old way to work or sleeping on the same side of the bed.

Other ruts create a freeze-frame situation; people stop moving and huddle in bottom of their ruts where they have no control over their own lives. The walls of their ruts become not only jailers but also protection from additional pain. In *When All You've Ever Wanted Isn't Enough*, Harold Kushner says it so well: "We can endure much more than we think we can; all human experience testifies to that. All we need to do is learn not to be afraid of pain. Grit your teeth and let it hurt. Don't deny it, don't be overwhelmed by it. It will not last forever. One day, the pain will be gone and you will still be there."[28] If you prefer a musical message, listen to Eagles Don Henley and Glenn Frey's "Get Over It."

We're talking to you if you fall into one of these categories:

- Those thousands of dejected applicants not accepted by their first choice colleges. (In 1996, 16,300 applied for 1,620 freshman slots at Harvard.) Despite what you think, your life is not ruined. Stop moping; find another college and get on with your life.[29]

- Those drowning in grief and abandonment due to the death of a spouse, child, or other loved one. Find a grief counselor or group, talk to others who are grieving, and look forward, not backward.

- Those with chronic drug or alcohol problems they blame on bad genes. Get counseling, join a group, get over it.

- Those with physical injuries or illnesses that make each day a challenge. Get on with your life as Stephen Hawking and Christopher Reeve have.

- Those with post-traumatic stress disorder from war or other inhumane trauma. Get help; even though PTSD lasts a lifetime, it isn't a life sentence—you can handle the effects and get on with your life.

- Those downsized after giving up everything for their jobs. Now that you are a lot smarter, deep-six the bitterness and blame—get over it.

- Those facing a change in lifestyle because of a physical problem. You can get on with your life.

We've lived too long and been hurt too often to imply you can solve your problems instantly by joining a group, reading a book, or seeing a counselor. To overcome the pain, you need to recognize that climbing out of life's ruts requires a can-do attitude; keep climbing and after a while you'll be looking over the top of your rut and seeing blue sky and a future. Then, keep looking to that future and stop looking backward. Because ruts are self-built, they can be self-filled.

Remember that wherever two pieces of steel are welded together, the welds become stronger than the individual pieces. As Ernest Hemingway wrote in *A Farewell to Arms*, "The world breaks everyone and afterward, some are strong at the broken places." The strong ones have climbed out of their ruts; their pain no longer rules their lives.

Following his heart attack at 42, Dr. Robert Eliot took a good look at his life and developed these rules to live by: First, don't sweat the small stuff; and, second, it's all small stuff unless it's worth dying for. Now, that's a get-over-it attitude!

People Who Have Gotten on with Life

Buck Macpherson, my wife, saw her five-year-old son struck by a speeding car in front of his school. Buck administered CPR, but J.J. died. Two years later, her husband was severely burned when another truck collided with his steel truck. Jim survived for nine days and died. Three weeks after that, Buck's father died of cancer; while not unexpected, it was too soon. Buck says that although she'll never forget, she needed to move on with her life.

Kirby Puckett, a 35-year-old Minnesota Twins center fielder and power hitter, was forced to retire in 1996 when diagnosed with glaucoma. One of baseball's most beloved players, Puckett commented: "Baseball has been a great part of my life. Now I have to close this chapter and go on with part two of my life." Puckett's statement proved that he is just as classy a life player as he is a baseball player.

Helen Keller could neither see, hear, nor speak as a child, but never let these deficits affect her interest in life, or understanding of people. She commented: "The hands of those I meet are dumbly eloquent to me. I have met people so empty of joy that when I clasped their frosty fingertips it seemed as if I were shaking hands with a northeast storm. Others there are whose hands have sunbeams in them, so that their grasp warms my heart. It may be only the clinging touch of a child's hand, but there is as much potential sunshine in it for me as there is in a loving glance for others."

Alexandre Dumas, a nineteenth-century story teller, overcame poverty, lack of education, censorship, and bigotry. When taunted about the black blood in his veins, Dumas replied: "Yes, of course. My father was a mulatto, my grandfather was a Negro, and my great-grandfather was an ape. You see, sir, my family began where yours left off."[30]

Carla McGhee, a professional basketball player, overcame an auto accident in October of 1987 that shattered all but two of the bones in her face, broke her hip, tore up her right arm, and punctured her vocal cords. Specialists said she would be lucky to walk without a limp; the following September, she reported for University of Tennessee basketball practice. After graduation, she played in Europe for four years and for the 1996 U.S. Olympic team. That team's coach, Tara VanDerveer, commented: "You wouldn't wish it on anyone, but the accident in a lot of ways has shaped her personality in a very positive way. She appreciates and makes the most of the time she has with people."[31]

Samuel L. Jackson admits that he has acted in films and on stage while addicted to drugs. He commented that seven years ago "I had to take charge of my life and stop throwing it away or die. I did that and the results have been phenomenal. A lot of people go through the same thing and don't come out the other side. I did. . . . The important thing for me to remember is that I'm still that person and I still have the potential to be that destructive to myself and the people around me. I have to remember one day at a time that I'm not that person. It sounds corny, but that's what it is."[32]

Julius Ancer was captured by the Germans as a young Jewish soldier in the Polish army and survived the death camps. After the war he and his wife boarded a ship for America; the ship sank and they lost everything but the clothes they were wearing. After working a number of minimum-wage jobs due to his minimal command of English, Ancer became a successful architect. Soon after he retired, his wife died. Before he could mourn her, a car ran a stop sign and hit Ancer. He celebrated his 78th birthday by swimming 78 lengths in his swimming pool. Adversity may slow him down a bit, but nothing stops Julius Ancer.[33]

The Bayliss Family paid their dues in radio in the Midwest. Then John and Alice Bayliss bought two stations in Southern California in 1981. Four years later, their dreams were falling into place when an unlicensed driver crossed the median on Interstate 5 and hit the Bayliss car head-on. Alice sustained severe head injuries that required years of recovery. John's internal injuries proved fatal. Twelve years later, Alice owns and operates KSMA-AM and KSNI-FM in Santa Maria. Her sons, John, Jim, and Joe are board members; in addition to supporting each other, they pay tribute to John Sr. each October. During a major media convention in New York City, the John Bayliss Broadcast Foundation sponsors a dinner and auction to raise money for college scholarships for future broadcasters. Alice says simply, "None of this would have happened without the strength of my three sons."

Having a responsible attitude can be excruciatingly difficult. Take for example, Bobby Powers, who instigated an attack on a black man in Boston's City Hall Plaza in the '70s. Powers and over a hundred whites were leaving an anti-busing meeting when he saw a black man in a business suit. Ted Landsmark was on his way to a contractors' meeting. Someone with Powers viciously jabbed at Landsmark with an American flag staff. The mob broke his nose and hit his face. The scene was captured in a photo that won the 1976 Pulitzer Prize.

Two decades later, Powers met with Landsmark to apologize. Powers carried guilt not only for Landsmark's injuries but also for the shame that scene cast on Boston. He said it felt like a "burlap T-shirt" he couldn't remove. Landsmark commented: "If Bobby's visit has any meaning to me, it's that change occurs over 20 years and reconciliation is possible."

Bobby Powers' reference to his burlap T-shirt shows the power of imagination. Chapter 3 takes a look at imagination as a wellspring of innovation and integrity.

ENDNOTES

1. Roger von Oech, *A Kick in the Seat of the Pants* (New York: Harper & Row, 1986), p. 125.
2. Liz Doup, "Buddhist Sect Opens Retreat to Serve Members Around Globe," *Columbus Dispatch*, May 25, 1996, p. 9J.
3. David Mahoney, *Confessions of a Street-Smart Manager* (New York: Simon & Schuster, 1988), p. 23.
4. Elwood Chapman, *Attitude: Your Most Priceless Possession* (Los Altos, CA: Crisp Publications, 1990), p. 72.
5. Adapted from Marian Thomas, *A New Attitude* (Shawnee Mission, KS: National Press Publications, 1991), pp. 39–45.
6. John Naisbitt, Speech at the Training '96 Conference and Expo, Atlanta, Georgia, January 29–31, 1996.
7. Diane Hales, "How Teenagers See Things," *Parade*, August 18, 1996, pp. 4–5.
8. Patricia Fripp, *Get What You Want* (Mansfield, OH: Bookcrafters, 1996), p. 25.
9. Naisbitt, Speech at the Training '96 Conference and Expo.
10. Rosabeth Moss Kanter, *World Class: Thriving Locally in the Global Economy* (New York: Simon & Schuster, 1995), p. 40.
11. "Duderstadt Urges New Role for Nation's Graduate Schools," *Michigan Today*, June 1996, p. 5.
12. Kanter, *World Class*, p. 41–51.
13. "Labor Secretary: Layoffs Falling Out of Favor," *Columbus Dispatch*, June 4, 1996, p. 2D.
14. Maggie Mahar, "Not So Magic Kingdom," *Baron's*, June 20, 1994, pp. 29–33.
15. Walt Disney Company, 1994 Annual Report, p. 21.
16. Adapted from "The 100 Largest Foreign Investments in the U.S.," *Forbes*, July 18, 1994, pp. 266–70.
17. Jim Massie, "The Downside," *Columbus Dispatch*, February 25, 1996, p. I1–2.
18. "Firms Reject Many to Hire the Skilled,"*Toledo Blade*, September 18, 1995, p. 25.
19. Bruce Weber, *New York Times Magazine*, April 28, 1996, p. 49.
20. Consolidated Edison Company of New York, Inc., 1996 Annual Report, p. 13.
21. Melanie Berger, "How to Remap Your Life," *Ladies' Home Journal* 109 (August 1992), p. 62.
22. Jim Massie, "Brennan Hopes to be an Inspiration to Youths," *Columbus Dispatch*, February 22, 1996, p. C2.
23. Tina Lassen, "Sold on Risk Taking,"*World Traveler*, March 1996, p. 45–50.
24. "Labor Secretary," *Columbus Dispatch*, June 4, 1996.
25. Consolidated Edison, p. 13.
26. Denis Waitley, *Time to Win* (Salt Lake City: Franklin Quest Co., 1993), np.
27. Ron and Mary Hulnick, "Nobody's Making You Mad but Yourself," *Your Personal Best*, January 1991, p. 7.
28. Harold Kushner, *When All You've Ever Wanted Isn't Enough: The Search for a Life that Matters* (New York: Simon & Schuster, 1986).
29. Weber, "Inside the Meritocracy Machine," p. 44.
30. Victoria Foote-Greenwell, "Alexandre Dumas: One for All,"*Smithsonian*, July, 1996, p. 112.
31. Bonnie DeSimone, "McGhee's Been One to Land on Her Feet," *Chicago Tribune*, July 10, 1996.
32. Frank Gabrenya, "Turning Points," *Columbus Dispatch*, July 21, 1996, 1–2G.
33. Harvey Mackay, "Winners Know: A Beating Isn't Necessarily a Defeat," *Detroit Free Press*.

3

Igniting Imagination, Innovation, and Integrity

Learn to listen. Opportunity sometimes knocks very softly.
H. Jackson Brown, Jr.

In the late 1890s when a Protestant bishop visited a small religious college, the college president asked him to stay for dinner. At the end of the meal, the mellow bishop confided that he was sure the millennium was coming; it was the end of the nineteenth century and everything that could or would be invented had been.

For a moment, the college president—who doubled as a physics and chemistry professor—hesitated for he realized the religious significance of the millennium. Then he quietly disagreed, pointing out that many things were still to be created. The bishop was not pleased; color rose to his face as he demanded to know just what had not been invented. The president answered he was certain that within fifty years men would be able to fly.

"Nonsense!" said Bishop Milton Wright, "only angels are intended to fly."

Later, his sons Orville and Wilbur proved him wrong.[1]

With marvelous resourcefulness like that of Orville and Wilbur Wright, our minds see what could or should be. Imagination is our creative ability to see mental images of something real or not yet real. Imagination causes ophthalmologists to spend their vacations in less-developed countries enabling the blind to see. Imagination causes caring retirees to volunteer to tutor reading and math students. Imagination causes college students to build houses with Habitat for Humanity.

A life-changing gift, imagination allows us to arise and don our better selves; the sky has no limits and the rainbow no end. Imagination comes as standard equipment from a merciful God; however, some people allow it to rust out from disuse. When we do not use imagination, we lose our childlike ability to see the technicolor world of what could be, dooming ourselves to lives of black and white reality.

Imagination is the basis of innovation and integrity; similarly, visualization and listening foster innovative thinking. By using visualization, we can create all the innovative changes we desire in our lives. By listening closely, we can learn about the life of another person. By imagining something entirely different than what is, we can innovate.

We develop integrity by allowing our imaginations to show us how to put our beliefs into action. This gift of seeing what could be is accompanied by a willingness to work or sacrifice for a better world. Without this vision, no one would take a stand for people or causes that seem impossible.

YOU MAY HAVE A WRONG ATTITUDE IF . . .

- Your random acts of kindness are all tax deductible.

- Your idea of saving money is surfing the Internet on company time.

- You decided finding a better way to do your job is not your job.

- You'll never start your own businesses—there's no one to blame when it fails.

- You sell Avon to co-workers during office hours so you all have time to go out for lunch.

- Your job is who you are, end of story.

- You enter the room and the fireplace logs hiss.

IMAGINATION

Former Chief of Staff General Colin Powell once commanded 75,000 troops along the Berlin Wall that separated East and West Germany. He commented, "In spite of all the armies and the weapons we had, it was not the armies that brought down the Berlin Wall; it was simply the idea.

When the ideas and the minds and hearts of men changed, that's when the wall came down. Ideas are more powerful than armies."[2] That's a powerful thought—if the German people had not imagined that the wall could fall, Germany would not be united today.

For years pilots have used airplane simulators to practice flying; during their training, astronauts also use simulators to drill and rehearse so that their actions become second nature. As a result of such practicing, an Apollo moon walker commented, "It was as if I had been here before, exhilarating, but not frightening nor unfamiliar."[3]

More recently, virtual reality enables people in wheelchairs to practice manipulating them in a computer-controlled environment where mistakes aren't painful. The lessons they learn, however, are real enough to fool their imaginations because human nervous systems cannot tell the difference between something experienced and something vividly imagined. That's why virtual reality is becoming a useful tool in training employees and educating students. Isn't it amazing that it has taken us this long to duplicate imagination? At last we are beginning to recognize its potential. Write down a change in the world that you can imagine:

```
┌─────────────────────────────────────────────────────────┐
│                                                         │
│                                                         │
│                                                         │
│                                                         │
│                                                         │
│                                                         │
└─────────────────────────────────────────────────────────┘
```

Visualizing

According to the Talmud, we see things as we are, not as they are. That's where imagination comes in; we can imagine our futures as we want them to be. What do you see in your future?

The lives of Carol Burnett, Nelson Mandela, Phil Jackson, and Peter Vidmar demonstrate the power of visualizing. Despite a difficult home life, Carol Burnett envisioned such a successful acting career that she even heard the applause. While being interviewed by James Lipton, host of *Inside the Actors Studio*, Burnett discussed growing up in an old apartment house in Hollywood. She and her grandmother lived in a cluttered room that served as kitchen, bath, bedroom, and living room. Her family was on relief and her alcoholic parents were divorced; her mother lived down the hall. Despite her environment, as a child Burnett knew she wanted to be an actor, so much so that she could see herself acting. Burnett warned, "If you see something—I don't mean if you wish for it or pray for it—if you *see* it, be careful; you're going to get it. If you visualize it, it's already there."[4]

Write down a change you can see in your life:

```
┌─────────────────────────────────────────────────┐
│                                                   │
│                                                   │
│                                                   │
└─────────────────────────────────────────────────┘
```

While imprisoned on South Africa's Robben Island—similar to our Alcatraz—Nelson Mandela nurtured his vision of freedom. The 46-year-old politician was living in a cell three paces long and six-feet wide. He was in the lowest group of prisoners and received the fewest privileges. Every six months he was allowed to see only one visitor, to write one letter, and to receive one letter. Faced with a life sentence for conspiracy to overthrow the government, some people might have felt hopeless, but not Mandela. His autobiography recounted this vision of the future that kept him going:

> I never seriously considered the possibility that I would not emerge from prison one day. I never thought that a life sentence truly meant life and that I would die behind bars. Perhaps, I was denying this prospect because it was too unpleasant to contemplate. But I always knew that some day I would once again feel the grass under my feet and walk in the sunshine as a free man.
>
> I am fundamentally an optimist. Whether that comes from nature or nurture, I cannot say. Part of being optimistic is keeping one's head pointed toward the sun, one's feet moving forward. There were many dark moments when my faith in humanity was sorely tested, but I could not give myself up to despair.[5]
>
> I thought continually of the day when I would walk free. Over and over, I fantasized about what I would like to do.[6]

After twenty-seven years in prison, Mandela strode out in 1990, still standing tall, still completely committed to his vision of multiracial democracy in South Africa.

Swifter, Higher, Stronger.

Long before the Chicago Bulls won the 1997 NBA championship, Coach Phil Jackson taught his players to visualize championship basketball. Jackson introduced visualization and meditation to his team when he became head coach. Coach Jackson practices visualization for 45 minutes with his team before each game. During this time he calls up situations that might happen so everyone is ready if they do occur. The first time the Bulls practiced meditation, Michael Jordan thought Jackson was joking. Jordan opened an eye to see if the other players were actually meditating. Much to Jordan's surprise, many of them were.

Echoing Phil Jackson, psychologist and triathlete Jacqui Lewis suggests: "Create your own imaginary situation (a race, a tournament, a competition) and rehearse it over and over until you can think of anxiety-producing situations without feeling any accompanying anxiety." Before he won his ninth gold medal, four-time Olympian Carl Lewis summed up how he planned to win it: "I have to be better than myself, mentally." That's mind over muscles.[7] Golfing great Jack Nicklaus believes half of a great shot is visualizing its success. Before every swing, Nicklaus imagines the ball's perfect flight.[8]

I (TB) have spoken to U.S. Olympic teams about the role that visualization plays in the athletes' success. In gymnastics, for example, coaches videotape an athlete's performances many times. Then they splice together a perfect routine for each athlete to watch over and over; later the Olympians have no trouble visualizing themselves performing their routines perfectly.

My friend, Peter Vidmar, is now a motivational speaker; in 1984 he was captain of the U.S. gymnastics team at the Olympic games in Los Angeles. I asked Vidmar how he used mental imagery. He explained that he visualized his routine from mounting the pommel horse to flying off and spiking. (Spiking is the last movement, where the gymnast lands on both feet with arms raised.) Every time, Vidmar would visualize doing his routine perfectly, hear the crowd roar, and look at the judges—10, 10, 10, 10, 10. And that's how he won the gold medal—18 months of constant preparation and visualization. List three sports that you enjoy that could be improved through your visualization:

For each example of someone using imagination successfully, there are thousands who have given up completely on themselves. Norman Vincent Peale told the story of walking through Kowloon in Hong Kong. When he came to a tattoo studio, Peale stopped to look at the various samples and was astonished to see *Born to Lose*. Curiosity took him into the small shop where he asked the Chinese tattoo artist if anyone actually chose that negative statement. The artist nodded. Peale shook his head and wondered aloud why anyone in his right mind would do that. The artist tapped his forehead and said that before it was tattooed on the body, *Born to Lose* was tattooed on the mind.[9]

Ready to use your own imagination? Then, listen up. That's right, listening sounds pretty simple but like visualizing, listening takes practice;

it is not something we do naturally as most of us would rather be talking. Visualizing emphasizes what you can become; listening helps you understand someone else's point of view. Imagine that right attitude!

CYA Journaling Exercise: After you decide what you want to visualize, write down a description of how you will see yourself. Add notes later about how your visualization is going.

Listening

As this story illustrates, good listening is more than just hearing words; expectations are all important: A twenty-something driver squealed his candy-apple red 3000 GT convertible around a curve on a narrow country road. Cruising along under a warm sun in his gleaming babe-mobile, he was ready for action. Something was going to happen; he could feel it in his shoulders. As a bright blue Corvette convertible approached, its driver's long blond hair whipped in the breeze. A definite babe alert! But why was she waving her long, tanned arm next to the car? Probably just a new pick-up tactic, he thought. Both drivers slowed slightly as they approached each other; the other driver kept motioning frantically and yelled "Pig!" Frowning, the young man thought why you feminist witch and put the pedal to the metal despite an oncoming curve. By the time he squealed around the curve, he had thought of several appropriate, though unprintable, answers to the woman's name calling. Just then, he saw a very large pig reclining in the road.

Not only do we see things as we are, we hear them as we are. The young driver's expectations in the preceding story affected his listening ability—he heard a word with several meanings and chose the wrong one. Listening is making a conscious effort to hear—to really pay attention to what someone else is saying. Listening is using your imagination to learn where that person is coming from. One of the differences between an order taker and a professional salesperson is that a salesperson listens to find out exactly what each customer wants. Once a customer begins considering a purchase, a true salesperson waits. That's because the opposite of talking isn't listening; its keeping still and waiting, which is often the key to making a sale. By not talking while the customer is considering a purchase, the salesperson does not derail that person's train of thought.

The rest of us should imitate good salespeople by really listening to others and allowing them to finish before reversing roles during a conversation. Wait to respond; this indicates that you have been listening and need a moment to collect your thoughts. An instantaneous response indicates that you have been planning your own comments and stopped listening to what the other person was saying minutes ago.

While talking to another person, we instinctively watch that person for listening attitudes indicating how much attention the other person is paying. These attitudes include:

- Finding nobody home: "Huh? You say something?"

- Rehearsing the monologue: "Well, of course, I would never tell you what to do, but . . . "

- Playing conversational ping-pong: "You talk, then I'll talk, then you talk . . ."

- Listening to W I I-FM: "What's in it for me?"

- Pretending to listen: "Oh, yes, that's just so interesting."

- Talking head: "And then, I . . . And then, I . . . And then, I . . ."

Practice, practice, practice is the secret to good listening. Practice these listening skills:

1.   Establish rapport by standing tall, establishing eye contact, and respectfully giving all of your attention to the speaker.
2.   Listen for what, where, when, with whom, and why. If you don't remember, ask questions to clarify the speaker's message.
3.   Remain calm, even if the speaker is angry or excited.
4.   Listen when someone recounts an important event that happened to him without trying to top it with your own story. Let the speaker have the stage.

When you are responding,

1.   Speak in a smooth, personal manner, using honesty, candor, and openness.
2.   Give appropriate feedback by paraphrasing the other speaker's message.
3.   Use vocal variety and body language.

On the next page, write down one of the preceding tips that you could use to improve your listening skills:

Employers, listen to your employees. Abraham Zaleznik pointed out that effective leaders are skilled listeners who take an active interest in the other person. Leaders suspend judgment until all the facts are known and use a "third ear" to discover what the person wants to—but doesn't or can't—say.[10]

Politicians, take a page out of statesman Benjamin Franklin's *Poor Richard's Almanack.* Franklin wrote that we attain true knowledge by using our ears rather than our tongues. He gave others time to talk, consciously allowing a silent pause afterward to be sure they had finished speaking. By listening so carefully, Franklin learned what was really important to others. Refusing to speak when he was angry, Franklin waited until he could think more clearly because he realized that softly spoken words often are heard more clearly than harsh loud epithets.[11]

Parents, really listen to your children. OK, so maybe when they're little they talk an awful lot; when they get to be teens, you'll wish they were still talking. By really listening, you prove to your children how important they are to you. Actor and producer Marlo Thomas remembers that her father, comedian Danny Thomas, listened to his children: "One of the most important things about my father—and the reason my sister and brother and I have such a love for him—is that he was a listener. If his kid said something, he heard it." That's a great legacy.[12]

CYA Journaling Exercise: Describe someone who is a really great listener.

Really listening has fallen victim to our busy schedules; we turn into talking heads that spew out recorded messages, making our conversations resemble rote multiplication table drills:

Two times two . . . **Four.**

Two times three . . . **Six.**

I love you . . . . **I love you , too, dear.**

Have a nice day. . . . **You, too.**

Can I help you? . . . **No, thank you, I'm just looking.**

How was your day? . . . **Great, I killed your pit bull.** . . . That's nice. . . . **And you're next.**

How can I help you? . . . **You can't, I'm beyond help.** . . . Okay, well you just let me know when you're ready.

Have a nice day. . . . **And you have a rotten one** . . . . Why thank you. You stop back, now. . . . **In your dreams.**

I love you . . . . **I love you, too.** . . . But I want a divorce. . . . **Oh, me too, darling.**

      In case you think we exaggerate, I (TB) was critiquing training in a fast-food chain not too long ago. The manager was certain his bottom line would improve because now his employees were asking, "Would you like a hot pie to go with that?" after taking each order. I suspected that these employees were just running their new hot pie tapes, so we did an experiment. On our first trip to the drive-thru order window, I placed my order for drinks and burgers. Just as the manager forecast, the order taker asked about hot pies. I politely refused. On our second trip through, I ordered two shakes and twelve hot pies. And the order taker asked, "Would you like a hot pie to go with that?" The manager went ashen. When we drove up to the window, the smiling employee realized what he had done and said, "Well, I guess you don't need another hot pie to go with the others." Describe a time when you responded like a talking head here:

```
┌─────────────────────────────────────────────────────────┐
│                                                         │
│                                                         │
│                                                         │
│                                                         │
│                                                         │
└─────────────────────────────────────────────────────────┘
```

Create Mental Pictures.
To increase the impact of your message, help your listeners create vivid mental pictures. When people can imagine as well as hear what you are saying, they respond, "I see what you are getting at, " or "I've got the picture." Examples I (TB) use: If you won $1 million and spent a dollar a second, it would take 11.6 days to spend your million. For $1 billion, it would take 31.7 years!

      Joel H. Weldon, one of this country's premier seminar presenters, uses this example: While discussing the national debt, you may notice that your listeners' eyes glaze over by the time you hit the words *$5 trillion*. To maintain interest, describe $1 million as a stack of $1,000 bills four inches high. Explain that $1 billion is a stack of $1,000 bills 333 feet high, the height of a 33-story building, and $1 trillion equals a stack 62-1/2 miles high, while $5 trillion equals a stack 312 miles high.

CYA Journaling Exercise: To become a better listener during the next month take these steps:

1. Make two lists of attitudes, behaviors, and habits that affect your listening ability. On the first, list the keepers and on the second, list behaviors you want to change.
2. As your listening skills improve, describe situations indicating you are becoming a better listener.

INNOVATION

Futurists have been trumpeting the creative revolution as the natural successor to the agricultural, industrial, and information revolutions. According to Marsh Fisher, co-founder of Century 21 International and inventor of IdeaFisher software, "The real true source of power in any company today is ideas, and the rest is housekeeping."[13]
As you try to keep up with our constantly changing world, you'll keep bumping into innovations; one example is high-definition television that will be replacing our current TV technology. Remember, it's not the content of an innovation that matters; it's people's attitudes toward innovation.
Innovative businesses are changing not only their products but also their methods of doing business:

- These days Sgt. Preston of the Yukon is wearing Mickey Mouse ears and the Royal Canadian Mounted Police couldn't be happier. In 1995 the Mounties signed a licensing deal to have Walt Disney Canada market their image. The Mounties wanted to end the sale of tacky, tasteless products as well as to make money to support such community-based policing projects as helping battered women and encouraging elderly Indians to work with youth.

- In Bristol, Rhode Island, John Merrifield needed to keep his boatbuilding business afloat during a recession when people stopped ordering yachts. So he changed course and diversified into building prototypes for defense contractors, making windmill blades, and making large-scale public sculptures. Today, Merrifield's sales total $1.5 million and increase 10 percent annually; half of his business comes from building sculptures; the rest from boatbuilding, windmill blades, and prototypes.

List four innovations you expect to see in the next five years:

1	
2	
3	
4	

Innovation Up Close and Personal.   Change is great as long as it does not affect us. You'll need something to write on and something to write with for our minidemo of the effects of innovation. Write the words *Change your attitude!* with your usual writing hand, then with your other hand. Looking at the words you wrote with your nonwriting hand, you may think them strange or misshapen.

Any first experience is threatening; we feel awkward, incompetent, and removed from our security comfort zone. Therefore, we need to minimize the risk of innovation with proper planning. In a family, moving to a new neighborhood or going on a long vacation can classify as an innovation because everyone is removed from a mutual comfort zone. At work, a new supervisor or a new job can demand more than we are comfortable giving. Again, planning makes all the difference.

Innovations that disrupt our comfort zones are never greeted with enthusiasm. When food companies first brought out cake mixes, the boxes stayed on the shelves. Puzzled executives did some investigating and discovered that women felt guilty just adding liquid to cake mixes. Everyone knew that real women baked from scratch, using a pinch of this and a cup of that. By using a comfort zone innovation, manufacturers changed their recipes so that cake bakers had to add an egg and liquid. This simple addition allowed the bakers to feel like they had made a contribution and cake mix sales took off.[14] Now when someone asked,"Did you make this yourself?" the baker could smile and say, "Of course!"

When there is no ego involvement, people are willing to expand their comfort zones as Edwin Perkins demonstrated. In 1914 he was selling bottles of flavored syrup called Fruit Smack in Hendley, Nebraska. Perkins wanted to expand his drink syrup business and cut down on the expense of shipping glass bottles of syrup. In 1927 he came up with an innovation that allowed him to reach both goals. Perkins removed the water and offered his beverage powder in envelopes labeled Kool-Aid. Perkins Products Company became part of General Foods Corporation in 1953.

Innovative Attitudes. For anyone who has been downsized or rightsized, innovation may be a four-letter word. As our writing exercise demonstrated, change creates uncertainty, which in reality is fear about our ability to change or sometimes management's ability to handle change. Peter Drucker suggests that innovation is a combination of attitude and practices. Employees with the right attitude expect change to be part of a company's environment. Management practices include looking for innovation and welcoming employees' suggestions for change. Also, innovation requires time and a separate space; a development department cannot be tacked onto an established unit. Drucker summarized:

> The innovative organization . . . that resists stagnation rather than change, is a major challenge to management, private and public. That such organizations are possible, we can assert with confidence; there are enough of them around. But how to make such organizations general, how to make them productive for society, economy, and individual alike, is still largely an unsolved task. There is every indication that the period ahead will be an innovative one, one of rapid change in technology, society, economy, and institutions.[15]

Create Innovation. Everyone has heard that cliche that we use only 10 percent of our brainpower. We're happy to tell you researchers have reworked that figure; current figures indicate that we use about one-hundredth of 1 percent (1/10,000) of our potential brain power during our lifetimes. This means that each of us possesses an almost unlimited inner creative resource. Robert K. Cooper suggested several ways to develop innovative attitudes and think more creatively:

- Establish and maintain an open mind and spirit of inquiry; ignore fear and familiar ways of thinking.

- Remove hidden obstacles to creative thinking; these include a lack of balance in your life and poorly handled stress (see chapters 5 and 7).

- Laugh more because humor can increase creativity and mental flexibility (see chapter 5).

- Reject old explanations and look for ways to improve the familiar.

- Ask creative questions.

- Listen carefully and pay attention.

- Expand your work expertise continually.

- Be willing to be uncertain.[16]

CYA Journaling Exercise: Reread Dr. Cooper's ways to increase innovative thinking; then choose one and explain how you are going to apply this idea to your life.

Then again, sometimes innovation doesn't quite work. A reporter driving through cattle country stopped at a farm auction to ask a rancher why he was selling out. The rancher answered, "Well, you see, we just love cattle. Its a business my whole family could get involved in."

"So what was the problem?" the reporter asked.

"Well, we couldn't decide what to call ourselves. I wanted the Bar X. My wife wanted the Flying W. My son wanted the Lazy Y, and my daughter just wanted to call it the Suzy Q. So we all got together and called it the Bar X, the Flying W, the Lazy Y, and the Suzy Q."

Looking around, the reporter answered, "Well, that's interesting, but where are all the cattle? Have you sold them?"

The rancher nodded and said glumly, "Well, they all died due to the branding."

Always begin with the end in mind; this brings us to a key ingredient of innovation—vision.

Vision

Epictetus, a Greek philosopher, wrote: "What concerns me is not the way things are, but rather the way people think things are." Centuries later, Johnny Carson proved old Epictetus right when he joked on his late night television show about a shortage of toilet paper in the United States. Fiendishly, Carson went into exaggerated detail about the dire consequences of the tp shortage. To his amazement and distributors' dismay, people took Carson seriously and bought up all the tp in sight. People who heard Carson's retraction later remained unconvinced; they knew there was a shortage, after all, the shelves were bare. This was a vision gone awry.

Personal Vision. Leaders must have a vision that they can convey to others; they must begin with the end in mind so they always know where they are going. Ordinary, everyday people need personal visions, too. Having a vision of your future enables you to make it come true through your actions. Your vision also keeps you afloat during hard times; describe three elements of your vision here:

```
┌─────────────────────────────────────────────────────┐
│                                                       │
│                                                       │
│                                                       │
│                                                       │
└─────────────────────────────────────────────────────┘
```

Sandra Shank Beckwith's vision is that of being a pathfinder: As one of three female students in law school at the University of Cincinnati in the 1960s, Beckwith knew each woman would be called on every day in every class. The women quickly learned to always come to class prepared, which probably made them better lawyers. Subsequently, Beckwith was the first woman elected judge of Municipal Court and later the Common Pleas Court in Hamilton County. Elected to the county commission, she later became president. Beckwith is now the first woman U.S. District Court Judge in Cincinnati. How did being first throughout her life affect her? She commented, "I think it carries with it something of an added burden. If you're first, you want to make a good impression so those who come after you don't have much pressure to perform well. . . . What I've found is that if you do the work and do it to the best of your ability and carry your fair share, you don't have a problem with the trust and respect of your colleagues."[17]

CYA Journaling Exercise: Write about your personal vision and don't be afraid to dream.

Family Vision. In addition to having a personal vision, create a vision for your family. In 1975 Thuc and Thanh Dinh escaped Saigon just ahead of the communist forces. When they settled in America, the Dinhs had little but their vision that each of their six children would graduate from college. As educated people, they believed that education was the key to success. Although he had been a journalist in Vietnam, Thuc Dinh took a job as a parking lot attendant and later became a stock handler at Xerox. Thanh, a literature teacher in Vietnam, stayed home with her family, then worked in a cafeteria, and later for a small computer company. The Dinhs worked opposite shifts so that their children were never left alone.

The whole family worked hard and saved for college.

In May of 1996, the Dinhs' youngest, Thuy, was the sixth to graduate from the University of Virginia. Thuy wrote about his parents: "Thinking back, I find it hard to believe that they were able to stick to it for so long, despite all the hardships. . . . They threw away all their dreams and accomplishments by leaving their homeland in 1975, and have instead given us the love and support to allow us to achieve our dreams."[18]

CYA Journaling Exercise: Write about your family vision; include important members of your extended family.

Political Vision. The mayor of your immediate community should have a vision for its development, as should your state governor, and the president of our country. When you agree with politicians' visions, support their visions for your community, state, and country. When you disagree, actively work for what you believe, that's what America is all about. In each case, the politician should remember the KISS principle in conveying a vision; keep it simple, stupid. List leaders who have vision:

1	4
2	5
3	6

To get a hands-on feel for his city, former Baltimore Mayor Donald Schaefer made wandering the neighborhoods a priority. His crews always knew when he had been wandering. That's when they received lists of potholes, dirty parks, or broken streetlights to fix or abandoned cars and dead trees to remove.

Great political leaders understand that their own right attitudes create an atmosphere that enables the right responses from others. For instance, in July 1940 Prime Minister Winston Churchill broadcast his vision to the people of Great Britain during World War II: "We shall defend every village, every town and every city. The vast mass of London itself, fought street by street, could easily devour an entire hostile army; and we would rather see London laid in ruins and ashes than that it should be tamely and abjectly enslaved."

Five weeks later, Churchill paid this tribute to the Royal Air Force: "Never in the field of human conflict was so much owed by so many to so few." Very often the politician with a vision is an eloquent cheerleader without pompons or a megaphone.

CYA Journaling Exercise: Write about your political vision for your city, state, or country.

Business Vision. Your employer must be able to tell you and other employees where the company is headed because the employees as well as the owners have their integrity on the line. Abraham Zaleznik defined ideal business leaders as focusing on imaginative ideas; taking risks; and being visionary, dramatic, trusting, hardworking, and fair-minded. Their goals are entrepreneurial and active.[19]

While traveling from coast to coast, I (TB) have noticed that some companies with visionary leadership, such as General Exposition Services, are increasing their training budgets. They are treating employees like the company's most important assets by making them more effective at their jobs. Once employees believe in themselves, they improve the quality of their service; this results in higher profits for the company. Best of all is a wholesale improvement in the right attitudes of staff and management.

In 1991 a major petroleum retailer realized that training could help it retain a more loyal workforce. Managers held seminars for employees to explain how they could be more service oriented. They also taught employees about new technology such as point-of-sale scanners and computerized gas pumps. That retailer's profit margins have improved by 14 percent since 1991.[20]

In each of the following businesses, the leaders have different, yet similar, visions for success: In 1971 Jack Kahl's vision was growing his business. He bought a company for a down payment of about $10,000 and renamed it Manco, Inc. Manco makes Duck Tape and related products; the first year his company grossed $800,000 from sales in three states. In 1976, Wal-Mart ordered $88,000 of Duck Tape, but more important, Kahl first met Sam Walton, who became his mentor: "Sam Walton . . . was the greatest entrepreneur this country has ever seen. He understood that the customer is the critical ingredient in the product/marketing mix. If you please them, you win the game." Today, Kahl still assesses any new product by its usefulness to the customer. In 1995, Manco sales totaled $130 million in an international market.

Kahl's vision made all the difference at his Avon, Ohio, firm because he shares it with his employees and the entrepreneurial community. Employees are called partners and own a third of the company's stock. At weekly partner meetings, they make suggestions about improving operations and new products. Kahl intends to retire when he is 60 to travel, teach, and write. When people ask how Manco can survive without him, Kahl answers, "This company is in one sense a democracy, with a tremendous upflow of new ideas from the bottom up. We almost invariably promote from within. . . . We've already got tremendous built-in continuity."[21]

CYA Journaling Exercise: Explain who you would nominate as the greatest entrepreneur in our country.

Tony Wells' story reminds us of the two frogs who fell into a bucket of cream. The first frog drank some cream, swam until he was tired, gave up, and drowned. The second frog kept thrashing around until he created a mound of butter high enough so he could hop out. Like the second frog, Wells knew he was going to succeed; the only question was how soon. When he was setting up computer applications for area firms, Wells saw a need that no one else saw—rentable classrooms for computer training. Banks refused to fund Wells' idea, so he took out a second mortgage on his house, totaled his and his wife's retirement funds, and borrowed on his credit cards and from relatives. Three years ago he set up two top-notch training rooms in Columbus, Ohio. Since then he has filled the rooms with personal computers and paid off his debts. Knowledge Development Centers has added two more training rooms and has franchises in Phoenix and Indianapolis. Additional centers in Detroit, Cincinnati, Kansas City, St. Louis, Orlando, and Rochester are on the drawing board.

Wells has joined the boards of the Goodwill Rehabilitation Center, Special Wish Foundation, and Adventures for Kids, in his effort to give back to his community. Despite his jam-packed schedule, Wells finds, "There's so much excitement, we survive on that natural high of having a successful idea."[22]

Along with Apple Computer and Hewlett-Packard Company, Minnesota Mining and Manufacturing (3M) has become known as a company that grows innovation. Employees are not only encouraged to work on projects that interest them but also given time and resources to produce a successful product. Many times a product is the result of an accident. For instance, forty-three years ago a lab assistant spilled a synthetic latex mixture for jet fuel lines on his tennis shoes. He noticed that any liquid he used to clean his shoes beaded up immediately. Later he noticed how clean the spilled area remained. It took three years for researchers to isolate the stain-resistant properties in the original mixture. Finally, in 1956 3M introduced Scotchgard, the world's first chemical fabric protector.

More recently, Post-It note pads resulted from a not-too-sticky glue developed by Spence Silver. Silver took a lot of teasing until Art Fry, who worked in another division, saw a use for this glue. Fry applied the glue to small pieces of paper he used as temporary markers in his church hymnal. Uncertain that they had a saleable product, someone suggested sending samples to 3M's secretaries, who found all kinds of uses for pieces of paper that would not stick forever. 3M has also developed Post-It Software Notes that pop up from a desktop dispenser.

Perfect Failures. OK, you say, all of this vision stuff can't be successful all the time. People do fail once in a while, don't they? Yes, they do and at 3M they are not only congratulated for trying but also usually get to keep their jobs. It's the same story at Ore-Ida; in fact, Heinz's frozen foods subsidiary treats failure with a boom. When an Ore-Ida employee makes a "perfect failure," management shoots off a cannon in celebration. A perfect failure is an experiment that failed, was learned from, and can be forgotten.[23] Ore-Ida and 3M employees don't mind taking risks because their companies recognize risk taking as necessary for innovation.

Dr. Gary McGraw, vice president of development at Eastman Chemical Company suggests that we redefine the idea of success: "Success in the innovation area is gaining knowledge. So if you are a creative person and you have a great idea and you do enough work on it to show that it won't work, then you are successful because you created some new knowledge. You've learned some new things. You taught the company some things."[24]

Danny Hillis of Thinking Machines Corp. believes the goal is to get workers to think in ways their managers cannot imagine. Because creative thinking is inherently risky, innovative organizations "have to allow people to take controlled risks. If you punish failure at the early stages too much, then people won't take risks. If you're doing anything truly innovative, a certain percentage of things have to fail. You can't say the person fails just because the idea failed."[25]

Some innovations are just plain common—or uncommon—sense. When Southern California Edison (SCE) faced a language problem, it recruited its bilingual employees to serve as spokespersons. After receiving training in communication, public speaking, and issues affecting the corporation, SCE workers began handling calls from Cambodian, Chinese, Hispanic, Korean, and Vietnamese customers who did not speak English.

In *Built to Last*, James Collins and Jerry Porras shot down some myths about visionary companies; they aren't for everyone:

- It doesn't take a great idea to start a great company; few visionary companies began with a great idea.

- The most successful companies do not focus on maximizing profits; they are guided by a core ideology—core values and a sense of purpose beyond just making money.

- Change is not the only constant; successful companies display a powerful drive for progress enabling them to change and adapt without compromising cherished core ideals.

• Visionary companies are great places to work, but not for everyone; they don't have room for those unwilling or unable to fit their exacting standards.

• The most successful companies do not focus on beating the competition; they focus on beating themselves.

• Highly successful companies do not make their best moves by brilliant complex and strategic planning; they use experimentation, trial and error, opportunism, and accident.

By the way, the companies these authors labeled visionary are 3M, American Express, Boeing, Citicorp, Ford, General Electric, Hewlett-Packard, IBM, Johnson & Johnson, Marriott, Merck, Motorola, Nordstrom, Philip Morris, Procter & Gamble, Sony, Wal-Mart, and Walt Disney.[26] List five core values that you would want your company to exemplify:

Core values:

Developing Vision When You're the Boss. Douglas K. Smith

suggests taking more personal risk when developing a vision for your company. "Use visioning as a behavior-driven change initiative itself. Instead of shaping the process with the single objective of identifying the best vision and strategy for the organization, craft an approach that has two goals: *both* identifying the best vision *and* maximizing the number of people, including yourself, who emerge from the visioning process having taken responsibility for change. The following actions can help you accomplish that":

1. Enlist the contributions of many, not just a few.
2. Ask how, not just why and what.
3. Demand that people wear two hats—yours and theirs.
4. Treat vision as something people live now, not just in the future.[27]

CYA Journaling Exercise: Describe your business vision for a firm you own or would like to own.

Social Vision. Social reformers also have visions that too often make headlines. The contentious, sometimes murderous, struggle over abortion jumps to mind. We are not here to praise either side. We do praise Zoe's Place, which we describe in chapter 4; they are putting their talk into action. As a member of the board of directors of the Child Abuse Prevention Council for Orange County, I (TB) am very concerned about all the children who are already here. We need to prevent cyclical child abuse in families. We need to concentrate on children already born who hunger for love, for homes, for food, for clothing, for a sense of self. Throughout this nation, some children go to decrepit schools that fall into the category of cruel and unusual punishment. Some children are afraid to go out to play. Some children suffer mental abuse in stressful, tumultuous home conditions. Some children receive only hate and learn only to hate. Our children are self-fulfilling prophecies; they are what they learn or don't learn.

One social reformer, Mother Teresa, had a most effective way of reminding her workers of their vision. She said,

> I have five sisters getting M.D. degrees and far greater numbers getting R.N., L.P.N., and M.S.W. degrees. But a funny thing happens. They come back from their education and they are concerned about titles, offices, and parking privileges. So . . . I send them to the Hospice of the Dying. There they hold people's hands, pray with them, and feed them. After six months of that, they typically get things straight again and they remember their vocation is to be a spiritual presence first and a professional presence second.[28]

That's one attitude adjustment technique that won't readily transfer to other situations, but it illustrates the need for visionaries to be practical.

Dick Anthoven, a white South African millionaire is another practical visionary. Three years ago he bought a rundown farm and winery called Spier in the wine country north of Cape Town. To run it he hired George Frans, a black wine manager who learned his trade by working in vineyards for free. Frans is delighted with his job because he believes in Anthoven's plan to give workers a better life and help them learn on the job. According to Frans, "The owner had this vision of what really we could do with this place. We're really getting down to doing what's right." About 80 percent of the winery's 280 workers are illiterate. In addition to learning to read, they are learning skills they can use later from experienced workers and managers. Frans believes that one day each of them will be a farm manager.

CYA Journaling Exercise: Write about your social vision and don't be afraid to dream.

INTEGRITY

As our astronauts circle the earth, they can identify only one structure built by humans—the Great Wall of China. Through the centuries, various emperors added to it until today the wall is 1,500 miles long; its height ranges from 20 to 50 feet; its width spans 13 to 40 feet. In the third century B.C., Emperor Shi Huangdi began the wall by ordering workers to erect a wall of earth and stone in northern China. Tired of his country being invaded by nomadic tribes from the north, this new wall was to connect older walls and form a secure border. When his wall was completed around 228 B.C., the emperor was certain that no enemies could breach a wall so thick and so high. Wrong! Three times in the first hundred years, enemy forces got through the wall. They did not go over it; they did not go through it; they simply bribed the gatekeepers. Imagine the wrath of an emperor powerful enough to order hundreds of workers to build the Great Wall yet unable to control the integrity of his gatekeepers. Write down some recent examples when a lack of integrity affected the security of a country, city, or business:

```
┌──────────────────────────────────────────────────────────────┐
│                                                                │
│                                                                │
│                                                                │
│                                                                │
└──────────────────────────────────────────────────────────────┘
```

Socrates said that persons with integrity were in reality what they appeared to be. This makes complete sense; before we can achieve the kind of lives we want, we must think, act, talk, walk, and conduct all of our affairs as if we were the persons we wish to be. To have integrity, we must be our own persons—invest in and insist on the integrity of our individual identities. Each of us must maintain our integrity because that is the only way we can trust each other. In the stories that follow, a mantle of integrity connects people from different times and places.

• Integrity is both who we are and what we do; Galileo Galilei was a man of integrity whose actions supported his beliefs. While teaching mathematics in Pisa around 1589, Galileo dropped rocks off the Leaning Tower in his spare time. He discovered that a two-pound rock and a ten-pound rock reached the ground at the same time. When he demonstrated this to the scientists of his day, they said that could not happen because everyone knew that weight affected speed. So Galileo offered to repeat the experiment.

Less than two decades later, Galileo announced that the earth was not the center of the universe; but again, everyone knew differently. Galileo's statement of fact caused him to be condemned to life in prison; in addition, Italian printers were forbidden to print anything he wrote. Although his sentence was commuted, Galileo spent the rest of his life under house arrest. His struggle exemplified scientists' need for freedom of inquiry. Today, most people think of Galileo as a pioneer of modern physics and telescopic astronomy, but we think of him as a man of integrity.

• A Russian poet said, "Silence when a person sees a fault, is a lie." *Common Fire: Lives of Commitment in a Complex World,* investigates why some people see faults, or things to improve, that others never see. After interviewing 100 people nationwide, the authors found that compassionate people share these traits: flexibility, strength of spirit, and a sense of humor.[29] We'd like to add that people committed to helping others also share integrity; they are acting out what they are and correcting society's faults.

• While imprisoned in a death camp, Viktor Frankl wondered why a few people survived when most died. Frankl discovered that those who survived had a future vision, a mission to perform, some important work to do.[30] Sculptor Alfred Tibor is a death camp survivor who had some important work to do. Tibor appreciates his freedom: "I am celebrating my freedom with my art, my life, and my existence. . . . And do you know another thing? I do not have bad days. If it's raining or if it's sunny, it's a good day because I am free. . . . Freedom is so gentle, if you're not carrying the freedom, you're destroying it. And where is freedom? It's inside of you."

When he's not working in bronze, marble, or alabaster, 76-year-old Tibor tells schoolchildren about living without freedom during the Holocaust and during the communist occupation of Hungary. Tibor hopes he is providing a voice "louder than the guys preaching the hate." Before he and his family landed in Miami in 1957, Tibor had survived concentration camps, prisoner of war camps, and the Hungarian Revolt. No wonder he loves freedom.[31]

Jot down the names of eight people who have integrity:

- In January 1896, Boston socialite Harriet Hemenway began to feel guilty for wearing feathers in her hats. Today this sounds a bit strange, but in the late nineteenth century hunters killed 5 million birds annually to satisfy the dictates of style. When Hemenway heard that the fashionable hat trade was fueling the wholesale slaughter of birds, she knew she had to risk alienating people—it just wasn't right. She and her cousin Minna Hall sat down with her Blue Book of Boston society. They checked off the names of fashionable ladies who wore feathered hats and might join a society for the protection of birds.

  Hemenway targeted two groups: First she met with the scientific and social leaders in Boston; during this meeting they formed the Massachusetts Audubon Society to "discourage buying and wearing . . . the feathers of any wild bird." Second, Hemenway held a series of teas for the ladies of Boston, where she urged them to forsake feathers and join the Audubon Society. Not long afterward, women in other states formed societies. Two years later the National Association of Audubon Societies was formed.[32]

- When people mention recruiting violations, Michigan State University is one of an increasing number of schools that leaps to mind. No one got too excited in the spring of 1996 when the media trumpeted conjectures about major infractions in the Spartans' football program. Shock waves resulted, however, when the whistle-blower was revealed: M. Peter McPherson, MSU president. McPherson believes "you can do things right and still succeed. What you basically have to do is decide who you serve and then constantly measure how well you are keeping up."

  McPherson's other changes on the MSU campus are the result of quiet persuasion: the Detroit College of Law moved to East Lansing from a decaying downtown location; MSU's bookstore was privatized to save $2 million annually; the state legislature increased its support of MSU. McPherson also announced a program under which every MSU student has a chance to study abroad for one semester without paying extra fees. He believes "knowing other languages and other cultures is going to be a key requirement for success in the 21st century, whatever you do." McPherson should know; after graduating from MSU in 1963, he served with the Peace Corps in Peru.[33]

•   When a disaster struck Lawrence, Massachusetts, on December 11, 1995, a Jewish Santa Claus came to the rescue. A fire at Malden Mills Industries, Inc., seemed like it would destroy the jobs of 3,000 local textile workers, who feared their charred company would close or move south. But they didn't worry for long.

Owner Aaron Feuerstein paid a Christmas bonus and three months' salary to each employee. More important, he pledged not only to rebuild but also to improve one of New England's last successful textile mills. Two weeks after the fire, Feuerstein's factory was back in partial operation, manufacturing Polartec and Polarfleece, which are used in outdoor wear. Within a month, most workers were back to work.

Feuerstein kept his jobless employees on the payroll until the company had taken a $50 million hit. In July 1996, he wrote to the 400 still waiting to return, advising them to look for other employment. Meanwhile Feuerstein extended their health benefits, provided extra training, and promised they would be given first crack at the new jobs, even if they were employed elsewhere.

Aaron Feuerstein claims he's not a mench and that he just kept paying his workers because he needed them. His business philosophy is simple:

> Once you break the workers' trust, I don't think you ever get
> it back. You'll never get the quality you need. Once you treat
> them like a cuttable expense, instead of your most important asset,
> you won't recover. I am firmly convinced the degree of loyalty our
> people have extended Malden Mills is equal to or greater than
> what we have done for them.

Sixteen months after the fire, the new $200 million, 600,000-square-foot, two-story building was complete and the plant was in full operation; all but about a hundred of the original employees had been rehired.

•   Amish communities traditionally pitch in to help when tragedy strikes. The Amish are opposed to most social welfare programs and prefer that communities take care of their members without government help.

When a driver rear-ended Mary Lambright's horse-drawn buggy, she died. Mahlon Lambright, her husband, refused a $212,418 wrongful-death settlement, explaining that the Amish community had provided him with food and clothing for his eleven children and raised money by having an auction. Community was more important than money to this Mondovi, Wisconsin, carpenter.

A few days before he became ten, Samuel Herschberger was almost torn limb from limb by a grinding machine. The accident happened in 1991 and in 1996 Samuel still had additional operations ahead of him. People from around the world read about the Sullivan, Illinois, family's six-figure medical bill and donated $250,000. Meanwhile, each weekend the Herschbergers raised money by serving home-cooked meals and giving guests horse and buggy rides in exchange for donations.   In 1996, Oba Herschberger thanked everyone for their donations, prayers, cards, and letters. Then he asked the public to stop sending money; accepting additional money would go against the traditional Amish ways of humility and reliance on community.

CYA Journaling Exercise: Write about someone you know who has integrity, explaining what that person has done.

•   When people daydream about what they would do if they won the lottery, very few consider buying a factory. Fortunately for the employees of Bettie Dawn Uniform Company of Mount Vernon, Missouri, Gerald Martens won the California lottery and bought that closed sewing plant. Martens not only rehired the twenty-five laid-off seamstresses but also plans to add more workers and upgrade the machinery. Martens said he liked producing nursing uniforms and hospital scrub outfits domestically because 80 percent are produced overseas. What he liked even better was putting people back to work.

•   Captain Scott O'Grady—the American pilot who was shot down in Bosnia and survived on bugs and grass until he was rescued—captured America's heart. Now in the Air Force Reserves, O'Grady is stationed at Hill Air Force Base in Utah. In between flying ten to fifteen days a month, he gives speeches. O'Grady takes his fame—but not himself—seriously. He believes, "Whether you deserve [fame] or not, you have a responsibility to act in a decent manner. And then when you benefit, work to benefit others." Accordingly, O'Grady has endorsed two charities, Make-a-Wish Foundation and St. Jude's Children's Hospital; he speaks to school groups as often as he can.   O'Grady says he is not a hero because "the only person I helped was myself, by surviving." O'Grady defines a hero as "A teacher helping students, parents helping their children learn right from wrong," and the 61 people who endured hostile fire to rescue him. OK Scott

O'Grady, you say you're no hero; but with all that integrity, you're a hero to us!

•   Chicago's Joseph Cardinal Bernardin died on November 14, 1996, after fulfilling his vow to show the nation that death was a friend, not something to be feared. After Bernardin announced his terminal condition in late August, a reporter asked if he didn't want to be with his family. Sixty-eight-year-old Bernardin replied, "You are my family." Even after discontinuing chemotherapy, he continued ministering to his family until two weeks before his death. Television coverage of his funeral indicated that Bernardin's family embraced a good part of Chicago and the world. From the dignitaries in the front pews to the nameless sidewalk throngs that watched his funeral procession, Joe Bernardin brought together divergent groups in death, as he did in life.

•   In 1996 Poland proved that it is a country with enough integrity to admit its mistakes. On July 7, Prime Minister Wlodzimierz Cimoszewicz led a commemoration honoring forty-two Jews massacred on July 4, 1946, in Kielce. Ironically, Europe's last pogrom occurred after World War II. Before the war, Poland had 3.5 million Jews; afterward, 250,000 survivors of the Holocaust returned to Poland. However, as a result of the Kielce pogrom, only 5,000 to 10,000 Jews now live in Poland. In 1946 Poland's communist government banned mention of the Kielce pogrom; only after that regime ended in 1989 did people begin to ask why. A dozen theories still fuel discussions, but little certainty exists. Months before the ceremony, the Polish government issued an official apology to Jewish leaders for this act of anti-Semitism, "our common tragedy."

•   Our last example is an organization with integrity: ORBIS International. This nonprofit, humanitarian organization fights blindness through health education and hands-on training for ophthalmologists, nurses, technicians, and health care workers in other countries. Each week volunteer doctors join ORBIS's medical team to operate and teach. I (DM) heard of this organization from my ophthalmologist, Dr. Larry Birndorf, an ORBIS volunteer.

    Since 1982, ORBIS has conducted 250 programs in 71 countries. In 1980 United Airlines donated a plane that became ORBIS's first flying eye hospital. United also trained ORBIS pilots and provided pilots and a full-time mechanic. Federal Express ships ORBIS's medical supplies without charge.

    When ORBIS first came to Romania, for example, only three doctors were trained to use an operating microscope. While a volunteer demonstrated a corneal transplant on an eleven-year-old Gypsy boy, Romanian doctors in the plane's classroom observed and discussed the procedure. Currently, twenty-five doctors now trained in microsurgery have helped about 4,000 Romanians to see again. We salute both ORBIS and the generous professionals who donate their time and skills.[34]

ORBIS is a perfect example of SMART goal setting; its goals are to alleviate suffering and to educate. ORBIS began by assembling the personnel and equipment; after that, the organization worked out the logistics and achieved its goal. We discuss goals and SMART goal setting in chapter 4.

ENDNOTES

1. Adapted from John C. Maxwell, *Developing the Leader Within You* (Nashville, TN: Thomas Nelson Publishers, 1993), pp. 142–43.
2. Colin Powell, Training '96 Conference and Expo in Atlanta, Georgia, on January 29–31, 1996.
3. Denis Waitley, *Time to Win* (Salt Lake City, UT: Franklin Quest Co., 1993), n.p.
4. Carol Burnett, *One More Time* (New York: Random House, 1986), pp. 44–46; and Julia Keller, "What Makes Stars Tick," *Columbus Dispatch*, June 4, 1996, p. 6B.
5. Nelson Mandela, *The Long Walk to Freedom* (New York: Little Brown and Co., 1994), pp. 341–42.
6. Ibid., p. 433.
7. John Hughes, "Head Games," *Orange County Register*, August 7, 1996, p. 1 (Accent).
8. George Leonard, "How to Become Much Better than Just Very Good," *Bottom Line Personal*, October 15, 1996, p. 2.
9. Adapted from John Maxwell, *Developing the Leader*, p. 101.
10. Abraham Zaleznik, *Restoring Leadership in Business* (New York: Harper & Row, 1989).
11. Michael Loren, "Lessons in Life from Benjamin Franklin," *Bottom Line Personal*, November 1, 1996, pp. 13–14.
12. Julia Keller, "Biography Makes Room for Memories of Danny Thomas," *Columbus Dispatch*, September 4, 1996.
13. Polly LaBarre, "The Creative Revolution," *Industry Week*, May 16, 1994, p. 12.
14. Sara M. Evans, *Born for Liberty* (New York: Free Press, 1989), p. 251.
15. Peter Drucker, *Management: Tasks, Responsibilities, Practices* (New York: Harper and Row, 1973), p. 803.
16. Robert K. Cooper, *The Performance Edge* (Boston: Houghton Mifflin, 1991), pp. 112–19.
17. Jim Massie, "Hall of Fame Members Undaunted by Obstacles," *Columbus Dispatch*, February 22, 1996, p. 2C.
18. "Vietnamese Couple's Son to be Sixth Child to Graduate from College," *Columbus Dispatch*, May 18, 1996, p. 3A.
19. Abraham Zaleznik, *Restoring Leadership in Business* (New York: Harper & Row, 1989).
20. John W. Jones, "Ensuring an Ethical Environment," *Security Management*, April 1996, pp. 24, 26.
21. William Troy, "Duck Pond," *Cleveland Magazine*, Inside Business supplement, January 1996, pp. 6–9.
22. Brian Williams, "Entrepreneur Puts Training to Work at Computer Centers," *Columbus Dispatch*, March 11, 1996, pp. 1–2 of Business supplement.
23. John Ivancevich and Michael T. Matteson, *Organizational Behavior and Management* (Burr Ridge, IL: Richard D. Irwin, 1996), p. 138.
24. Polly LaBarre, "The Creative Revolution," *Industry Week*, May 16, 1994, p. 15.
25. Ibid., p. 16.
26. James C. Collins and Jerry I. Porras, *Built to Last* (New York: Harper Collins, 1994),

pp. 7–10.
27. Douglas K. Smith, *Taking Charge of Change* (Reading, MA: Addison-Wesley Publishing, 1996), p. 289–91.
28. Quoted in the *Catholic Spirit*, February 29, 1996.
29. Cheryl and James Keen and Laurent Parks Daloz and Sharon Daloz Parks, *Common Fire: Lives of Commitment in a Complex World* (Boston: Beacon Press, 1996).
30. Stephen R. Covey, A. Roger Merrill, and Rebecca R. Merrill, *First Things First* (New York: Simon & Schuster, 1994), p. 103.
31. Alice Thomas, "Hungarian Preaches Freedom," *Columbus Dispatch*, July 15, 1996, p. 3C.
32. Joseph Kastner, "Long Before Furs, It Was Feathers That Stirred Reformist Ire,"*Smithsonian*, July 1994, pp. 97–104.
33. Jack Lessenberry, "McPherson Is a Surprise Success at MSU," *Toledo Blade,* July 14, 1996, p. 7.
34. *Orbis Observer*, Spring 1996, p. 1.

4

Nourishing Goals for Greatness and Graciousness

"Would you tell me, please, which way I ought to walk from here?" asked Alice.
"That depends a good deal on where you want to get to," said the cat.
"I don't much care where," said Alice.
"Then it doesn't much matter which way you walk," said the cat.
LEWIS CARROLL

People with the right attitude focus on their goals, just as actor-turned-activist Christopher Reeve does as he lobbies for those with spinal-cord injuries. Focusing on increasing research funds and insurance caps gives him the energy to achieve his goal. Those who lack that ability to focus on goals remain forever bound to stationary wheelchairs by their thoughts of failure. Let's face it. Like Alice, many people refuse to set goals for themselves because they risk failure; even if no one else knows about their goals, they risk really wanting something and not getting it. Oh, the pain of it all. If this is your problem, CYA by continuing to read about setting realistic goals and achieving them and then rereading the "Risk" section of chapter 2. Ninety-five percent of achieving a goal is knowing what you want and figuring out how you are going to get it. The rest is activating your plan on a daily basis, that's the follow-through part.

Gracious people are the icing on humanity's cake, the oil on our squeaky wheels, the balm for our souls. They pursue goals motivated by a love of others. Graciously they feed and shelter the homeless, baby-sit for single parents, and visit shut-ins. No Howard Sterns in this chapter; instead, we introduce some wonderful people. (Not that you're not wonderful in your own way, Howard.) Somehow, gracious people manage to float above problems that scuttle the rest of us because they are so busy being grateful for, and using, their gifts.

People who rise even further above seemingly impossible situations possess greatness that is always goal driven. These impatient characters see something that needs changing and they just do it. The people we profile in this chapter are change catalysts for nations and the world. Great people have buildings named after them; gracious people don't and couldn't care less; both achieve their goals.

YOU MAY HAVE A WRONG ATTITUDE IF . . .

- You went to Disney World but they wouldn't let you in.

- Your idea of forgiveness is revenge.

- You don't trust anyone of a different race, religion, or culture.

- Your grandkids ran away from home the only time you baby sat.

- You were asked to leave the neighborhood by Mr. Rogers.

- You laugh at people who share their dreams and claim they just lucked out when they achieve them.

- You think a compliment is something owed you, and somebody sure owes you big time.

GOALS

Need some motivation to establish even one goal for yourself? Consider this: The University of North Carolina at Chapel Hill surveyed 4,000 retired executives whose average age was 70. Researchers asked these former titans of industry what they wished they could have done differently. The most frequent answer was something like, "I would have taken charge of my own life, set my own goals, and not let anyone else do it for me." In other words, these executives would have created happier environments for themselves. Have you noticed that more people rust out while receiving geriatric care than wear out while happily pursuing goals? Denis Waitley describes people without goals as spectators in the arena of life, doing the wave and cheering for those who participate.[1]

To be honest, choosing goals is easy; it's the follow-through that's the killer. Actually taking yourself seriously is difficult stuff; goal setting must have top priority in your life and at times, you'll need to make sacrifices. Indiana University basketball coach Bobby Knight commented, "Everyone wants to be a winner, but hardly anyone wants to prepare to be a winner." That's a pretty good attitude statement for a man better known for throwing chairs and screaming.

Goal setting is one of the eight ways to change attitudes that we introduced in chapter 1. A study at UCLA revealed that 93 percent of all communication is nonverbal; this means it is subconsciously sent and subconsciously received.[2] When you first set a goal, therefore, your subconscious begins working with the single-mindedness of a honey bee in search of nectar. Your subconscious makes sure you attain any goal you establish; conversely, if you send your subconscious mixed messages, it delivers whatever you order.

Pitfalls in Achieving Goals

Bobbe Sommer suggests that one pitfall in establishing goals is keeping a *yabbit*; this pitiful critter is a lousy pet because its mother is a *when-I* and its father an *if-only*. When we talk ourselves out of taking action and setting a goal, we use excuses that begin with: yeah, but; if only; or, when I. *Yeah, but* I'll be so much older than all those kids taking management classes. *If only* I had more time, I'd teach my children how to fish like my dad taught me. *When* I retire, I'll take up painting miniatures again.

Another major detour on the road to goal setting is Can't Boulevard. As we pointed out in chapter 1, self-talk is part of our original equipment package. Hearing a you-just-can't-do-anything-right message repeatedly can cause you to camp out permanently on Can't Boulevard. Only you can change the self-talk and move to Can-Do Parkway. Remember, acting as if changes your thinking and subsequently, your actions.[3]

Postpone Gratification. Still another pitfall in goal setting is the necessity of delaying gratification. If you chase a goal, you're giving up time and money that could be spent on other fun things. As a steeplechase participant in four Olympics, Henry Marsh knows about giving up time and money to pursue a goal; his motto is "Don't sacrifice what you want most for what you want now."

In the 1960s, psychologist Walter Mischel performed an experiment at Stanford with preschoolers and marshmallows. Each child had to choose between receiving one marshmallow immediately, or two marshmallows in about 20 minutes. A follow-up study a decade or so later revealed the one marshmallow kids turned into stubborn, indecisive, stressed teens. The two marshmallow teens were more socially competent, self-assertive, and better able to cope with frustration. Choose to be a two-marshmallow goal seeker.[4]

If you want to do your own follow-up study, write down a time when you didn't delay gratification and another time when you did in this box:

I was a one-marshmallow kid when I
I was a two-marshmallow kid when I

Excellence, success, and happiness all require stick-to-itiveness. Alan Loy McGinnis, author of *The Power of Optimism,* quotes Irwin C. Hansen, CEO of Porter Memorial Hospital in Denver. "You don't need talent to succeed," insists Hansen. "All you need is a big pot of glue. You smear some on your chair and some on the seat of your pants, you sit down, and you stick with every project until you've done the best you can do."

Postponing pleasure to produce excellence makes the pleasure that much more of a reward. It also leaves a residue in your memory to promote similar activity next time.

CYA Journaling Exercise: Explain how delaying gratification has worked for you or a friend in the last year.

Goal Setting by Default. Goal setting by default is like driving from Miami to New York by way of DesMoines. Bobbe Sommer points out that everything you have done in your life has occurred because it was someone's goal. Most of us graduated from elementary school because our parents sent us to school, not because we set a goal for school. If you cannot remember ever personally setting a goal, you'll want to figure out just who has been setting your goals for you. Imagine how much more effective you would be if you were gliding beelike through the air toward a goal, instead of ricocheting around achieving goals set by default.[5]

Stephen Covey points out that sometimes "we set goals and work to achieve them, but either the circumstances change or we change. A new opportunity surfaces, there's a shift in the economy . . . we get a different perspective. If we hold on to our goals, they become masters instead of servants. But if we let them go, we often feel uneasy or guilty that we did not keep our commitment."[6]

As we mentioned in chapter 2, change happens. And when it does, we can use twister Chubby Checker as a guide for managing change while achieving a goal. Checker was all of four years old when he decided he wanted to be on the stage (his goal). In the 1960s, Checker was on the stage teaching the world the twist—that's a dance, young people—when the Beatles and other British groups hijacked popular music.

Keeping his goal in mind while his theater dates evaporated, Checker wrote to clubs in various cities to announce he was available (his minigoal). In a few years, he was playing 278 dates a year and had his own band that could play twisting, not rock, music (his minigoal). In 1980 Checker took stock again; he reasoned that most of his early fans were now businesspeople and marketed himself for business banquets and conventions (his minigoal). In the 1990s he went back to the clubs and theaters, this time to entertain young people (his minigoal). In the spring of 1996 Checker made his Broadway debut in *Grease* (his minigoal). Goal seeker Chubby Checker has shown us how to do more than the twist. Young people today can expect a minimum of five to seven career changes; they may want to emulate Checker's twisting, turning approach to success.[7]

Sometimes goal seekers become myopic, mistaking having a goal for having a life, which we discuss in the last chapter. Goal seeking isn't a once-in-a-lifetime happening; it is a continuing process that we use to improve our lives and to update our attitudes. So, live today as today, not as a rehearsal for tomorrow.

Ready-Fire-Aim Goals. Thorough planning is key to achieving the goal you desire, as Stephen Covey points out with this story: When Mikhail Gorbachev was president of Russia, he made alcohol illegal so that his people would not drink so much. Unfortunately, he had forgotten the lesson of Prohibition in America—sobriety can't be legislated. Instead of becoming more productive, people replaced alcohol with narcotics. Gorbachev's goal of reducing alcohol consumption was achieved with a side effect worse than the problem itself.

Taking a ready-fire-aim approach means you'll likely shoot yourself in the foot.[8]

Deciding on a Goal or a Series of Life Goals

As we discussed in chapter 3, your personal vision is based on your values; these in turn determine your life goals. List the values that guide your life in the box on the next page.

My values:

To reach your goals, break them up into short-range goals or minigoals that are flexible; these minigoals take less time to accomplish and offer options for doing things. Minigoals are like stepping-stones leading to your goal. Denis Waitley suggests setting your core values in concrete and putting your short-range goals in pencil or on a computer disk so they can be revised as needed. Finally, there is stuff—that's what you do to achieve each minigoal (see figure 2). Next, let's look at the SMART way to set a goal.

SMART Goal Setting. Is your goal reasonable for you right now? For example, a sandwich generation person with parents and children to care for may have little time for a large, involved goal. A smaller goal, however, is still possible. To be sure that your goal is attainable, make sure that it is

> Specific and a stretch
>
> Measurable and malleable
>
> Action-oriented and anticipated
>
> Realistic and reachable
>
> Time-conscious and timely

- **Specific goals** are personal, present-tense goals, such as *I am learning to inline skate this fall.* Specific goals give you a smaller target than *I am improving the world.* Narrowing that global wish down would result in *I am tutoring reluctant readers at the Eleventh Avenue School from September 5 through June 15.* Stretch goals pull you out of your present comfort zone—as a nontutor—to a new level of achievement as a volunteer tutor.

- **Measurable goals** allow you to document your progress by checking amounts and dates, such as *Within six months, I am accepting a job that pays $10,000 more than my current position.* For goals that are

Figure 2   **Goal**   =   **Minigoals**   +   **Stuff**

GOAL BASED ON YOUR VALUES	Minigoal 1	*Daily life stuff that moves you closer to minigoal 1.*
	Minigoal 2	*Daily life stuff that moves you closer to minigoal 2.*
	Minigoal 3	*Daily life stuff that moves you closer to minigoal 3.*
	Minigoal 4	*Daily life stuff that moves you closer to minigoal 4.*

not as easily measured, such as *I am looking at my job more positively,* write in your journal what you are doing daily or weekly to achieve your goal. Malleable goals are as pliable and resilient as modeling clay.

• **Action-oriented goals** can be divided into the specific actions, or minigoals, because they comprise your plan of action to achieve your goal. If your goal is to learn archery, you may set these minigoals: buy the equipment, find a teacher, go to the lessons. The minigoal of buying equipment can be divided into stuff: deciding if you want a new or used bow, investigating the brands, and checking on brands by calling the local archery club. Anticipating goals helps you stay on course as you visualize what you want—to become an archer.

• **Realistic goals** allow you to establish a comfort zone within the bounds of risk and safety. If your goal is to buy a new car, how much debt risk will you be comfortable with? Would purchasing a gently used car allow you to satisfy both your debt risk and your need for financial safety? Some risks are not worth taking. You may decide that a new BMW is not realistic for you right now and choose a used

Taurus. Reachable goals provide a reality check—are you able to pay the price?

- **Time-conscious goals** allow you to do three things: First, to decide if you can achieve a goal or complete a list of minigoals at this time without destroying the balance in your life. Your goals should complement your life, not add conflict; is this the best time to pursue this goal? Second, time-conscious goals allow you to complete one goal before undertaking the next. Third, they allow you to schedule just enough time to achieve your goal; with too much time you'll get bored.

Write Down Your Goal and Minigoals

Now is the time to identify what you currently want out of life. Whatever you do, don't confuse life goals with a wish list. Goals are action-oriented (In September I am enrolling at State U to finish my degree in biology); wishes are passive (Wouldn't it be nice if I won the lottery?). In chapter 1 you wrote down an attitude that you wanted to work on, so you may want to base your goal on that attitude. For example, if you want to decrease your chronically angry attitude, a goal may be: I am becoming more calm and reasonable each day. Write your goal here:

My current goal is

CYA Journaling Exercise: Explain how you are using SMART goal setting to determine your goal.

Planning to Achieve a Goal. Proper planning prevents poor performance. Planning includes writing down your goals, minigoals, and stuff. Taking time to write out a plan helps you visualize your goal and see what you must do to get there. Use a pen and pad, spreadsheet, or wall chart—anything that gives you a picture of how you are going to achieve your goal. Consider what could go wrong with your plans. Create a checklist for each step—for the stuff, minigoals, and goal. That way you will also have a clear agenda for yourself for each step. Write down the minigoals and stuff you need to do to achieve the goal you just wrote:

MINIGOAL 1	STUFF
MINIGOAL 2	
MINIGOAL 3	
MINIGOAL 4	

Celebrating a Goal Accomplished

Celebrate! Congratulatory self-talk is definitely in order. Each time you complete part of your goal-seeking agenda, reward yourself. Small rewards are OK for stuff, slightly larger rewards for doing minigoals, and bigger rewards for achieving your goals. Enjoy the realization that by setting and achieving a goal, you have done something most folks don't have the guts and perseverance to do.

While working on this book, I (DM) rewarded myself after completing minigoals. In the past, when I rewarded myself before doing any work, little was accomplished. Recently, my reward for accomplishing a minigoal was two chocolate almond biscotti and a large daily special coffee at our local coffeehouse.

So, what will your reward be when you achieve your goal? Write it down in this box.

My rewards for finishing minigoals are
My reward for reaching my goal is

Successful Goal Seekers

Successful goal seekers come in all shapes and sizes, and from all over the world. In chapter 3, I (TB) described how gold medalist Peter Vidmar and the other U.S. Olympians used visualization as part of their training. While we were talking about winning the gold, Vidmar mentioned that he always stayed focused on his goal. "I knew I wanted the gold medal. I found out that you cannot work out constantly, but you can focus mentally on what you want. Obstacles are what you see when you take your eye off your goal." That really makes sense, so be careful; don't allow other people to cause you to take your eye off your goal. You know that a runner who turns because of a noise in the crowd has a good chance of crashing into a hurdle. Ignore distracting obstacles while focusing on your goals. List two obstacles that could distract you from reaching your goal:

Obstacle 1
Obstacle 2

Zoe's Place. Zoe's Place is a hospice in Liverpool, England, for children under three who are terminally ill or severely disabled. The Life organization runs this home as part of its campaign against abortion and euthanasia. Manager Nicky Goldberg explained, "It is no good saying life is precious and expecting people to struggle on. Zoe's is our answer. We give parents support and time to consider."

Karen and Roy Tyndall are grateful for the respite Zoe's provides. Their daughter, Fiona, has cerebral atrophy that prevents her brain from developing. Karen Tyndall said, "She was so tortured, I was at the end of my tether. . . . The love and attention she has received at Zoe's Place has saved us—and helped her improve." In Zoe's homelike atmosphere the emphasis is on fun and physical contact. Goldberg said, "The babies badly need to be cuddled. That is often their only form of contact." Zoe, by the way, means *gift of life* in Greek.[9]

Evelyn Glennie. From childhood, Evelyn Glennie knew exactly what she wanted—a career as a musician. When the nerves in her ears deteriorated, she was twelve; by learning to lip read, Glennie continued attending regular schools. A native of Scotland, Glennie calls herself a fairly determined person who sometimes turns stubborn. Perhaps that is why she was the first student in solo percussion (marimba, timbales, snare drums, cymbals, congas, bass drum) at London's Royal Academy of Music. Because she was the Royal Academy's first deaf student, the media made Glennie the subject of TV documentaries that created curiosity; concert organizers hired her for lunchtime recitals and later concerts. Over a decade later Glennie has performed all over the world; in fact, she keeps percussion kits at her home in London, in Japan, Europe, and the United States. At first, she worried about finding enough solo percussion music; now composers are writing pieces for her.[10] Glennie believes she is the first full-time solo percussionist in classical music; one of her six recordings won a Grammy.

Don't Take Your Eyes Off the Goal

As Hyrum W. Smith explains in the following excerpt from his book, some goals are so important that we cannot fail to attain them. To set the scene, Smith was drafted into the Army in 1965 and sent to Fort Polk in Louisiana:

> A great deal of our training was to teach us how to stay alive in combat. This was an important goal for the army—if too many lives were lost, we would lose the war. But for me as an individual, survival was an absolutely essential goal. If I failed at this goal, nothing else would matter. . . .
>
> The interesting thing to me . . . was the number of guys who were asleep [in class]. About half were sleeping. This was training that would be essential for them if they wanted to reach the most critical goal in their lives at that point, and they were sleeping through it. . . . The Viet Cong [had] developed a number of . . . ingenious devices that were intended to maim or kill and the army did its best not only to find better ways to identify these booby traps but also to train the troops in how to spot them and avoid them. . . . .
>
> Because my friend had stayed awake in those training sessions he developed the ability to recognize those punji stick pits and other booby traps from twelve to fifteen feet away. He was very serious about achieving his primary goal, so serious he devised his own methods for keeping himself and his men alive. He carried in his pocket Popsicle sticks with a ribbon attached to each of them. He would go in front of the squad, and as he identified the trip wires and mines and pits, he would put Popsicle sticks next to them. When the rest of the squad would come by, they would see his little warning signs. Because of this, he brought his men back for eleven months without a failure. His squad developed an intense love and respect for him because he helped save their lives.
>
> In the eleventh month, however, he took his eye off the trail for just a second, and he missed seeing a three-wire mine. His

foot brushed one of the wires and the mine exploded. That tiny
margin of error cost my friend his life. There wasn't enough left of
him to send home. . . .

His death brought home to me that some goals are far more
important than others. This is because some values are more
important than others. If you are walking along a booby-trapped
trail in the jungle . . . there's no margin for error. With some goals,
you simply can't afford to take your eye off the mark for an instant,
and you most certainly can't afford to fall asleep.[11]

Choosing Your Next Goal

Achieving goals helps you to grow and stretch. As Elwood Chapman says,
"Goal-oriented people are more positive than others. The primary reason
for this is they are so involved in reaching their goals that they do not
have time to dwell on negatives. It is a credible formula. Once they reach
one challenge, they create another. A goal becomes a positive factor. A
realistic, reachable goal motivates you to reach your potential."[12] Write
your next goal:

My next goal is

GRACIOUSNESS

Give graciously of your time and talent to yourself, your family, your
friends, and community—in that order. Be sure to start with yourself. John-
Roger and Peter McWilliams suggest developing an attitude of gratitude for
everything in your life. Yes, be grateful for the wonderful, the good, the
awful, and the terrible things in your life. What?, you say, why be grateful
for the terrible things?

There are two reasons; the first is that everything is in our lives for
a purpose; sooner or later we learn that purpose. For example, Richard
Bloch recognizes that people can both learn from and survive cancer. The
founder of H&R Block tax preparation service, Bloch is a lung cancer
survivor. To motivate others to fight cancer, Bloch and his wife, Annette,
have been building cancer survivor parks in cities of more than 1 million in

North America. So far, they have built eight parks at $1 million each. Cancer-free for 16 years, Bloch hopes that the survivor parks convey his message: "Cancer is a word, not a sentence. There is life after cancer." At the center of each park is a list of five-year cancer survivors in the area and a 5,000-pound granite ball supported by jets of water in a fountain. Due to its well-balanced support, the massive ball moves at the touch of a finger, reminding people that despite cancer's power, intervention can change its course.

The second reason to develop an attitude of gratitude for everything is the joy this attitude creates; your mind has little room for negative thoughts. This means making time to appreciate everything—especially the everyday things such as a telephone. In addition to answering calls from telemarketers, we share joy and sorrow and connect with friends over the phone. Be grateful to inventor Alexander Graham Bell, the local phone company, those who lay fiber cable or string lines, those who put phones together, and so on and on.[13]

Rex Hudler has an attitude of gratitude for the game of baseball. Thirty-five-year-old Hudler is grateful to still be playing baseball; he'll go anywhere and do anything to play. In 1997 Hudler played for the Philadephia Phillies. During nineteen seasons, he has played in two countries for sixteen major and minor league teams at seven positions. At first, Hudler felt slighted that managers saw him as a part-time utility player. Then he changed his attitude and realized that being so versatile was his greatest asset, along with his legs, his zest for the game, and his spunk. Hudler views his job as a baseball player as a reward for hard work, dedication, and desire. "I'm just tickled to be out here and have a job. I'm having more fun playing baseball than I've ever had."[14]

CYA Journaling Exercise: Describe how you have shown your attitude of gratitude in the past, or how you will in the future.

Gracious Corporations

Savage & Associates believes in giving back to the community as well as to its employees. With sales totaling $442 million in 1994, Savage is one of the nation's top 100 financial planning firms nationwide. The firm is active in the Toledo, Ohio, community because President Robert Savage believes that unless his people care about the community, they cannot care about individuals who need financial planning. Even competitors describe Savage & Associates as a highly professional and ethical organization.

In addition to its community service, Savage is noteworthy because of its attitude toward employees. Robert Savage says, "We think of people as coequals, the whole place is really built on that. I think it makes more sense: if people are happy, they perform better." The firm attracts the best young people it can find, therefore, and tries to keep them happy. Of Savage's sixty senior employees, fifty-eight joined right out of college; the youngest has been there fifteen years. Lots of right attitudes, Savage.

Dayton Hudson Corporation also demonstrates corporate graciousness by donating 5 percent of its pretax profits to the community. Regardless of its annual profit picture, since 1946 Dayton Hudson has given more than $350 million to arts organizations and social action groups. Operating 1,032 stores in 34 states, this retailer planned to invest $23 million in those communities in 1996.

Some of Dayton Hudson's projects in Michigan have been to help restore Detroit's Opera House, support arts-centered education in Detroit schools, help people find and prepare for jobs in JobPlus, operate a Career Exploration Program for high school students, and contribute to the Battle Creek Zoo's bald eagle aviary.

Dayton Hudson's Retiree Volunteer Association has 1,400 members who contribute 61,000 hours a year to nonprofit organizations. That's definitely a gracious attitude.

CYA Journaling Exercise: Describe a gracious company with which you enjoy dealing.

Gracious People

Gracious people set goals to help others in their communities. Graciousness is a gift to those who have it, a blessing to those who cross their path, and a right attitude in short supply. In 1995, 93 million people in the United States volunteered 20.3 billion hours—one billion more than in 1993—according to a Gallup Organization study. Forty-eight percent of all Americans volunteered in 1995; and 37 percent of those increased the time they spent volunteering.

In the business community, 82 percent of corporations sponsor volunteer programs for their employees and 26 percent actually give employees time off to volunteer.[15]

Headlines never tout "Graciousness Gains Ground in Grand Rapids," or "Brooklyn Relaxing under Graciousness Siege." With graciousness, the little things count. For example, Joel Weldon, a well-known motivational speaker, suggests sending brief thank-you notes to people who have contributed to our lives whether they are clients, friends, relatives, or associates.

- Actor Richard Dreyfuss believes everyone has an individual responsibility to help improve the world. In 1991 along with corporate and entertainment executives, Dreyfuss began a volunteer action center, L.A. Works. The center is similar to an interactive bulletin board that matches people in need with people who want to do something. Each year L.A. Works provides more than 75,000 volunteer hours to over 650 southern California community-service organizations.

- Despite well-publicized in-your-face NBA stars, graciousness also can pop up on a basketball court. After home games, the starting center for the University of Dayton in 1995 was surrounded by young autograph seekers. Chris Daniels obliged his young fans, enjoying them as much as they idolized him. One evening, a young boy hung back before working up the courage to ask for an autograph. Daniels agreed, but only if the boy signed an autograph for him, giving an instant shot of self-esteem to a mentally challenged youngster. Perhaps Daniels remembered how he felt as an eighth-grader, when he was told that he would never graduate from high school due to a learning disability.

  When Daniels's final buzzer rang, he had earned a degree in communications management and was a fifth-year senior pursuing a second degree in sociology. He ranked second in the nation in field goal percentage at .679, and hoped to use his 6-foot-10, 238-pound frame playing basketball in Europe. When he died at twenty-two of a cardiac arrhythmia in February 1996, Daniels left a legacy of graciousness—except when he was rebounding. We should all have such a learning disability.[16]

- Barber Eugene Parker gives free haircuts to forty or fifty senior citizens every Thursday; he's been doing this since 1994. The Cleveland barber claims he's just plain selfish: "You know, I get so much more out of doing this for older folks than I could ever give them. I learn so much from these folks who worked and suffered to get me where I am today. And it really makes me feel good to know I can pay them back even a little. . . . I could look around and see how little is done for the older folks. I wanted to do something and giving haircuts is what I know best."[17]

- Two of my (DM) favorite gracious people are George and Bonnie Estill of Maysville, Kentucky. While I was working in Northern Kentucky, I called home to check on my mother, who lived alone.

She was so disoriented I panicked and called George, a doctor, to see what I should do. Even though it was his day off, he insisted on picking me up and driving up to see mom; it was a four-hour round trip. Almost as soon as she answered the door, George made a sixty-second diagnosis, dehydration and overmedication, and took mom back to Kentucky so he could keep an eye on her. After she left the hospital, mom stayed with George and Bonnie who helped her get used to the idea that she could no longer live alone. What a caring attitude the Estills share!

CYA Journaling Exercise: Describe someone who has been gracious to you and your reaction.

Gracious Katie

Despite life's ups and downs, people with the right attitude remain gracious. I (TB) do a lot of volunteer work with Make-A-Wish Foundation, which makes dreams come true for children with life-threatening illnesses. The work is very draining because we all get so involved with the children and their families. After we receive a name, we immediately swing into action because some of these kids do not have time for us to be too tired or too busy to visit them.

With my partner, I went to interview Katie Bell, a golden-haired, beautiful eight-year-old with breathing difficulties, a heart murmur, and other major problems. She couldn't thank us enough for coming by and hesitated to ask for anything. Finally, she confessed she really would like an Apple computer similar to those her class used in school. Katie hadn't been able to attend school very often, and she wanted a computer to help her keep up. With all her medical expenses, her parents couldn't afford a computer.

We had wonderful help from Apple Computer, Inc., and delivered the whole system to her four days later. She was in bed when we arrived. After we had strung streamers through the house, set up the computer, and brought in a birthday cake, her father carried her down. The expression on her face I will never forget.

The very first things Katie printed out on her new printer were thank-you cards for my Make-A-Wish partner and me. Her note to me had a kitty on the front. Two days later Katie died. I carry that card with me to help me get through tough days when I want the world to stop changing for a while.

Paying Forward

Legendary football coach Woody Hayes often mentioned that we have an obligation to pay forward, or help those who follow us. Hayes lived this idea by visiting hospitalized vets in Vietnam, being there for his boys—former football players—when they needed help, visiting kids at Children's Hospital, and being kind to neighborhood children who called him Coach. Oscala McCarty, Bonnie St. John Deane, Kevin and Sherry Hall, and Jake Garn also are paying forward by contributing their time and money to help young people and service groups.

• Although Osceola McCarty had to drop out of the sixth grade to help care for her mother, she believes in paying forward. Once she dreamed of becoming a nurse; instead, for 75 of her 88 years, McCarty washed and ironed clothes at $1 or $2 a bundle. And, she saved her money.

Recently McCarty donated most of her life savings to provide scholarships for deserving black students. The University of Mississippi received $150,000 from her; after raising matching funds, the school now has a $300,000 endowment for scholarships. On June 23, 1996, McCarty received an Essence Award; during her acceptance speech, she mentioned that she just wanted to "do somebody some good." Scholarship recipients have been assuring her that she certainly did just that.[18]

• Bonnie St. John Deane also pays forward by talking to middle-school classes about setting goals and never letting obstacles cause them to give up. As a child in San Diego, Deane felt scared about her future; she often thought, I have only one leg. What are my chances of ever having a date, let alone falling in love? She saw herself as a handicapped kid who rode a special bus.

Deane skied for the first time when she was fourteen and knew immediately she wanted to race. She wrote goals for herself that included attending ski school in Vermont. Four years later, she won two bronze medals and a silver medal for downhill skiing in the 1984 World Winter Games for the Disabled in Innsbruck, Austria. She assures middle-schoolers that "winners aren't people who never make mistakes. They are the ones who pick themselves up and finish the race." That's how she won a silver medal; after she fell on an icy patch during her final slalom run, she wanted to cry and bury herself in the snow. Instead, she got up, finished the race, and received a medal.

After that, Deane earned a degree from Harvard University, was a Rhodes Scholar at Oxford University, worked as an international financier, and is a mother. Her middle-school audiences are most impressed, however, when she demonstrates that an artificial leg doesn't keep her from running and even dancing the macarena, a Latin line dance.[19]

•   In addition to hiring both of us to work at Franklin nine years ago, Kevin Hall helped Franklin reach its present level of success in the productivity and leadership training area. Hall's attitude continues to be "Focus on success and success will focus on you."

Hall retired in 1993 to fulfill a dream he shared with Sherry, his wife—to work full time with and for young people, helping diamonds in the rough learn how to create their personal purposes and balances.

The Halls have established Focus Foundation; Focus stands for Furnish Our Community Uncommon Service. Its purpose is to provide a year-round place for young people to create a map of their lives and answer the question, How can I best serve others? The foundation is building a lodge in the mountains on the Utah–Wyoming border.

•   Three years after Kevin Hall hired us, we attended a Franklin meeting. When I (DM) noticed a politician was one of the keynoters, I was disappointed. This meeting was supposed to be a reward for great work. Why bore us with a politician? Wrong attitude!

That politician was the retired senator from Utah, Jake Garn; he is also a retired Navy and Air National Guard jet pilot and a retired Reserve Air Force brigadier general. For four years, Garn served as mayor of Salt Lake City, and for eighteen years he was a U.S. Senator.

Garn recounted his experiences in space for one swift hour. On April 12, 1985, the fourth anniversary of the first space shuttle's ascent, Garn flew on the *Discovery*. With passion, conviction, interest, entertainment, and wonder he spoke of "one of the most sacred and humbling experiences" of his life. "From 300 miles in space as you look on the planet we share, you see that the way we treat each other does not make any sense." Jake Garn's space trip deepened his conviction to serve others. At age 64 he continues to work in the private sector and serves on as many not-for-profit boards as he can. I asked Garn to what he attributed his attitudes of service and adventure. He answered it was the way he was raised and added, "My mother never had a bad day. She wouldn't allow it."

List two gracious actions you will take in the next week.

First gracious action
Second gracious action

Airborne Graciousness

Documenting our current need for graciousness are the burgeoning wrong attitudes of some airline passengers. Flight attendants have had enough high-altitude food fights and they aren't taking any more caustic comments or physical abuse from passengers. As complaints by flight crews multiply, every once in a while the airline employees win a round: Mobbed by passengers after a canceled flight, airline reservationists were doing their best to rebook passengers quickly when, a demanding passenger abruptly pushed to the front of the line. Pounding on the counter, he shouted, "You have to get me on this plane." Barely looking up, the reservationist remained accommodating and unrattled, while continuing to help another passenger.

Her inattention made the demanding one's tirade became even more incensed and insulting. "Do you know who you're talking to?" he shouted. "Do you know who I am?"

With that, the reservationist calmly picked up the intercom microphone and announced, "We have a passenger who doesn't know who he is. Will someone who knows this passenger please come forward to identify him." The other passengers erupted in applause.[20]

Our next book will be about customer service attitudes. If you have had really good or simply awful service experiences, please share them with us. Send a description of your experience to us at either of the addresses on the copyright page and let us know if we can mention your name.

GREATNESS

A gentleman out for a walk happened upon a construction site; he strolled up to a bricklayer and said, "Hi, how's it going?"

"Fine," answered the worker as he kept working.

"What are you doing?" asked the gentleman.

Without looking up, the worker said, "Can't you see? I just lay brick."

The gentleman walked a little farther and came to another worker. He said, "Hi, what are you doing?"

The worker said, "Well, I'm a bricklayer helping to build this wall."

"Well, that's good," said the man with a smile. He walked a little farther and came to a third worker. Again he said, "Hi, what are you doing?"

The third bricklayer smiled and said, "Thanks for asking. I'm building a cathedral."

What a difference a person's perspective makes! A person who is part of a great plan focuses on possibilities, not trivia or problems. This difference in perspective is the key to greatness that often requires self-sacrifice or giving up the personal comforts of life for an overwhelming goal that changes humanity.

One requisite for greatness is self-confidence. Walt Disney's brother tells this story of Walt when his fifth-grade teacher asked her students to color a garden scene. As the students were doing this, she walked around to check on their progress; stopping at Disney's desk, she commented, "Walt, that's very pretty, but flowers don't have faces on them." Disney stopped only long enough to reply, "Mine do!" and happily continued his work. If you have visited Disneyland or Disney World, you've probably noted that his flowers still have faces.[21]

Greatness is ordinary people who have the strength of character to do extraordinary things. Yes, ordinary people—you and me. Greatness does not depend on age, economic background, race, or gender. It depends on the inner fire that drives an impatient person to focus on changing injustice now. Dorothea Lynde Dix was an impatient person. While teaching Bible studies in Boston's women's jail in 1841, she noticed a group of women huddled in the back of the room. Chained together, disheveled, and in rags, they were not criminals—they were lunatics. Prison guards considered them a lower form of life; in earlier decades, these women would have been thought to be possessed by the devil.

Outraged by this inhumane treatment, Dorothea Dix began investigating the treatment of the insane; she visited almshouses, jails, and houses of correction in Massachusetts. Then she wrote a memo to the state legislature, describing what she found. Its title says it all: The Present State of Insane Persons within This Commonwealth, in Cages, Closets, Cellars, Stalls, Pens! Chained, Naked, Beaten with Rods, and Lashed into Obedience. Next, Dix wrote letters to the press to arouse public interest.

Continuing her campaign to treat the mentally ill in hospitals instead of warehousing them in jails, she toured the country. In each of the seventeen states she visited, Dix used the same approach: investigate, use the press to arouse the public, and present evidence to government officials. By 1847 she had visited 500 almshouses, 300 houses of detention, and 18 penitentiaries as well as countless hospitals and asylums. In each state she met fear and ignorance toward the mentally ill, not to mention reluctance to take a mere woman seriously.

Between 1854 and 1857 Dix carried her compassionate message to England, the Vatican, Scotland, France, Italy, Scandinavia, Holland, Turkey, and Russia. Returning home, Dix lobbied Congress to create the first national mental hospital in Washington, D.C. For six years she urged

Congress to fund national mental health care through a land grant bill that President Franklin Pierce vetoed. For the rest of her life, Dix continued to raise money for hospitals, to inspect them, and to instruct care givers.[22]

Great Teens

Eleven-year-old Trevor Ferrell was just an ordinary kid watching television reports about homeless people sleeping on the street despite the cold weather. That night he persuaded his parents to drive to downtown Philadelphia where he gave the pillow and blanket from his own bed to a man sleeping on an iron grating.

Even when Ferrell's parents returned with him the following night with more blankets and hot coffee, he wasn't satisfied. He put up posters asking for winter clothes and blankets for the homeless. Soon the people of Philadelphia had filled the Ferrell garage with clothing, blankets, and a van to deliver all the donations. They also contributed time and money. How many lives did one eleven-year-old's greatness change?[23]

At thirteen, Canadian Craig Kielburger is one of the youngest lobbyists to appear before the Canadian Parliament or the U.S. Congress. He has taken up the fight that a young Pakistani, Iqbal Masih, started. A former child laborer, Masih was allowed to return to his village when others intervened on his behalf. Bravely, he often spoke at rallies about the evils of child labor and described his experiences as a rug maker. When he was fatally shot near his home, Masih was just twelve.

Kielburger started Free the Children after learning that more than 200 million children were working twelve to sixteen hours a day in difficult conditions. Since then, Kielburger has spoken all over the world against international child labor violations. When he traveled in Asia for seven weeks, he was surprised to see children working out in the open, sometimes in life-threatening environments. Separated from their parents, young workers spend their childhoods working to pay debts that are two generations old. Back home in Canada, Kielburger spoke at schools and showed his pictures of Asian child laborers.

When interviewed on "60 Minutes," Kielburger was planning a trip to Brazil to visit shoe factories, sugar cane fields, and charcoal factories. His parents have suggested that he stop his crusade so he can have a childhood, but Kielburger refused. He believes that once you see a problem, you have a responsibility to do something. Why not me, he asks.[24]

Airborne Greatness

During World War I, all U.S. military pilots were white men; no blacks or women were perceived to be smart enough to join this elite group. Charles

Alfred Anderson, the father of black aviation, helped change politicians' and military leaders' perceptions; so did the Ninety-Nines, a group of persistent females.

In 1929, twenty-year-old Charles Anderson bought a plane and then "had to depend upon any pilot who was kind enough to advise me and fly with me. . . . After being chased from various airports, I finally found a friend in Ernest Buehl, who served in the German Air Force in World War I."[25] Due to his difficulties in finding someone to train him, Anderson later started a civilian pilot training program at Howard University. By the time he joined Tuskegee's civilian pilot training program as its first black instructor, he had accrued 3,500 flight hours. One of his early duties was to take First Lady Eleanor Roosevelt for a plane ride; she became a strong supporter of blacks in aviation.

When Tuskegee's program became part of the Army Air Corps, candidates desiring to be the first black military pilots came to Alabama from all over the United States. Over several years, Anderson trained 992 Tuskegee Airmen, 66 of whom were killed in action. Black fighter pilots flew 1,578 missions and were best known for escorting heavy bombers—they never lost one. Thirty-two Tuskegee pilots were shot down and taken prisoner.

Both overseas and at home, the Tuskegee Airmen lived on segregated bases; integration came to the armed forces in 1949. Undoubtedly, the Tuskegee Airmen's record helped change public opinion. When he died in 1996 at 89, Charles Alfred Anderson must have felt very proud of their accomplishments.

In 1929, woman pilots banded together as the Ninety-Nines to overcome the perception that they were freaks; they elected Amelia Earhart as their first president. Despite the efforts of the Ninety-Nines, airlines continued to hire female stewardesses to serve passengers and male pilots to fly planes—a practice that continued into the seventies.

During World War II, Jacqueline Cochran founded and directed the Women Airforce Service Pilots (WASPs) who delivered planes within the United States. Although the Soviet Union and Germany had a few woman pilots flying bombers, the United States restricted the role of women in the war effort to ferrying planes around in the nation and teaching men to fly. Despite the Ninety-Nines' persistence, not until 1993 did the armed forces have women pilots—that's ten years after astronaut Sally K. Ride was the first woman in space.[26]

In this box, fill in two qualities that you share with great people.

First quality of greatness
Second quality of greatness

Nobel Peace Prize Winners

In recognition of their greatness, three national leaders have received Nobel Peace Prizes in recent years. In 1993, Nelson Mandela and Frederik W. De Klerk from South Africa shared the prize; in 1983, it went to Lech Walesa of Poland; and in 1991 Aung San Suu Kyi from Burma won it.

Nelson Mandela. A Xhosa herdboy and former rabble-rouser has turned into a statesman who orchestrates extraordinary changes. Nelson Mandela, now president of South Africa, was imprisoned in 1964 by the South African government for sabotage, treason, and conspiring to overthrow the government. After serving twenty-seven years of a life sentence, Mandela was released and immediately began trying to create a multiracial democratic government in South Africa.

The day that he was freed, Mandela appeared at a rally in the square before Cape Town's City Hall. Had he been filled with bitterness, Mandela could have inflamed the gigantic crowd. Instead, he spoke to the people using words filled with forgiveness and conciliation: "Friends, comrades and fellow South Africans. I greet you all in the name of peace, democracy and freedom for all! I stand here before you not as a prophet but as a humble servant of you, the people. Your tireless and heroic sacrifices have made it possible for me to be here today. I therefore place the remaining years of my life in your hands."[27]

The following day, Mandela held a press conference; after commenting that "I might be out of jail, but I am not yet free," Mandela was asked about the fears of white South Africans. He replied: "I know that people expected me to harbor anger toward whites. But I had none. In prison, my anger toward whites decreased, but my hatred for the system grew. I wanted South Africa to see that I loved even my enemies while I hated the system that turned us against one another."[28]

After being elected president of South Africa, Mandela reflected about his years in prison:

> It was during those long and lonely years that my hunger for the freedom of my own people became a hunger for the freedom of all people, white and black. I knew as well as I knew anything that the oppressor must be liberated just as surely as the oppressed. A man who takes away another man's freedom is a prisoner of hatred, he is locked behind the bars of prejudice and narrow-mindedness. I am not truly free if I am taking away someone else's freedom, just as surely as I am not free when my freedom is taken from me. The oppressed and the oppressor alike are robbed of their humanity.[29]

Lech Walesa. Lech Walesa also sought freedom for his country, Poland. Walesa was an electrician at the Lenin shipyards in Gndansk when he founded the Solidarity labor movement. Solidarity was the first independent social and political movement in Eastern Europe after World War II. Unhappy about widespread corruption, graft, and waste in the communist government, Solidarity staged several strikes at the shipyards during the summer of 1980. After enduring months of labor unrest, the government met the strikers' demands. One of those demands was to allow workers to form independent trade unions and to strike.

Because he was spearheading a drive for a national referendum to establish a noncommunist government, Polish authorities put Walesa in prison and outlawed Solidarity, forcing the union underground in 1982 . When his union became legal in 1988, Walesa once again lobbied openly for political concessions. In 1989 the government agreed to various political and economic reforms.

After Poland's first free election in forty years, Walesa helped form a Solidarity-led government; in 1990 Walesa was elected president. Despite accusations that he sometimes acted like a dictator while implementing radical economic reforms, Walesa shared power with Premier Hanna Suchocka in 1992–93. After the initial shock of converting to a market system, Poland's economy began to stabilize. Solidarity's era ended in 1995, however, when Walesa was ousted as president by Aleksandr Kwasniewski, a former communist.

To put pressure on lawmakers to approve pensions for former government officials, Walesa made a well-publicized return to the Gndansk shipyards, where he threatened to become worker number 61878 making $250 a month. Lawmakers voted Walesa a pension at the end of May 1996.

Aung San Suu Kyi. Unlike Nelson Mandela and Lech Walesa, Aung San Suu Kyi has not been the head of a government. She has, however, dedicated her life to fighting for democracy in Burma, just as her father did. Burma was a British colony until 1948. Suu Kyi's father, Aung San, helped overturn British rule by organizing the Anti-Fascist People's Freedom League. Shortly after being chosen to run the government, he was assassinated.

In 1990 the military government placed Suu Kyi under house arrest; in 1994, it drew up guidelines intended to bar Suu Kyi from politics. Unfazed by opposition, she has organized the National League for Democracy. When Suu Kyi's house arrest ended in July 1996, her supporters —roughly 4,500 strong—held weekly rallies. The government once again placed Suu Kyi under house arrest. A new law allows the military to confiscate the property of anyone who threatens the stability of the state; Suu Kyi could not only lose her home but also go to jail for up to twenty years. Surely Suu Kyi understands the risk she is running by resisting the military, and yet a streak of greatness makes her continue her pro-democracy activities.

CYA Journaling Exercise: Write about someone you consider a hero.

Greatness in Adversity

Sometimes greatness sneaks up on people in the form of adversity. Desmond Doss and Christopher Reeve have had their lives changed by adversity and risen gloriously to the challenge.

Do you know a Medal of Honor winner? Not many of us know any of the 178 winners still alive; so here's the story of a skinny little medic, as President Harry Truman called him. Desmond Doss lives on Lookout Mountain in Georgia. In May 1945 Doss carried a stretcher instead of a gun; he was a conscientious objector despised by some members of the 1st Battalion, 307th Infantry, 77th Infantry Division.

On May 1, 1945, the Japanese watched his division climb to the top a 400-foot escarpment on Okinawa before they opened fire and seventy-five men fell. Everyone took cover—except Doss who carried each wounded soldier to the edge and lowered him down in a litter, under fire all the while. The next day he survived more heavy fire to rescue a wounded man 200 yards ahead of the lines. On May 4, Doss was showered with grenades as he treated four wounded and dragged them to safety.

On May 5, he ran through small-arms fire to rescue an artillery officer for whom he applied bandages and administered plasma. Then he crawled to within 25 feet of the Japanese position to save an infantryman and carry him 100 yards to safety.

On May 21, Doss was seriously wounded by a grenade while treating wounded. Instead of calling for help and endangering another medic, he waited for five hours. As the litter bearers were carrying him to safety, he rolled off when they came to a more seriously wounded soldier, instructing the bearers to take him. While Doss waited for them to return, a shell fractured his arm. Doss saved himself by binding his arm to a rifle stock and crawling 300 yards to an aid station. Months later, when President Harry Truman pinned the Medal of Honor on Pfc. Doss, he said he'd rather have this man's medal than be president of the United States.

During the next fifty years, Doss paid a price for his greatness. He spent more than five years in veterans hospitals due to service-related tuberculosis; gradually, the medication he took destroyed his hearing. Doss was so weakened by his injuries that he could not work a full day and has lived on disability pay. We hope he finds comfort in having stuck to his nonviolent beliefs while triumphing over the violence that surrounded him.[30]

CYA Journaling Exercise: If you were giving out medals for heroism, to whom would you give one? Why?

Another Superman's luck hasn't been too good these days, but his spirit is tremendous. Paralyzed from the neck down in a horseback-riding accident in May 1995, Christopher Reeve is not only recovering but also has become a spokesperson for people with spinal cord injuries. Reeve believes that "when you're pushed, you find reserves in yourself." Despite his severe injury, his upbeat attitude has inspired others in wheelchairs as well as the able-bodied.

Reeve has taken on the government and the insurance industry. When he asked the government to increase spinal-cord injury research, President Bill Clinton promised to budget an additional $10 million. Recently, researchers have helped paralyzed rats walk and Reeve believes paralyzed people are next. He asked the insurance industry to increase the typical $1 million caps on catastrophic care, pointing out that severely injured people should not have to worry about using up their insurance. Reeve has some personal goals, too; his short-term goal is to stop using a ventilator to breathe; his long-term goal is to throw away his wheelchair by the time he is fifty, in 2002.

Reeve is indeed Superman in a wheelchair only temporarily. He has directed one film and plans to act in another. He has appeared on Capitol Hill, at the White House, at rehabilitation center openings, at the Academy Awards, and anywhere he can help people with spinal cord injuries. Reeve has met the adversity with greatness and a sense of humor. You'll find out why humor is so important in the next chapter where we also discuss health and habits.

ENDNOTES

1. Denis Waitley, *Time to Win* (Salt Lake City, UT: Franklin Quest Company, 1993), n.p.
2. Bobbe Sommer with Mark Falstein, *PsychoCybernetics 2000* (Englewood Cliffs, NJ: Prentice Hall, 1993), p. 165.
3. Ibid., 155, 158.

4. Daniel Goleman, "What's Your Emotional IQ?" *Reader's Digest,* January 1996, p. 49.
5. Sommer, *PsychoCybernetics 2000,* p. 155.
6. Stephen R. Covey, *First Things First* (New York: Simon & Schuster, 1994), p. 138.
7. Mary Campbell, "'Around and Around and Up and Down' Describes Career Path," Associated Press, May 20, 1996.
8. Covey, *First Things First,* p. 138.
9. Sue Leeman, "Tiny Tots Find Hugs at Hospice," Associated Press, May 13, 1996.
10. "60 Minutes," November 17, 1996; Mary Campbell, "Despite Her Hearing Loss, Percussionist Never Misses a Beat," Associated Press, April 22, 1996.
11. Hyrum W. Smith, *The Ten Natural Laws of Successful Time and Life Management* (New York: Warner Books, 1994), pp. 89–91.
12. Elwood N. Chapman, *Life Is an Attitude: Staying Positive When the World Seems Against You* (Menlo Park, CA: Crisp Publications, 1992), pp. 115–16.
13. Adapted from John-Roger and Peter McWilliams, *You Can't Afford the Luxury of a Negative Thought* (Los Angeles: Prelude Press, 1991), pp. 591–92.
14. Dick Fenlon, "If It Had More Hudlers, Baseball Would Be Cured," *Columbus Dispatch,* June 9, 1996, p. 1F.
15. Survey for Independent Sector conducted by the Gallup Organization, May 4–June16, 1996; J. Mathews, "AT&T to Pay Employees for Volunteering," *Boston Globe,* September 22, 1996, p. E3.
16. "An Ovation for a Giant,"*University of Dayton Quarterly,* Spring 1996, pp. 3, 10, 11.
17. "Elderly Don't Get Fleeced at His Shop," *Columbus Dispatch,* March 24, 1996, p. 13.
18. "Essence Awards," Fox Broadcasting System, June 23, 1996.
19. Nancy Smeltzer, "For Disabled Woman, No Mountain Too High," *Columbus Dispatch,* September 12, 1996, p. 5B.
20. Ann Chadwell Humphries, "Treating Employees with Respect Reaps Rewards," *Columbus Dispatch,* September 2, 1996, p. 25.
21. Dale E. Galloway, *The Awesome Power of Your Attitude; It Can Make You or Break You* (Portland, OR: Scott Publishing Company, 1992), p. 145.
22. Robert M. Goldenson, *The Encyclopedia of Human Behavior* (New York: Doubleday & Company, 1970), p. 341–42.
23. Gerald G. Jampolsky, *One Person Can Make a Difference* (New York: Bantam Books, 1990), p. 45.
24. "60 Minutes," Columbia Broadcasting System, July 21, 1996.
25. Charlie and Ann Cooper, *Tuskegee's Heroes* (Osceola, WI: Motorbooks International, 1996), p. 39.
26. David Roberts, "Men Didn't Have to Prove They Could Fly, but Women Did," *Smithsonian,* August 1994, p. 72–81.
27. Nelson Mandela, *A Long Walk to Freedom* (New York: Little, Brown and Company, 1986), p. 493.
28. Ibid., p. 495.
29. Ibid., p. 544.
30. John Lang, "July Fourth Should Be Heroes Day," *Columbus Dispatch,* July 4, 1996, p. 5B.

5

Enjoying Humor and Healthy Habits

Happiness is good health and a bad memory. INGRID BERGMAN

Laugh at yourself first, before anyone else can. ELSA MAXWELL

In the spirit of Mark Twain who commented, "Nothing so needs reforming as other people's habits," we are ready to help you review and improve your habits.

Your attitudes are habits; although your habits are not written in granite, they seem to be. By reviewing your current habits, you can winnow out the bad habits and consider adopting some new right-attitude habits. Of the many ways of facing life, habits of happiness, forgiveness, perseverance, and being the best that we can be have some of the largest paybacks.

Later in this chapter we discuss two life-affirming habits, taking care of your health and developing a sense of humor. We also discuss physical, emotional, spiritual, and social health. Because stress affects all aspects of health, we list a variety of ways to overcome it; one of those ways is by seeing the humor in life.

All of us need to increase laughter in our lives because humor and exercise release endorphins that create a sense of well-being, a definite right attitude.

YOU MAY HAVE A WRONG ATTITUDE IF . . .

- You're up to your neck in concrete and your co-workers go get more.

- You fried your kid's pet rabbit and told her it was chicken.

- You don't bother to take care of your health; that's why you have health insurance.

- You tell people who think life is funny they're just plain crazy.

- Your mental health is your business; no fool is messing with your mind.

- Your face looks like a road map on which all roads head south.

- You think most people in the world are apathetic, but who cares.

HABITS

Your life is a series of habitual activities that make up your daily routines. Habits are learned behaviors that are relatively fixed and hard to change; they occur repeatedly in specific situations. Habits are comfort zone actions (sometimes inactions) that we learn to do automatically; some are good for us, such as fastening a seat belt, and others aren't, such as eating too much.

When you open the daily paper, for example, you may be in the habit of scanning the headlines and then turning to the sports or comics. Other no-brainer activities are leaving for or returning home from work. We are on automatic pilot at times like these. Someone could have repainted our houses and we would not notice because we look and don't see. It's the same with driving or busing to and from work. In chapter 3 we gave several examples of automatic conversations. The same thing can happen with habits—our bodies act while our minds are elsewhere—but that does not have to happen. During 1996, the two of us gave more than 300 Franklin Quest Time Management Seminars. Even though giving this seminar could become an autopilot activity for us, we do not let it because we value each opportunity to teach people how to make the best use of their time.

Our values and the way that we look at life are composed of lots of little habits, things that we learned from others or discovered on our own. Some habits save time, such as planning a home improvement project before beginning it. Other habits are time wasters, such as rearranging the groceries in the cart when you and your spouse shop.

Focusing on Your Habits

So what's to change, you say? Well, sometimes our habits have a sound track full of negative self-talk that has become as innocuous as elevator music. For instance, your waking up habits include a whole series of automatic activities accompanied by your sound track. When you awake, do you groan, "Oh, God, another day," or smile and say, "Thank you, God, for another day." When you think of going to work, do you smile or frown? Do you drive or ride to work dreading to arrive? Or, do you switch on your autopilot like a clone of the Dunkin Donuts donut maker, who mutters, "gotta make the donuts"? Worse yet, do you drive or ride home dreading to arrive?

Many people have developed an I-have-to habit. They habitually complain, "Oh, I have to see Pat's teacher tonight," "I have to buy birthday presents after work, and I hate to buy presents," "I have to go to the opera tonight, what a drag." As a result, they sound like children being coerced by their parents; in reality, they have agreed to do each of these things. This leads us to ask, just who is in charge, anyway? It's time to own your actions and deep-six an I-have-to habit. If you agree to meet your children's teachers, accept the responsibility without complaining. If you are the teacher and just hate meeting parents, CYA and read "Emotional Health" in this chapter.

Breaking Bad Habits

As you review your habits by being more aware of your daily no-brainer activities, chances are you will find you are human and have a few bad habits. Let's say that when you are driving, you have a habit of using a phrase your mother wouldn't like for anyone who gets in your way. Or, perhaps you must always do at least two things at once. Better yet, write down a bad habit you really want to replace:

```
A bad habit I want to replace is
```

You have just completed step one, identifying the habit you want to change.

- Step two is to decide when to change. During the next blue moon is not an acceptable choice; now is preferable.

- Step three is setting a definite, very specific goal. If your bad habit is a heavy-duty one, such as drinking and driving, this step must include a decision to change, such as not hanging out with the same friends in the same places.

- Step four is to choose a substitute habit to replace the bad habit.

- Step five is to relax and visualize yourself doing your substitute habit in a peaceful, pleasant place.

- Step six is to persevere and practice the new habit as often as possible. As we mentioned earlier, you only stumble when you are moving, so don't worry about slip ups.

- Step seven is to reward yourself when you begin automatically choosing the alternative to your former bad habit.[1]

If you are skeptical about changing a bad habit, you may have a feeling of deja moo (that's French for I've heard that bull before). Bad puns aside, your determination to change is what makes the difference; only you can change your habits. Think of the substitute habit as a new shoot trying to replace a weed that's three feet tall and wide, with roots as thick as Arnold Swarzenegger's arm. That's why you must tend to the new habit daily. Just as your bad habit is learned behavior, the substitute habit becomes learned behavior the more often you do it.

Acquiring New Habits

When you live with other people, their reminders may prompt you to acquire new habits, "Don't drink out of the milk carton," "Put your dirty dishes in the dishwasher," or "Stop taking money out of my wallet." Sometimes people can apply pressure to be sure your habits kick in: "Don't even think of bringing the car home with less than half a tank of gas," "If you can drive, you can wash the car every two weeks," "If you insist on brewing your own beer, be sure you clean up, too." Acquiring new habits requires the discomfort of leaving a familiar comfort zone, as the following story shows:

During a church service, a chunk of ceiling plaster fell on the chairman of the finance committee. The minister stood by the altar thinking thank you Lord, thank you. That chunk was just the right size; light enough not to brain him and large enough to get his attention.

After the service, the chairman asked the minister if the finance committee could meet in the rectory right away. "I just noticed that our ceiling is in terrible shape; it's probably a danger," he said.

"Yes," smiled the minister, thinking *I've been telling you that for over a year.*

The committee met briefly in the rectory, invited the minister to join them, and announced that they made four decisions. The minister smiled and nodded, "Good, good, let's hear them."

The chairman said, "First, we must build a new church." The minister nodded enthusiastically.

The chairman continued, "Second, we would like to build a new church on the site of our old church because this is our place."

"Fine, fine," the minister beamed, "when do we start?"

"Well, third, we want to use a lot of the materials in the old church in the new church," said the chairman.

"Yes, we have some great windows," the minister agreed.

"And the last thing, we want to worship in the old church until the new one is built."

It's hard to break old habits, and it's hard to become aware of a self-defeating sound track you take for granted. It's also important because your attitude is a habit that reflects how you see life. According to writer Paul Meier, "Attitudes are nothing more than habits of thought and habits can be acquired. An action repeated becomes an attitude realized." Go around thinking to yourself, life stinks and then you die, and that's going to be the sum total of your life. Instead, you could develop the following habits that support a right attitude.

Habit of Happiness Within minutes of an earthquake or serious fire that destroys blocks of homes, TV reporters appear, thrusting their microphones into tear-stained, smoke-blackened faces. In answer to the inane "How do you feel?" some people sob that they have lost everything and don't know how they will go on. Others say the important thing is that their families are still alive and most of what they lost can be replaced. One fellow waved at the remnants of his hurricane-leveled home, with a boat and dock where the living room was, and said cheerfully, "Well, I guess that's what insurance is for, isn't it?" Fortunately, most of us do not undergo events that test our habits of happiness, but like the people who do, we determine how happy we will be in each and every situation. Before reading about some happy and unhappy people, write the name of the happiest person you know in this box:

The happiest person I know is

- Dale E. Galloway tells the story of Grandma Nichols, an elderly woman who had many visitors because she was so radiant and happy. As he came to know her family, he learned about Grandma's very difficult life; for more than ten years she cared for her invalid husband, a demanding, contentious man. Grandma's married children also had troubles and heartbreak. Even so, love radiated from Grandma Nichols to everyone in the family. Amazed at her attitude, Galloway asked for her secret. She laughed, it was no secret: When she got up each morning, she had two choices, to be happy or unhappy.[2]

• In *The Power of Positive Thinking*, Norman Vincent Peale tells about meeting a couple in a railroad dining car. The woman was dressed in expensive furs, diamonds, and jewelry. Wrinkling her nose as though she smelled a dead fish, she proclaimed regally that the car was not only dingy but also drafty, the service was abominable, and the food tasteless. Her easy-going husband cringed at his wife's critical attitude.

To change the subject, he asked Peale's occupation, mentioning he was a lawyer. Then he said that his wife was in manufacturing which surprised Peale, who asked what she manufactured. Her husband replied, "Unhappiness, she manufactures her own unhappiness."

• The story is told that an advisor to President Abraham Lincoln suggested a certain candidate for Lincoln's cabinet. Lincoln immediately refused, saying, "I don't like the man's face." "But, sir," the advisor said, "he can't be responsible for his face." Lincoln looked him in the eye and answered: "Every man over forty is responsible for his face."[3]

CYA Journaling Exercise: Describe two people you know who are happy and two who are unhappy. Explain which duo you resemble.

Habit of Forgiveness Following the Civil War, Confederate General Robert E. Lee visited a friend's home in Kentucky. While showing him the grounds, his hostess pointed to a limbless, battered tree trunk standing on the front lawn, saying: "Before the Union Army came through here, General, that was a such a magnificent magnolia tree. After those northerners blasted it with their artillery, only the poor old trunk is left. What do you think about that, sir?"

Expecting him to sympathize and criticize the Yankees, she was amazed when Lee answered: "Cut it down and forget it."[4] Lee's what's-done-is-done attitude was a healthy way to look at life.

We don't have to look to the atrocities of war for examples of life-shattering injuries. When hurt by death, divorce, disappointments, setbacks, criticism, or deception, we desire revenge with all our hearts. Many times, however, we need to cut our losses and accept reality. Forgiveness is the result of admitting that life is not always fair; injustices occur and we can do nothing about them. Forgiveness is a way of getting on with life for your own sake as well as for others. Forgiveness is not letting hate, revenge, and violence rule your life. One of the most difficult injustices is accepting the senseless loss of a son, as Zalinda Dorcheous did.

In August of 1979 Zalinda Dorcheous's twenty-year-old son was murdered. When the murderer became eligible for parole, she fought it with all the anger and hate in her body. Gradually she began to realize that "it was possible to look at things differently. I couldn't live the rest of my life with anger and pain. I chose not to do that anymore."[5] For reasons she did not understand, she began meeting weekly with her son's killer and she began working on forgiveness. Dorcheous's goal changed from keeping her son's murderer in jail to helping him be released from prison.

Dorcheous believed forgiveness was a necessity, not an option: "I was destroying myself through my hate and bitterness. My body was falling apart, and it seemed that all the hate inside me was attacking my own body. For example, my hair was falling out. I had bladder and gallbladder difficulties. I had a terrible rash on my hand that would not go away."[6]

Dorcheous testified at the parole hearing for her son's killer and when he was released from prison in July of 1989, she was there to walk him out. She also had lined up a job for him.

Like Zalinda Dorcheous, Peter and Linda Biehl have discovered, "It's liberating to forgive. We can sleep at night and we feel totally at ease. You can't do that if you're harboring hate and anger." In July of 1997 the Biehls flew to Cape Town to testify for their daughter's murderers before South Africa's Truth and Reconciliation Commission.

Amy Biehl was a 26-year-old Fulbright scholar from Newport Beach, California. In 1993, she was working with voter education programs prior to the country's first all-race elections. The day before she was to return home, Biehl was driving three black friends home when four young men stoned, beat, and then stabbed her to death.

When the Biehls met the parents of the murderers, they shook hands and said: "We are parents, too. We are in solidarity with you. We are not opposing amnesty." Peter Biehl told the mother of one young man, "It gives me great hope that he has an opportunity now to really achieve something in his life and to be a contributing member of this great new country."

Just as hard to forgive as a person who kills a loved one is someone who has injured us with apparent malice. On December 20, 1974, Chris

Carrier stepped off his school bus and disappeared; despite a community search, he seemed to have stepped off the face of the earth. Six days later, a hunter found a dazed boy wandering in the Everglades—seventy-five miles from Carrier's Miami home. He had been poked with an ice pick, burned with cigarettes, partially blinded by a bullet, and left for dead.

More than two decades later, from his bed in a rest home the prime suspect confessed that he had kidnapped the ten year old. Carrier described visiting his kidnapper: "When I look at him, I don't stare at my abductor and potential murderer. I stare at a man, very old, very alone and scared. . . . He's never been able to live without memories and pain. From that perspective, he has paid his price, served his time."

Carrier reassured his abductor, David McAllister, that he was not permanently scarred by the horrendous experience. He is married, has two children, and graduated from a seminary. Carrier visits daily to read the Bible with McAllister. Definitely a right and courageous attitude. Write the name of someone you need to forgive here:

> For my own good, I forgive

Forgiveness Research. Psychologist Redford Williams is an expert on anger; his research at Duke University suggests that unwillingness to forgive can harm the heart that holds the grudge. During twenty years of research, he found that anger over long periods is associated with high blood pressure, high cholesterol levels, and increased clumping of blood-clotting cells. Chronic feelings of hostility harm the immune system and increase the risk of infectious disease. A study described in *Circulation* (November 1995) determined that outbursts of anger doubled the chance of a heart attack in the two hours following the outburst. Williams recommends forgiveness rather than hostility.

Harold G. Koenig, also from Duke, described a patient who was involved in a lawsuit against his brother for nine years. Unable to forgive his brother, this patient had consequently developed high blood pressure, had difficulty sleeping, was periodically depressed, and had little energy. Koenig commented that it takes a lot of energy to hold onto that anger.[7]

Surgeon Bernie Siegel claims that our greatest disease is lack of love for children. He cites a study by Internist Caroline Bedell Thomas of Johns Hopkins Medical School and follow-up studies that conclude the "psychological patterns and attitudes formed in early life were found to continue to have a significant influence on people's physical health as they aged." This means babies who are ignored or actively rejected or punished for showing emotions may shut down and blame themselves for the lack of attention. Later in life, these stoic, self-denying persons possess the most commonly cited psychological factor in developing cancer.

Siegel's solution is taken from computer jargon: garbage in, garbage out. Siegel suggests that those with loveless childhoods put the garbage out and let the love in; letting the painful feelings out permits healing inside. As difficult as it may be, the walking wounded need to get over the pain and hurt and get on with their lives for their physical and emotional well being.[8]

CYA Journaling Exercise: Write about someone you have forgiven or need to forgive. Describe the steps you have taken or will take.

Habit of Perseverance Prince Michael of Greece was devastated when he heard of Elisa Izuierdo's battering and murder at the hands of her mother. Prince Michael had paid Elisa's tuition to the Montessori Day School in New York City, where he met her and was charmed by her smiles and laughter. Prince Michael said, "I was overwhelmed by despair, a despair that was amplified by my feelings of powerlessness. As the weeks went by, despite my grief, I began to believe that this unspeakable tragedy could have a hidden meaning for me. That it was setting me on an unknown path. Where that path would lead me, I could not tell."

A few months later, he and his wife met Mother Teresa in Calcutta, India. Prince Michael observed her at a center for abandoned children and "saw that the path I had been on since [Elisa's] death had led me here, and its purpose became clearly visible. I saw that in her work, in her very being, Mother Teresa brings hope where there would not be any hope left. Now I understood that each one of us must follow her example. We must hope—and act."[9] Write the name of the most persevering person you know in this box:

The most persevering person I know is

Florence Rogers has acquired the habit of perseverance in the face of devastation. Rogers is the CEO of the Federal Employees Credit Union (FECU) in Oklahoma City; she joined the firm in 1971 when assets totaled $1 million. Today they total $78 million. When the Alfred P. Murrah Federal Building exploded on April 19, 1995, at 9:02 A.M., eighteen of her thirty-two employees fell to their deaths. At 4:30 P.M., still bruised and bloody after being rescued from a ledge, Rogers met with her board of directors to discuss rebuilding FECU from scratch.

Examiners expected a bank run at FECU; Rogers and her staff worked to avoid this by taking action to retain their customers' trust. They announced that FECU would reopen at a temporary location within two days. This meant finding a site, setting up telephone and computer connections, and retrieving data stored off-site. The only data lost were for April 18 and took all summer to reconstruct. According to Rogers, "Our members were so awed and overjoyed they could use their ATM cards two days later, they wouldn't have left us for anything."

Rescue workers found most of the $200,000 in cash lost in the explosion. To be sure no one even momentarily considered defaulting on a loan, Rogers sent out a newsletter explaining that all records had been retrieved or reconstructed. The most difficult part was replacing the workers who died; ironically, most of the applicants she interviewed had known someone who was injured or killed in the bombing.

Rogers persevered, working twelve-hour days and remaining strong for her staff; she left the office only to attend funerals. "I got through most of the funerals without crying because I knew I had to do the job. I know the eighteen we lost would want us to go on," she explained. Months later, Rogers felt a sense of closure: "I have been so busy putting my shop back together, I don't have time to feel angry. My priorities are my family, my staff, and the members of my credit union."[10]

CYA Journaling Exercise: Describe how someone's perseverance has affected your life.

Habit of Being the Best You Can Be Psychologist William James wrote to a friend about humanity's penchant for just getting by: "Most people live, whether physically, intellectually, or morally, in a very restricted circle of their potential being. They make use of a very small portion of their possible consciousness and of their souls' resources in general, much like a man who out of his whole bodily organism, should get into a habit of using and moving only his little finger. Great emergencies and crises show us how much greater our vital resources are than we had supposed."

Jean Driscoll, a native of Milwaukee, uses more than her little finger; she has the habit of being the best that she can be. Born with spina bifida, Driscoll was not supposed to walk, but she did until she was fourteen when a hip injury forced her to begin using a wheelchair. Some expected Driscoll to take special education classes and be dependent on her parents forever. Today Driscoll has a master's degree in rehabilitation administration and is self-supporting. She says: "For most of my life, too many people placed limitations on me. Well, I'm making a living at a sit-down job, but it happens to be wheelchair racing."

Driscoll is five feet tall and weighs 110 pounds; she benchpresses 200 pounds, and can power her wheelchair at about 16.5 mph when racing. While training six days a week, she logs about 130 miles on the road and at the track. Her mental toughness is equal to her physical strength. Driscoll learned to concentrate when she was a child by trying to keep her balance on crutches.

At twenty-nine, Driscoll is the best wheelchair racer in the world. With iron-woman stamina, she has set records in races ranging from sprints to endurance events. Since 1992 she has been winning gold and silver medals at the Paralympic Games; in 1996 she took the gold in the 10,000-meter race, clocking 24 minutes, 21 seconds to break her former record. How does Driscoll do it? She says: "If you're willing to take risks, to dream big and work hard, you'll meet goals you never thought you could. So many people have a fear of failure. It paralyzes them." Interesting analogy and attitude![11]

Like Jean Driscoll, each of us is a package of abilities, some of which are not obvious; hopefully, we are right-attitude packages. Get in the habit of being the best you can be by using all your abilities, walking your talk, and talking your walk. Reading this book and sighing, "I'll start tomorrow," won't cut it—CYA.

CYA Journaling Exercise: Discuss what actions you would need to take to become the best that you can be.

HEALTH

One of inventor Thomas Edison's gifts was forecasting human needs; this is what he said about future health care: "The doctor of the future will give no medicine but will interest his patients in the care of the human frame, in diet, and in the cause and prevention of disease." Following Edison's lead, we look at the human frame (exercise), diet, why people get sick, and how they could avoid it.

Everywhere you turn today, the media remind you to exercise and eat a low-fat diet, so we are simply going to point out that taking care of your health is part of a right attitude. Want to live long enough to see your grandchildren marry? Then remember that for every hour you exercise, you extend your life by two hours according to Dr. Larry Gibbons. The Centers for Disease Control estimate that in the United States 250,000 deaths per year are due to a lack of regular physical activity.[12] Today, two out of every three American adults do some form of exercise; couch potatoes are missing out on these benefits of exercise:

• Increases blood flow to the brain, which improves mental performance and causes the brain to secrete endorphins that block pain, counter depression, and promote a sense of well-being.

• Increases oxygen metabolism, which increases endurance and causes the lungs to completely fill and empty.

• Stresses the bones for proper bone metabolism.

• Improves muscle tone and increases strength.

• Requires the heart to beat faster and harder; lowers blood pressure and maintains the flexibility of heart walls.

Mary Bowermaster's life documents how much exercise benefits us; when she was fifty-eight, she learned that she had breast cancer. "I went through some really bad times," Bowermaster recalls. "When they tell you that you have cancer, I can tell you that it's very devastating to your life." While she was recovering from a mastectomy and radiation treatments, her husband suggested that she train for the Senior Olympics to rehabilitate her body. Once she began, she didn't want to stop.

At seventy-eight, Bowermaster plans to compete in track and field as long as she can. She has won more than 250 track and field medals at international, national, and local meets. Bowermaster credits her athletic ability to her good genes. When asked how she keeps fit in the winter, she commented, "I run up the steps. I shovel snow. I feel wonderful. I feel like I'm 55. I don't know what old is."[13]

Eating low-fat meals is second healthy habit; doctors suggest that fat calories should not exceed 30 percent of the total calories consumed each day. High-fat diets contribute to heart disease (the leading cause of death), cancer, stroke, diabetes, and gastrointestinal diseases. A third healthy habit is learning how to manage unavoidable stress.

Stress

To rock and roll entertainer Bo Diddley, there is no "stress like riding an airplane. Think about it. You have no idea if it's gonna fall outta the sky. That's stress. Stress is worse when your booty is up in somebody else's control."[14] That falling out of the sky image is what stress is for most of us—its anytime we are not in control.

Imagine for a moment that you spend your life in planes; most of the time you are the pilot, at other times you are the passenger. When you are the pilot, you experience good stress because you feel a sense of awe, happiness, peace, contentment, relaxation, and power. When you are the passenger, the pilot is always a stunt pilot wannabe. You experience bad stress because you do not control your feelings of frustration, helplessness, fear, anxiety, panic, fatigue, anger, and powerlessness. Throughout your life, you alternate between flying and being flown—good and bad stress. Although we want to spend all of our time in control, no one does; all of us can be stress managers, however. List times when you are a pilot and other times when you are a passenger:

I'm a pilot when	I'm a passenger when

At about age two, we begin wanting to control our lives. Then at thirteen or fourteen, and definitely by sixteen, we lobby for more control; we want to drive so we have some freedom. Stress results when we do not control our lives; success results when we control our lives. Of the $3.2 billion worth of prescription drugs purchased in the United States in 1995, the top thirteen drugs were prescribed for stress, or the results of stress, rather than for contagious diseases. And yet, stress is nothing more than perception.

When you meet a tiger, 1,500 chemical changes take place as your body produces an instinctive fight or flight response. Your desire for survival tells you to run or, perhaps, run faster. Whenever you meet a tiger, regardless if it's real or imagined, your body gets ready by making these changes:

- Your brain becomes more alert to deal with the situation; under continuing stress, this leads to mental exhaustion and headaches.

- Due to alarm warnings from your brain, your pituitary gland activates the adrenal glands to start pumping adrenaline and corticosteroids, preparing your body to take physical action.

- Your heart pumps faster and blood pressure rises.

- Your immune system shuts off immediately because it is unnecessary to meet the emergency.

- When you tense up, muscles tighten, your arteries constrict, and blood thickens from a consistency of water to molasses in less than three minutes making your heart pump harder. Your body produces platelets so blood will coagulate quickly if you are wounded.

- Your mouth has a bitter taste. Your skin perspires more.

- Your liver sends extra glucose into the bloodstream so you have energy.

- Your body produces four times as much acid in the digestive tract when your heart starts pounding. This makes sure nothing stays in the digestive tract, enabling you to face the tiger without a heavy stomach.

All of these physical changes make you strong at a time of crisis; afterwards, if your body is exhausted, you may develop a cold or the flu. In this box, list your tigers, or sources of stress, and petty annoyances:

Tigers	Petty annoyances

And now the kicker—if we continually sweat the small stuff, our bodies react to the frequent stress of petty annoyances rather than returning to a rest state. Our bodies remain in a state of vigilance—the blood is a little thicker, the heart beats a little faster, there is more acid in the digestive tract, the immune system is in more of an off position than it is on.

Our bodies' reaction to stress is why the top five drugs sold in 1995 thin the blood, the next five reduce the heart beat, and the next three treat ulcers. The more stress we are under, the more exercise we need to flush out the chemicals that accumulate in our bodies. These chemicals give our sweat a bitter taste. Have you ever noticed the difference between a tear of joy and a tear of pain? A tear of pain is bitter and alkaline making your eyes red when you cry. A tear of joy is a sweet tear, lacking the chemicals.

By developing the following life management habits, you can help your body move out of that semialert stage that causes racing hearts, thick blood, and acid stomachs:

- Become an endorphin production expert by increasing your laughter and exercise times. Set aside thirty minutes for vigorous physical exercise on the days you eat. In *The Joy of Stress,* Loretta LaRoche says that children laugh 400 times a day while adults are lucky to have 15 good laughs. Smile and laugh more; find positives in each situation.

- Refuse to sweat the small stuff. So what if MIT found that the world knowledge base is doubling every nineteen months. Is this a high priority concern for you?

- Change your attitude about waiting. Read a book, skim reports, close your eyes and relax. Reassure yourself that *This isn't so important,* rather than grousing, *This always happens to me. How could I be stupid enough to think someone would be on time?*

- Monitor your emotions and express your feelings by saying what you feel or writing down how you feel in your journal. Remember to own your emotions by using I-statements such as *I'm angry.* rather than you- or he/she-statements such as *He makes me so furious.*

- Use relaxation techniques when you are stressed (see chapter 1 and the "Spiritual Health" section in this chapter). Become still, meditate, and center your thoughts each day. Visualize yourself in a comfortable, serene place.

- Treat yourself with care and concern during the most stressful times of the year: holidays, family gatherings, income tax season, shopping for clothes or big-ticket items, and during vacations. Plan nonstress breaks.

- Realize that although men and women experience the same physical response to stress, they cope in different ways. Men react most often with anger and hostility. Women become submissive in stressful situations and tend to internalize stress, sometimes triggering autoimmune diseases. Both could benefit from talking out problems with a friend; such talking sometimes helps people find their own answers.

Ten More Steps to Lower Stress. In *A Survival Guide to the Stress of Organizational Change,* Price Pritchett and Ron Pound suggest these ways to lower stress. Note that this is a do-it-yourself job:

1. Set personal goals to give yourself a sense of purpose. (See chapter 4.)

2. Manage time by setting priorities and eliminating unrealistic goals. Do one thing at a time. Don't put things off. Delegate whenever you can. (See chapter 6.)

3. Make time to play, have fun, and recharge. Keep your evenings and weekends free. (See chapter 7.)

4. Count your blessings daily; make thankfulness a habit. (See chapter 4.)

5. Say nice things when you talk to yourself. Don't blame yourself for things over which you have no control; you can't teach a duck to catch a mouse. (See chapter 1.)

6. Eat right because hunger increases stress. Cut down on caffeine, which increases tension.

7. Get enough sleep.

8. Simplify. (See chapter 7.)

9. Forgive. Grudges are too heavy to carry around.

10. Practice optimism and positive expectancy. Hope is a muscle—develop it.[15] (See chapter 1.)

CYA Journaling Exercise: Discuss the major source of stress for you. List the steps you are planning to reduce stress in your life.

Emotional Health

Your emotional health has a lot to do with how physically healthy you are. Emotional health results from optimizing your inner-most feelings, from dealing with conflicts, and from viewing difficulties as challenges, not disasters. These six actions are excellent emotional health habits:

- Accept yourself. Deal with the world without constant inner battles. Not every battle is worth winning; accept what you can't change. When you find something that can and should be changed, accept that responsibility.

- Accept others. Dealing with others' faults is a test of one's maturity. Accepting others helps you deal with their faults and allows you to criticize without venom. Not getting along with people is a sign your emotional health needs work. (For help in understanding people, see the "Color Code" section in chapter 6.)

- Keep your sense of humor and use it as a plane to shave off the rough edges of life. Your humor reflects your attitude toward others; don't joke at the expense of others.

- Appreciate simple pleasures, no matter how often repeated. Stay excited over things even if they seem ordinary to others.

- Enjoy the present. Although you can provide for the future, you cannot control or foresee it. Venture fearlessly into new projects and new places.

- Welcome work. Enjoy work in all its aspects, including the trivia and the routine. Learn to live with these rather than living in a state of constant resentment.[16]

CYA Journaling Exercise: Choose one of the emotional health habits you want to acquire and describe how you will do so.

Denis Waitley noted scientists are discovering that disease is not necessarily caused by germs and viruses acting alone. All people have germs, but not everyone becomes ill. In addition to hereditary and environmental factors, there is strong evidence that the cause of many illnesses is closely linked with the way an individual reacts to life.[17]

Sixteen-year-old Melissa Anderson knows how to react to life and injuries. After being struck by a riderless motorcycle, Anderson was rushed to UCI Medical Center in Orange County, California. When doctors removed her ruptured spleen and repaired her damaged liver, they weren't finished. The accident punctured her lung, broke her collarbone and right leg, and caused her brain to swell. Doctors expected Anderson to be hospitalized for months.

Once she regained consciousness, Anderson had other plans; she wanted to go home.Twelve days later she did. "When I want to do something, I just go for it. I worked on getting out of there," she explained. Her doctor, Michael Lekawa, said Anderson's "attitude and willingness to get up and move around despite pain speeded her recovery and prevented side effects such as pneumonia, embolisms, or kidney failure." He added, "The will to recover causes hormonal changes in the body that encourage healing. I absolutely believe that a strong attitude to do well and survive helps you out."[18]

Researchers claim that your right attitude is a medicine and they can back up their claim. Physical and emotional health are interrelated; a person with good emotional health can work, love, and play without much internal stress. But things have a way of getting tough, and when they do your emotional health determines your ability to cope. Emotional health is as important as physical health because it helps you visualize, imagine, and anticipate full recovery from illness. You also can reward yourself for recovering. Good emotional health should be a goal in your life; activities such as hobbies, reading, watching old movies, enjoying nature, gardening, or listening to music can help your emotional health.[19]

In *There's a Lot More to Health Than Not Being Sick*, Bruce Larson writes, "Doctors have been telling me for years that you can't kill a happy man. Then I press for an explanation and they suggest that unhappiness often precedes illness. Happy people rarely get sick and tend to recover quickly when they do get sick. The unhappy person is a target for any and every kind of illness."

In *Ageless Body, Timeless Mind*, Deepak Chopra points out that our bodies eavesdrop on our minds and respond accordingly, which is why it is not a good idea to sigh, "Oh, I'm sooo fat." As mentioned in chapter 1, positive self-talk is critical to establishing a right attitude of emotional and physical health.

Chopra cited a study by doctors at Tufts University; it involved adults between eighty-seven and ninety-six who began a physical fitness program. Some of these frail people needed help just to get out of bed or perform other simple tasks. Eight weeks later their muscles came back "by 300 percent, coordination and balance improved, and an overall sense of active life returned." Chopra noted that by going to the weight-training room these people showed that they believed in themselves; despite their infirmities, they had some right attitudes.

Social Health

We offer a new twist on the old Barbra Streisand hit: People who need people are the healthiest people in the world. In the seventies, Professor

Leonard Syme at the Berkeley School of Public Health documented the value of social support when he compared populations of Japanese men living in California and Japan. Those in Japan lived longer; those in California had less social support and two to five times as much heart disease.

In the sixties, Doctors Stewart Wolf and John Bruhn studied men in two Pennsylvania towns: Roseto and East Stroudsburg. They found that men in Roseto had 80 percent less heart disease. A close-knit group of Italian immigrants founded Roseto; as a result, the men had companionship and the close social ties that were lacking in East Stroudsburg, a more fragmented town. But that's not the end of the story. In the seventies, things changed in Roseto as the younger generation moved from their old neighborhood to the suburbs. By the mid-seventies, Roseto men had fewer social ties and the town's mortality rates were the same as other communities.

Another important social connection is marriage. Single, widowed, or divorced persons have a death rate twice that of married people. On average, women tend to live seven years longer than men because they have more close social ties.

The bottom line is that close social ties—spouses, friends, relatives, and community organizations—enhance the immune system. Social interactions condition the immune system so people experience less illness and recover more quickly from diseases they can't avoid. Jot down the names of people who contribute to your social health:

Social health helpers:	

During the 1984 Olympic games in Los Angeles, millions of people were treated to a beautiful example of close ties—one that Kodak replayed as an Olympic moment during the 1996 games. One of the top runners in the world was Jim Redman, a gifted black man expected to sweep the races he entered. The gun went off and Redman moved ahead; then with about 100 yards to go, he came crashing down with a torn hamstring. Redman slowly limped toward the finish line, determined to finish the race despite excruciating pain. As people ran to help him, Redman waved them off—he didn't want to be touched. Meanwhile a man sprang from his seat in the stands, ran down, catapulted over the railing, and ran toward Redman. He was wearing a cap that said Just Do It, and a T-shirt that asked Have You Hugged Your Kid Today? When he saw others trying to stop the intruder, Redman reached out to him; together they finished the race. That man was

Redman's dad. When the media asked why he let his dad help him, Redman said, "I trust my dad." What a great attitude statement.

CYA Journaling Exercise: So, how's your social health? Describe possible improvements.

Spiritual Health

Herbert Benson, a Harvard Medical School professor, began researching mind-body response about twenty-five years ago due to a request from people practicing transcendental meditation (TM). When scientific evidence supported the health benefits of TM, Benson investigated whether a change in thinking could heal stress-related diseases.

In *The Relaxation Response,* Benson reports that the mind works like a drug, especially among people who had strong faith in God or a Higher Power. "Eighty percent of the patients, when given a choice of a word, sound, or a prayer to repeat, chose prayer. I discovered I was teaching prayer," Benson said. Priests, rabbis, theologians, and spiritual healers agreed with Benson's findings. "We have our own HMOs—healing ministry outreach," said Samuel Solivan, professor at Andover Newton Theological Seminary.

Today's cost-conscious health organizations are looking into research that repeating a prayer can lower the heart rate, breathing rate, and brain wave activity—and sometimes even help a person avoid surgery. Benson points out, "The supposed gulf between science and spirituality in healing does not always exist."[20] In the following box, explain how you would like to benefit from the mind-body response:

I hope to benefit from this mind-body response:

Centering Yourself The following meditation is based on Benson's relaxation response. Begin by choosing a place where you will not be disturbed and a time when your metabolism is low—before breakfast or in the late afternoon. Plan to meditate for twenty minutes. Then choose a word that expresses your love of God to use while meditating. If you prefer, you can use the word *one.*

- Sit in a comfortable straight-backed chair, feet together on the floor and hands in your lap, with your eyes closed.

- Relax your mind and body by using deep breathing or by tensing and releasing groups of muscles, beginning with your feet and moving up to your face.

- Say a brief prayer stating your desire to open your heart to God or your Higher Power. Then sit in silence. Whenever distractions come, gently say your word each time you exhale.

- At the end of twenty minutes, say the Lord's Prayer or a prayer of thanks that helps you return to the world.

Walking Meditation David and Deena Balboa are directors of the Walking Center in New York City. They recommend taking these steps for a walking meditation:

- Release yourself from any target heart rate goal or fitness walk objective. Walk where you can maintain a sustained rhythm without interruption, such as a track or peaceful pathway.

- Consciously relax your shoulders. Keep your head erect to avoid contracting your windpipe and shortening your breath.

- Lower your eyelids to shut out external visual stimuli.

- Allow your arms to move. You will naturally begin breathing more deeply, which automatically releases tension.

- Take a few really deep breaths. When exhaling, allow yourself to sigh gently but audibly to release tension and emotion.

- To clear your mind, focus on your breathing, not to control it but simply to watch it. Become aware of the swing of your arms and how you move your feet.

- Periodically check your shoulders to make sure they're dropped and relaxed.

George Bowman of the Cambridge Zen Center in Massachusetts adds that by focusing on your breathing and your body while you're walking you reach a state of mindfulness. Your mind is open and aware in the moment, free from regrets or anxieties. "Pay attention to the rise and fall of the feet, of the breathing, until you reach a place where the mind quiets. Until, in the most fundamental sense, you're just walking."[21]

CYA Journaling Exercise: Describe someone that you believe is spiritually healthy.

HUMOR

Humor can get us through some tough situations--such as being stranded in space. When asked what she missed most during the six months she was in space, Astronaut Shannon Lucid answered, "Obviously, I better say 'my family' because they would feel really bad if they thought they came in second to some real gooey desserts."

A laugh a day tunes up your immune system, according to the American Association of Therapeutic Humor (AATH). "Laughter is like morphine in that it reduces the perception of pain," said Kathleen Passanisi, past president of AATH. "It also strengthens the heart, improves circulation, and boosts the immune system, proving that . . . laughter is the best medicine." A physical therapist and professional speaker, Passanisi added that laughter deflects stress. AATH members don't recommend memorizing one-liners; they say go for the day-to-day occurrences that offer moments of humor, like this story:

When a orthopedic surgeon and a plumber went deer hunting a few years ago, both bagged deer. The doctor went to great pains as he always did when he field dressed his deer. He did a thorough, perfect job; he was, after all, a surgeon.

Loading their deer into the surgeon's truck, the hunters headed for a butcher shop to have the deer processed. As they waited in line, the man checking in the deer stopped when he saw the surgeon's deer. Then he walked over and took a closer look. Finally, he asked who the deer belonged to. The surgeon held up his hand.

Making a grandiose gesture to the deer, the check-in man announced to all the hunters in line: "Gentlemen! This is the way a deer should be field dressed."

Then he looked at the surgeon and said, "You, sir, must be a butcher." We don't know if the surgeon laughed, but we know the plumber did.[22]

Laughing Clubs

Members of India's eighty Laughing Clubs International believe they are lowering their blood pressure, stimulating their immune systems, developing more energy, and sleeping better at night. They meet at 7 A.M. every day in various parks to warm up by shouting "ho-ho, ha-ha" over and over. Next they put their arms in the sky and laugh heartily for twenty seconds. Then they do deep breathing and have a period of silent laughter with the mouth closed. More deep breathing and silent laughter with the mouth open follow; the final round is for guffaws.

People living near the parks aren't laughing about this; in fact some have filed noise pollution complaints with the authorities. We suggest they CYA by joining the laughing clubs. When writer Mary Roach asked members what they got from belonging to a laughing club, they answered weight loss, pleasure, and a chance to meet people.[23]

Write your favorite joke or pun here:

My favorite joke or pun is about:

Humor Research

Researcher Lee Berk brought laughers into his laboratory at Loma Linda University in California. Half of the subjects watched a video of a stand-up comedian while the other half, or control group, sat quietly in another room. Blood samples were drawn every ten minutes from both groups. The control group showed no physiological change. The video watchers showed decreased levels of cortisol, a hormone that suppresses the immune system, and "significant increases in various measures of the immune function." This means laughing activates:

•   T cells that battle infection

- B cells that produce disease-fighting protein

- Natural killer cells that attack tumors and microbes

- Immunoglobulin A antibodies that patrol the respiratory tract

- Gamma-interferon that is a key immune system messenger

Berk concluded that "laughter creates its own unique physiological state with changes in the immune system opposite to those caused by stress." He summed up the benefits of laughter this way: "Blessed are those who laugh, for they shall last." Dr. Stanley Tan, also of Loma Linda, and Berk have shown that laughing lowers blood pressure, increases muscle flexion, and triggers a flood of beta endorphins—natural morphinelike compounds.

At the State University of New York at Stony Brook Medical School, psychiatrist Arthur Stone studied a group of ninety-six men over a three-month period. While the men kept track of their emotions, Stone measured the antibody thought to be the body's first defense against cold and flu viruses. He found that positive social interactions raised the men's antibody levels more and for a longer time than negative events did.

Psychologist Peter Derks of the College of William and Mary at Williamsburg, Virginia, and his colleagues mapped the brain activity of subjects while they listened to jokes. Having discovered that the entire outer layer of the brain is involved when people laugh, they believe it could boost the immune system.

The bottom line to all this research is that laughter increases disease-fighting cells and proteins in the blood and increases our immunity to infections.[24] Even common sense tells us that no one can be anxious and tense while laughing; we recommend that you develop the ability to laugh at the humor of life.

A member of a laughing club explained its benefits like this: "We human beings have small, small irritations. You perhaps do not like my mustache, maybe it irritates you. I used to feel this—so irritated. But this laughter gave me more and more relaxation. And that took away the irritations."

To develop the habit of humor, take these six steps:

1. Start each day with a laugh.

2. Choose positive friends who have a sense of humor. Negative people are downright depressing.

3. Spend more time with other people. Laughter researcher Robert Provine found that people laugh thirty times more often in social settings then they do alone.

4.   Share stupid pet tricks and jokes; keep running jokes alive.

5.   Look for opportunities for fun, such as learning something new with a friend.

6.   Develop the fine art of comic complaining—exaggerate, overstate, and most of all, poke fun at yourself. Keep your comic juices flowing.[25]

CYA Journaling Exercise: Write about the funniest thing that happened in your life.

Flipside Technique

Elwood Chapman suggests using the flipside technique to develop a way of finding the humor in life. The idea is to flip a negative event over to find the humor in it. One well-known example would be Sir Thomas More who angered King Henry VIII and was sentenced to be executed. As he ascended the scaffold, More commented: "See me safe up: for my coming down, I can shift for myself." Placing his head on the block, he drew his beard aside, commenting, "This hath not offended the king."

Most of us do not like to dream of death—especially our own. Mother Teresa saw the flipside as reported by Prince Michael of Greece who was charmed by her sense of humor, which equals her optimism. "The other day," she said, "I dreamed I was at the gates of heaven, and St. Peter said, 'Go back to earth, there are no slums up here.'"

Elwood Chapman defines a sense of humor as an attitudinal quality, or mental focus, that encourages an individual to think about those lighter aspects others may not see in the same situation. Taking life too seriously pulls all of us down. Despite how they look at first glance, most things aren't the end of the world. Learning to laugh at the human predicament can make your life easier.

Chapman points out that we need to develop the habit of humor to create a right attitude. Developing a sense of humor just requires practice; sometimes humor can lead you from the problem to a solution.[26] For example, a problem one man had was a pit bull that hated to walk; whenever he saw the leash, Brutus sat and planted his feet. Considering this a test of wills, the man dragged Brutus along for weeks. Then, he stopped, realizing he was creating a bottomless pit.

Hospital Humor

Humorist James Thurber observed that humor is "emotional chaos, remembered in tranquillity." Life is just too long not to laugh, yet you have to hunt for humor in a hospital. And, the hunt is worth the effort. When you laugh, your brain releases endorphins that create a high. A hearty five-minute laugh will keep you on a high for close to sixty minutes afterward. Norman Cousins documented the positive effects of laughter in his books about overcoming illness. He watched Marx Brothers movies and "Candid Camera" episodes to overcome a life-threatening form of arthritis. Cousins pointed out that laughter and other positive emotions such as love, hope, faith, will to live, cheerfulness, creativity, playfulness, confidence, and great expectations block the apprehension and panic that accompany serious illness. Such negative emotions can torpedo healing. Surgeon Bernie Siegel and many others also documented the positive effects of laughter.

Comedian Steve Allen plays some tough audiences around the country—cancer patients and their families. As a survivor of colon cancer, Allen knows what he is joking about. Throughout his travels, Allen encourages hospital officials to set up humor rooms stocked with books, tapes, albums, and cartoon collections that allow patients and their friends to have brief interludes of fun at the hospital.

Allen's routine consists of answering questions from the audience. When asked about his daily habits now that he has overcome cancer, he responded that he eats more wisely than before. His exercise consists of getting up at the crack of dawn, stuffing up the crack, and going back to bed. On a more serious note, he suggested that cancer patients fine-tune their attitude toward death. "If we talk about it, exchange ideas about it, that'll make us feel better. It's important to put that card on the table."

When asked what sustained him through his illness, Allen answered his wife, Jayne Meadows. He went on to complain that "she spends far too much money on clothes. About six months ago, she lost her American Express card, and so far I've not reported it to the police."

Pro golfer Paul Azinger has a way of joking about cancer, too. While undergoing chemotherapy for shoulder cancer, he soon tired of awaking to a pillow covered with hair. So, he invited his children and their friends to a scalping party. The children enjoyed pulling off the hair and bald Azinger no longer worried about hairy pillows. Azinger's cancer is in remission; he is once again physically fit with a full head of hair, and his golf game continues to improve.

George Burns celebrated his 95th birthday by performing in Las Vegas, telling a standing-room-only crowd: "You can't help getting older, but you don't have to get old." How's that for a right attitude? Another of our favorites was "I've reached the point in life where I can get a standing ovation for just standing." When asked what his doctor said about his drinking and cigar smoking, Burns answered: "My doctor's dead. Anyway, I don't inhale."

When George Burns died at 100, he left a rich legacy of humor and a wonderful example of aging gracefully. His career as an entertainer spanned 90 years of humor; treat yourself to some of Burns' movies, especially the ones with Gracie Allen, his wife. George Burns received an Oscar for *The Sunshine Boys* in 1975, when he was 80.

Humor at Work

When you leave for work each day, take your sense of humor with you. Researchers have found that people who enjoy work are more satisfied with their jobs, less anxious, more creative, more highly motivated, and sick less often.[27] Again, the choice is yours—you can find humor in life or not bother to look. Ken Lodi suggests that humor "makes life's head-on collisions with disappointment nothing more than a brief sideswipe. We feel less burdened by life's challenges and therefore are able to persevere."[28]

Before I (TB) became a motivational speaker, I was an executive vice president for a savings and loan. One of my employees was a floater—Suzanne filled in as a teller, supervisor, or safe deposit person whenever someone was sick. This was a stressful job because from day to day Suzanne never knew where she would be working. I noticed that she usually had a smile on her face indicating everything was OK. The few times Suzanne arrived in a bad mood, she got out of it really quickly.

When I asked her about her cheerful attitude, she said that she did a lot of things to keep herself upbeat. "I have found that when you are working with other people's money, sometimes they are not very nice. They get irritated very quickly. When the customer from hell comes in and irritates me to where I want to scream, I drop my pen. This allows me to bend down, mutter under my breath or snarl, and take a deep breath. Then I can come back up and smile again."

I told her that was great. "Yeah, it works real well," she said and laughed, "except one time. At one branch I opened a teller window where I got one rotten customer after another. I suspected they came in a bus and were drawing straws to see how soon they could hassle me. Finally, after the fifth one, I found myself thinking, take your business elsewhere. So I dropped my pen. After a few deep breaths, I resurfaced with my smile in place, the customer asked, 'Feel better?'

"I answered, 'Well, yes I do.'

"'That's nice,' she answered. We finished the transaction and I had to get a safe deposit box for the next customer. After locking my drawer, I turned around to see the back wall—it was all mirrors."

Suzanne wasn't the only one with a sense of humor at that S&L. One day an elderly lady walked by my desk, which was right out in front, and graciously presented her savings book to a teller. The lady had opened an account the previous day and wanted to be sure her money was still there. The teller came over and explained to me that the lady wanted to see her money. When I mentioned to the teller that we had no way of recognizing the money the lady deposited, she smiled.

"That won't be a problem, Tom, she marked each $100 bill." Instantly I had visions of going through all the $100 bills. And then I heard what my teller said.

I asked how the lady marked her money. The teller said each bill had a red dot in the top right corner. Picking up a red pen, I proceeded to the vault. After I added red dots to a small stack of bills, the teller took them out for our depositor's inspection. Fortunately she did not have to see the entire $10,000 deposit. I would have run out of ink.

I was blessed with a very good team at that savings and loan; they were constantly thinking of ways to improve our service. We discuss teamwork as well as thinking, trusting, and saving time in the next chapter.

ENDNOTES

1. Alma E. Guinness, ed., *ABC's of the Human Mind* (Pleasantville, NY: Reader's Digest Association, 1990), p. 162.
2. Dale E. Galloway, *The Awesome Power of Your Attitude; It Can Make You or Break You* (Portland, OR: Scott Publishing Company, 1992), pp. 63–64.
3. Adapted from John C. Maxwell, *Developing the Leader Within You* (Nashville, TN: Thomas Nelson Publishers, 1993), p. 103.
4. Galloway, *The Awesome Power*, p. 133.
5. Gerald G. Jampolsky, *One Person Can Make a Difference* (New York: Bantam Books, 1990), p. 22.
6. Ibid., pp. 26–27.
7. Gurney Williams III, "Sweet Revenge," *Columbus Dispatch*, August 29, 1996, pp. 1–2E.
8. Bernie Siegel, "The Greatest Disease of Mankind Is Lack of Love for Children," *Your Personal BEST*, January 1991, p. 10.
9. Prince Michael, "All the Lives We Touch," *Parade*, August 11, 1996, pp. 4–5.
10. Michael Warshaw, ed. "Never Say Die," *Success*, July–August, 1996, pp. 39–40.
11. Jill Lieber, "Paralympian Simply Aims to Be the Best," *USA Today*, August 22, 1996, pp. 1–2C.
12. *Parade*, July 2, 1995.
13. Jim Massie, "Bowermaster, 78, Has No Plans of Slowing Down," *Columbus Dispatch*, February 22, 1996, p. 2C.
14. Anthony Bozza, "Bo Diddley," *Rolling Stone*, July 11–25, 1996, p. 31.
15. Price Pritchett and Ron Pound, *A Survival Guide to the Stress of Organizational Change* (Dallas: Pritchett Publishing Co., 1992).
16. Adapted from Mortimer R. Feinberg and John J. Tarrant, "Gaining Maturity to Accomplish More," *The Selling Advantage* 8, no. 183, pp. 1–2.
17. Denis Waitley, *Time to Win* (Salt Lake City: Franklin Quest, 1993), n.p.

18. Anne C. Mulkern, "Girl Hit by Motorcycle Has Beaten Long Odds," *Orange County Register*, July 5, 1996, pp. M1, 4.
19. Elwood Chapman, *Life Is an Attitude* (Menlo Park, CA: Crisp Publications, 1992), pp. 33–41.
20. "Researchers Say Those Who Pray Keep Illness at Bay," *Columbus Dispatch*, March 20, 1995.
21. Mark Bricklin et al., *Positive Thinking for Positive Living* (Emmaus, PA: Rodale Press, 1990), pp. 39–40.
22. Franz Bibfeldt, *The Problem of the Year Zero* (Chicago: University of Chicago Divinity School Press, 1996), p. 50.
23. Mary Roach, "Can You Laugh Your Stress Away?" *Health*, September 1996, pp. 93–94.
24. Studies of laughter from Roach, "Can You Laugh Your Stress Away?" pp. 94–95; and Delthia Ricks, "Laughter Boosts Body's Immunity, Experts Show," *Columbus Dispatch*, November 10, 1996, p. 7B.
25. Adapted from Mary Roach, "Can You Laugh Your Stress Away?" pp. 93–96.
26. Elwood N. Chapman, *Attitude, Your Most Priceless Possession* (Los Altos, CA: Crisp Publications, 1990), pp. 33-34.
27. Marian Thomas, *A New Attitude* (Shawnee Mission, KS: National Press Publications, 1995), p. 13.
28. Kenneth J. Lodi, *Tapping Potential: Achieving What You Want with the Abilities You Already Have* (Chicago: University of Chicago Divinity School Press, 1996), p. 42.

6

Appreciating Time to Think and Trust

During my 87 years I have witnessed a whole succession of technological revolutions. But none of them has done away with the need for character in the individual or the ability to think. BERNARD M. BARUCH

When Minnesota Twins center fielder Kirby Puckett was forced to retire due to an eye injury, he commented, "Don't take it for granted. Tomorrow is not promised to any of us, so enjoy yourself."[1] As time management specialists, we could not have said it better: Appreciate and use each of your 86,400-second days. Make your 86,400 seconds count because your tomorrows are no more guaranteed than Kirby Puckett's. To help you make better use of time, in this chapter we discuss a time saver—incorporating yourself.

Thinking is a wonderfully productive way to spend time; so often we avoid serious thinking because vegging out in front of TV sitcoms is easier, or doing the wash, more urgent. Just like your abs, your brain needs exercise; use it or lose it applies to both.

Developing trust is a way to make the best use of your time. Employee trust allows companies to use teamwork to manufacture their products; but more important, teamwork is a habit of thinking and trusting that works on each level of society.

YOU MAY HAVE A WRONG ATTITUDE IF . . .

- You were stung by a swarm of killer bees; they all died.

- You often sigh at work and plaintively ask, "Is it Friday yet?"

- You know where Jimmy Hoffa is buried.

- You're waiting until you retire to improve your attitude.

- Your co-workers and company haven't done anything right since hiring you.

- You can stand still to change a lightbulb because the world revolves around you.

- You moved five years ago and the Welcome Wagon still hasn't found your new home.

TIME

Voltaire, a French writer, told the story of Zadig, who was asked this riddle by the grand magi, "What, of all things in the world, is the longest and the shortest, the quickest and the slowest, the most divisible and the most extended, the most neglected and the most regretted, without which nothing can be done, which devours everything that is little and enlivens all that is great?"

> Without hesitation, Zadig answered, Time! Nothing is longer since it is the measure to eternity; nothing is shorter, since we lack it for all our projects. There is nothing slower to one who waits, nothing quicker to one who enjoys. It extends to infinity in greatness, it is infinitely divisible in minuteness. All men neglect it; all regret its loss. Nothing is done without it. It buries in oblivion all that is unworthy of posterity; and it confers immortality upon all things that are great.[2]

Voltaire's definition of time is on target, that's what makes using our time so frustrating.

Value-based time management involves managing your life, rather than watching it go by in your rearview mirror. The key factor in managing our lives is time; for most of us, there is never enough. A 1995 Gallup survey revealed 45 percent of Americans believe they have too little time for themselves, their spouses, and their children. Pollsters found that 58 percent of 18 to 29-year-old adults, 66 percent of 30 to 49 year-olds, and 34 percent of adults over 50 do not have enough time. The baby boomers lack time because seven out of ten are married and six out of ten have children under 18. If you are feeling guilty and sleep deprived about now, join the crowd. If you lack time for friends and other personal relations, or for household chores, join the 45 percent and 41 percent of Americans with the same problems.[3]

Say, you are given an extra eight hours one day. Describe how you would spend it:

I would spend an extra eight hours

How can you manage time more wisely? One way is by taking a good look at your 360-degree life in chapter 7. A second way is by organizing information. The information age brought more reporting requirements to most workers and more information to everyone. Before you drown in paperwork or E-mail, decide what you want to keep and don't waste time with the rest. Handle paper just once—make sure anything you don't want to keep goes straight from your in-box or mail box to the recycling bin. Sort your E-mail with the same fearless efficiency.

Establish places for information you need to keep, placing that which you use most frequently close at hand. Once you have organized your material, work on one project, such as paying bills, at a time. But, you ask, who has time to organize? The question is who doesn't? CYA and organize.[4]

CYA Journaling Exercise: Discuss steps you can take to become more organized.

A third way to handle time is to recognize the tradeoff between time and income. Paying to have the windows or car washed may give you more time with your family. Or, looking at the flipside, these activities could be family chores that generate teamwork.

Real estate mogul Ralph Burnet's firm in Minneapolis combines real estate sales, title insurance, a mortgage company, an insurance agency, and a relocation service. Burnet explains: "Time is a precious commodity. Our whole bent is one-stop shopping, working on how we can give people more time. For twenty years, the talk was about disposable income. Well, now it's disposable time—people don't have enough. They want a full-service provider and are willing to pay for it."[5]

A fourth way to save time is to incorporate yourself. Does this mean you have to become a stuffy corporation? No, but how does efficient entity sound?

I, Incorporated

One of my (DM) favorite quotes is Peter Drucker's definition of time:

> Everything requires time. It is the only truly universal condition. All work takes place in time and uses up time. Yet most people take for granted this unique irreplaceable and necessary resource. Nothing else, perhaps, distinguishes effective executives as much as their tender loving care of time.

Whether executives or not, all of us must learn to take tender loving care of time, and one way to do that is to incorporate. I, Inc., is a most effective time-management tool that forces you to answer two basic questions: Who is really in charge of me? and What are my goals? By accepting leadership and having clearly defined goals, you indicate that your time has been well-spent; these qualities are requisites for a successful life. Over the long term, your results are in direct proportion to the quality and effort you invest. In all areas of life, you get what you pay for.

CYA Journaling Exercise: List five ways you can take tender loving care of your time.

Incorporating yourself as I, Inc., imbues a sense of purpose and focus by encouraging you to become your own general manager, goal setter, activities director, and schedule coordinator. Each of us has to take charge of what's going on—to have a plan. Too many people are willing to just let things happen because planning takes too much effort. For example, we estimate that 80 percent of hospital beds in this country are occupied by people who didn't plan their health.

Incorporate yourself by taking these steps:

- First, draw up a certificate of incorporation electing yourself as sole owner, using a form similar to figure 3. Incorporation establishes you as a self-directed entity with definite goals.

- Second, accept time as the necessary and finite resource worth spending only on people, places, events, and things important to

Figure 3 A Certificate of Incorporation

FIRST.   The name of this corporation is—————————————————————.
SECOND. Its registered office in the State of ————————————— is to be located at—————————————————————————————————
in ——————————————, County of————————————. The registered agent in charge thereof is ————————————————————
at —————————————————————————————————.
THIRD. The nature of the business and, the objects and purposes proposed to be transacted, promoted, and carried on, are to do any or all the things herein mentioned, as fully and to the same extent as natural persons might or could do, and in any part of the world, viz: "The purpose of the corporation is to engage in any lawful act or activity for which corporations may be organized under the General Corporation Law of ———————————————————————."
FOURTH. The amount of the total authorized capital stock of this corporation is ————————————— shares of ————————————— Par Value.
FIFTH. The name and mailing address of the incorporator is as follows:
Name: —————————————————————————————————
Address:—————————————————————————————————
SIXTH. The powers of the incorporator are to terminate upon filing of the certificate of incorporation, and the name and mailing address of the person who is to serve as director until the first annual meeting of stockholders or until their successors are elected and qualify is as follows: Name ————————————————————
Address:—————————————————————————————————
SEVENTH. The Director shall have power to make and to alter or amend the By-Laws; to fix the amount to be reserved as working capital, and to authorize and cause to be executed, mortages and liens without limit as to the amount, upon the property and franchise of the Corporation.

   With consent in writing, and pursuant to a vote of the holders of a majority of the capital stock issued and outstanding, the Director shall have the authority to dispose in any manner, of the whole property of this corporation.

   The By-Laws shall determine whether and to what extent the accounts and books of this corporation, or any of them shall be open to the inspection of the stockholders; and no stockholder shall have any right of inspecting any account, or book or document of this Corporation, except as conferred by the law or the By-Laws, or by resolution of the stockholders.

   The stockholders and directors shall have power to hold their meetings and keep the books, documents, and papers of the Corporation outside of the State of ———————————————————, at such places as may be from time to time designated by the By-Laws or by resolution of the stockholders or directors, except as otherwise required by the laws of ——————————————————.

   It is the intention that the objects, purposes and powers specified in the Third paragraph hereof shall except where otherwise specified in said paragraph, be nowise limited or restricted by reference to or inference from the terms of any other clause or paragraph in this certificate of incorporation, but that the objects, purposes, and powers specified in the Third paragraph and each of the clauses or paragraphs of this chapter shall be regarded as independent objects, purposes, and powers.

I, THE UNDERSIGNED, for the purpose of forming a Corporation under the laws of the State of ————————————————, do make, file, and record this Certificate and do certify that the facts herein are true; and I have accordingly hereunto set my hand.

Dated at: —————————————————————————————
State of —————————————————————————————
County of —————————————————————————————

you. By accepting the finite quality of time, you can eliminate those frantic last-minute scrambles that result from half-hearted commitments and make your home resemble a sitcom.

- Third, know yourself inside and out. The leader of a corporation must know the organization intimately to utilize its resources for success; so must you.

- Fourth, be open to the risk of change. The risk you take may involve developing a new right attitude toward your present activities, or changing your life entirely.

- Fifth, plan. Think of your plans as dreams with deadlines or stepping-stones to visions. Your I, Inc., plan is exciting and effective not only because it is about your success but also because you make all the decisions. If the following planning suggestions sound familiar, you have been paying attention while reading the preceding chapters:

  P   Prepare by writing your own specific, measurable, accountable, realistic, and timely goals. Set priorities based on your vision for each facet of your life: family, business, social, educational, and religious. Omitting any facet is self-defeating because that throws your life out of balance.

  L   Look for the necessary people, places, and things to achieve your I, Inc., goals. Be sure to schedule your priorities instead of trying to prioritize your schedule.

  A   Assign and coordinate your schedules and deadlines based on planned priorities. Always start at the end and work back so you have enough time. Remember, work expands to fill the time available for its completion.

  N   Now, begin expecting results that lead to your success. Entertain no questions or doubts about your success.[6]

TRUST

Even though it is fast becoming an endangered attitude today, trust is one of the most important parts of a right attitude—that's why I emphasize it when I (TB) teach. Throughout the country, signs of increasing distrust are rising crime rates and increased civil litigation; people are less trustful of their partners, manufacturers, doctors, hospitals, and businesses.

Surveys also confirm that people are becoming more distrustful:

- When asked if most people could be trusted, 58 percent of those surveyed in 1960 said people could be trusted; however, in 1993, only 37 percent thought other people could be trusted.

- When asked in 1974 how often they spent a social evening with a neighbor, 72 percent answered more than once a year. In 1993, only 61 percent spent at least one social evening with a neighbor each year.[7]

- In the business community, although employees are paid according to their performance, executives' compensation does not appear to be tied to performance. For example, Ronald Compton, chairman of Aetna Life & Casualty, received a 1996 compensation package of $6.64 million, a 485 percent jump over 1995. Half the companies surveyed by Towers Perrin in 1995 had variable pay plans tied to a division's performance. Using this dual system of payment erodes employees' trust and creates the perception of inequity. Ironically, trust is essential to the long-term survival of any business enterprise.[8]

- The twenty-fifth anniversary of the Watergate debacle created a media frenzy in 1997. Talk shows, news programs, and radio shows dissected this benchmark of government scandal while poll takers discovered that trust in government is down. Trust in the presidency has slipped from 73 to 62 percent and trust in Congress plummeted from 71 to 54 percent. While surveying trust for USA Today and CNN, the Gallup Organization also found trust in the media dropped from 68 to 53 percent.[9]

In addition to such surveys, part of our American mythology proudly proclaims we are rugged individualists. That myth is directly traceable to our Founders—just read the Declaration of Independence and the Constitution. Yes, we are creative individuals showing initiative and unwillingness to bend to authority. But we are so much more than a collection of Clint Eastwoods—we also have a Jimmy Stewart side, a communal tradition tied to cultural and religious beliefs.[10] In short, even though we are independent cusses, we help each other out. As we discuss in the next chapter, we must be both trusted individuals and trusting helpers to achieve 360-degree lives.

Appreciating Trust

Trust is learned and later earned; most of us learned to trust as babies. Our parents and caregivers showed their love by their actions; because they loved us, we trusted them. At the same time, because others believed we were trustworthy, we learned to trust ourselves. As we grew older, we figured out that we could trust those caregivers and teachers who kept their word; they were the ones who truly loved us.

As a member of the council against child abuse, I (TB) have noticed too many of our kids trust neither themselves nor others; this lack of trust programs them for very difficult lives. Constantly on guard, they wait for the hostility that violated their basic ability to trust to be repeated; and too often they get what they expect. If you share this problem, you need to start developing self-trust.

Self-trust is a basic ingredient of living; it enables you to set goals and to value your instincts. It helps you accept your mistakes without hating yourself for not being perfect. Trust allows you to build rapport with others and to develop good relationships, especially in family and school situations. Trust is also important in communities and in the workplace, where it is "the expectation that arises within a community of regular, honest, and cooperative behavior, based on commonly shared norms on the part of other members of that community."[11]

We have two suggestions for those who have trust problems; and if the surveys are correct, that's about two out of three readers. First, use the Hartman Color Code to discover your dominant traits and limitations. Looking at both sides of your personality can help you understand yourself better, enable you to trust yourself, and make you more accepting of your limitations. You will also begin to notice color code characteristics in others. By using the color code, you can respond more appropriately to each personality type; you'll argue with Reds, who love a good debate, but not with Whites, who retreat rather than argue.

Our second suggestion is to appreciate the importance of teams—to trust teamwork in families, communities, and business. Companies large and small are finding new ways to produce the same goods with fewer workers; their technology has not changed as much as the employees' ability to work together.

Personality Color Code

To begin, we need to mention that we don't care what your favorite color is. Nor do we have any interest in which colors are most flattering for your skin tone. Our personality color code section is just a sampler, similar to software samplers designed to whet your interest. The basis of our personality discussion is Taylor Hartman's *The Color Code* and *The Character Code* (published by Scribner Book Companies in 1998 and available at your local bookstore).

In *The Color Code*, Dr. Hartman describes four personality types, their gifts and limitations, and how to deal with each type. In *The Character Code*, Hartman describes how to use your understanding of the color code to overcome your own limitations and build character in yourself and your children. We recommend both books highly.

As you most likely remember from Psych 101, the most popular personality theories are

1. Freudian—we are born irrational and bad.

2. Humanist—we are born rational and good.

3. Behaviorist—we are born neutral.

Hartman has developed a fourth theory. He believes we are born with both the gifts and limitations of a personality type. Within the red, blue, white, and yellow personality categories Hartman has identified, these gifts and limitations determine how people react and act throughout their lives. Thumbnail sketches of each category's strong points, limitations, wants, and needs follow.

As you are reading, you will probably recognize people you work for or with, your spouse, your children, and possibly yourself. Keep in mind that

- We all have the power to overcome our limitations and to acquire the gifts of other colors.

- No one has all of the characteristics of a specific color.

- Most of us have characteristics from more than one color; the trick is to figure out your motivating color.

By understanding these four personality types, you can save yourself much time, grief, and frustration; more about applying the color code after the descriptions.

Red Personalities

Gifts: Red personalities have the gift of vision; they see clearly what could be. Not surprisingly, they seek power. Reds need to look good academically and to always be right; they would rather be respected than loved. They want to receive approval, to hide their insecurities, to please themselves, to lead, and to find challenging adventures.

Reds are logical, focused, decisive, assertive, and direct; they are the movers and shakers of society, the lifeblood of humanity. Known for their dominant natures, they are powerful leaders, responsible delegators, and extremely loyal to their organizations. Competitive and bold, Reds are resourceful and self-reliant, self-motivated and directed, active and productive.

Limitations: Reds can be arrogant, selfish, and must always be right. To get their own way, they may use bullying, fast-talking (debate style), and absolute denial of any personal wrongdoing. Impatient and insecure, they can be difficult to live with and work with unless they get their way.

They are sometimes argumentative, taxing, calculating, demanding, insensitive, critical, disagreeable, manipulative, tactless, and stubborn. Pragmatic and profit-based, Reds hate incompetence and lack both compassion and any need for intimacy.

In dealing with Red attitudes, be sure to:

1.   Present issues logically and include facts and figures.

2.   Demand their attention and respect.

3.   Be direct, brief, and specific in conversation; verbalize your feelings.

4.   Be productive and efficient.

5.   Offer them leadership opportunities and support their decisive natures.

6.   Promote their intelligent reasoning where appropriate.

7.   Respect their need to make their own decisions in their own ways.

In dealing with Red attitudes, don't ever:

1.   Embarrass them in front of others or use physical punishment.

2.   Argue from an emotional perspective or be slow and indecisive.

3.   Forget to use an authoritarian approach.

4.   Expect a personal and intimate relationship.

5.   Attack them personally or take their arguments personally.

6.   Wait for them to solicit your opinion.

7.   Intrude on their alone time.

People I know who may have Red personalities:

Blue Personalities

Gifts: Blue personalities have the gift of compassion and want to save the world. They are motivated by intimacy. Blues need to be morally good, to be understood, and to be appreciated. Always appropriate and admired in any situation, they want acceptance, to reveal their insecurities, to please others, to be autonomous, and to be secure. Blues are reliable, self-disciplined, steady, ordered, and enduring.

They value intimate relationships and creative accomplishments more than material possessions. They enjoy culture, beauty, and emotional sincerity; they are most comfortable in creative, productive environments. Blues are loyal and nurturing people who value connectedness, who listen with empathy, and speak with zeal. Because they are purposeful, dedicated, and self-sacrificing, Blues expect other people to do the best they can. Committed and obedient, they support law and order.

Limitations: Blues can be self-righteous and have unrealistic expectations. Blues have been known to carry around unnecessary guilt, to whine, and to be perpetually discontented. Too sensitive and demanding, Blues may be complex and worrisome; their perfectionism can cause depression.

Lacking trust, they may suspect others and be skeptical of them. Blues can be bitter, resentful, and unforgiving. Moody, rarely playful or spontaneous, they sometimes become their own worst enemies.

In dealing with Blue attitudes, be sure to:

1. Emphasize their security in the relationship; be sincere and genuine.

2. Be sensitive and soft spoken in your approach.

3. Behave appropriately and be well mannered.

4. Appreciate them and promote their creativity.

5. Allow them to gather their thoughts before expressing themselves.

6. Be loyal and limit their risk level.

7. Do a thorough analysis before making a presentation.

In dealing with Blue attitudes, don't ever:

1. Be rude or abrupt, or make them feel guilty.

2. Promote too much change or push them into making quick decisions.

3. Expect spontaneity or demand immediate action.

4. Abandon them.

5. Expect them to bounce back easily or quickly from depression.

6. Demand perfection (they already expect too much from themselves).

7. Expect them to forgive quickly when crossed.

People I know who may have Blue personalities:

White Personalities

Gifts: White personalities, who have the gift of clarity, see things more clearly than the rest of us. They seek peace. Whites need to feel good inside, to be understood, and to be respected. Gentle and even-tempered, they want to be accepted, to hide insecurities, to please themselves and others, to be independent, and to be contented.

Whites are tolerant and capable, the nicest people to know unless you need a decision made. Peaceful, diplomatic, and patient, Whites stuff and stuff and stuff anger before they finally explode. Rarely ruffled and having little ego need, these easygoing people are impressionable, blendable, kind, and accepting.

Limitations: Whites often use silent aloofness and intellectualism to shield them from others. Known for habitually hiding out, they also can be silently stubborn; they smile in agreement while doing whatever they want. Passive, easygoing Whites may be hard to motivate; they don't like pressure or pushing. They can be doubtful and dependent, unmotivated, aimless, misguided, boring, and lazy. They are sometimes indecisive, insecure, and nonassertive; withholding their feelings, these unproductive dreamers can be timid and emotionally unsure.

In dealing with White attitudes, be sure to:

1. Be loving and sensitive, simple and open.

2. Be firm, patient, and gentle.

3. Provide boundaries for them to operate within.

4. Introduce options and ideas for their involvement.

5. Accept their individuality.

6. Be casual, informal, and relaxed.

7. Look for nonverbal clues to their feelings; listen quietly.

In dealing with White attitudes, don't ever:

1. Expect them to always need others to play or work with.

2. Force verbal expression or confrontation.

3. Be domineering or too intense.

4. Overwhelm them with too much.

5. Speak too fast.

6. Take away their daydreams or be unkind.

7. Demand leadership.

People I know who may have White personalities:

Yellow Personalities

Gifts: Yellow personalities have the gift of enthusiasm; they know how to enjoy themselves and to be entertaining. They seek fun. Yellows need to look good socially, to be popular, and to be praised. They want lots of approval, to hide insecurities, to be noticed, to be free, and to enjoy playful adventure. Carefree and trusting, charismatic Yellows are happy and naive; they love life. These popular fun people are spontaneous, enthusiastic, playful, and exciting.

Limitations: Yellows can limit themselves with their superficiality and avoidance; they are attractive but may run when anyone tries to get close. These flip chatterboxes refuse to have serious discussions, focused commitments, and deep emotional expression. Self-centered and uncommitted, Yellows can be irresponsible, disorganized, incomplete, impulsive, and undisciplined.

In dealing with Yellow attitudes, be sure to:

1. Be positive and praise them.

2. Adore them and accept their playful teasing.

3. Touch them physically.

4. Remember they are tender and enjoy their charismatic innocence.

5. Promote playful activities for and with them.

6. Remember they hold feelings deeply.

7. Allow them opportunity for verbal expression.

In dealing with Yellow attitudes, don't ever:

1. Be too serious or sober in criticism.

2. Push them too intensely or expect them to dwell on problems.

3. Ignore them or forget they have down times also.

4. Demand perfection or attack their sensitivity.

5. Give them too much rope or they may hang themselves.

6. Classify them as just lightweight social butterflies.

7. Totally control their schedules.

People I know who may have Yellow personalities:

About now, Red readers are asking, "So, what is the point?" Blue readers are concerned about whether the color categories can possibly decrease homelessness. Whites are waiting patiently for the explanation, and Yellows are wondering if they're having fun yet.

The point is that by using these categories, you can understand what motivates your attitude and other people's attitudes. What really motivates you? A desire for power, intimacy, peace, or fun? By understanding the color code, your attitude can compliment others' attitudes more effectively in appropriate ways. Once you realize that your boss is a Red, you won't expect him to stop changing and you can help other employees accept his vision for the company. If you realize your child is a white, you will help her overcome her lack of assertiveness. If you realize you are a blue with a typical unforgiving attitude toward people who have hurt you, you can work on getting over it and getting on with life.

If you have not figured out which color you are, read the descriptions of each color over until they become familiar. One day as you think about the characteristics of each color, you will know what color you are. (Or, to be more accurate, you can take the personality profile test in Hartman's books.) Remember that even when people have characteristics of two colors, one color is always dominant. If you have figured out what color your personality is, write it down here:

My personality color is

Using the Color Code

Work Situations

- If you heard your employer shouting about someone stealing a file folder or disk, would you

1. Slink off to the rest room to wait out his tantrum (White response).
2. Go in and try to cheer him up (Yellow response).
3. Rush in and find the lost item on his desk, saying, "Someone must have hidden it under this stack of contracts" (Blue response).
4. Scream from your adjoining office that you did not lose that file or disk (Red response).

- You accidentally dropped your computer password in the elevator and a computer hacker used it to wipe out the company's files. Would you

1. Deny dropping the password (Red response).

2. Confess contritely in your resignation letter after cleaning out your desk (White response).
3. Admit you are at fault and offer to resign (Blue response).
4. Deny even knowing the password (Yellow response).

Home Situations

- When your Red child's assignment is to explain a poem about apples to the class, would you

1. Be jolly while assuring her that she can explain the poem about apples and juggling several for her (Yellow response).
2. Tell her to get the assignment finished ASAP (Red response).
3. Bake apple tarts for all of her classmates (Blue response).
4. Say nothing, because you know she will do a good job (White response).

- Your two Yellow children hate to clean their rooms. Would you

1. Ask them to clean up the rooms sometime during the day (White response).
2. Tell them to start cleaning now if they want to live until lunch (Red response).
3. Explain how it pains you to see their rooms so messy, especially since you are constantly cleaning the house to be an example to them (Blue response).
4. Tell them to go play for a while and then come in and clean their rooms (Yellow response).

As we mentioned, this is just a sample of a fascinating theory. We both believe in Taylor Hartman's Color Code so much that we teach it; we do walk our talk. One of us is Blue with a little Yellow and the other Yellow with a bit of Blue.

___

CYA Journaling Exercise: Discuss your color, your strong points, and your limitations. How will you use this knowledge?

___

Trusting Teamwork

Teamwork is synonymous with sports. According to Michael Jordan of the Chicago Bulls, "Talent wins games, but teamwork and intelligence win championships. I'd rather have five guys with less talent who are willing to come together as a team than five guys who consider themselves stars and aren't willing to sacrifice." After winning three NBA championships, we suspect Jordan knows what he's talking about.[12]

Within team sports, the rapid, continuous action of an ice hockey team is the best example of teamwork contributing to the right attitude for success. Although hockey players play multiple and interchangeable roles, everyone passes, shoots, plays defense, and still has a primary role. Team and individual successes depend on how well individuals blend together, how much they trust each other. In this section we look at teamwork at work, at home, in the community, and between friends.

Teamwork in the Top Three Inches. Author H. Norman Wright tells the story of a Wyoming sheep herder who spent much of his time observing animals. Each winter, packs of hungry wolves swept into the valley and ferociously attacked herds of wild horses. To defend themselves, the horses formed a circle with their heads inside; they kicked furiously with their hind legs, driving the wolves away. Undaunted, the wolves moved on to attack a herd of jackasses that had been turned loose by their owners. The jackasses also formed a circle, but with their heads toward the wolves. When they kicked furiously, they kicked each other and were soon eaten alive.

Like the wild animals, people have a choice between being as smart as the horses or as stupid as the jackasses. They can kick the problem together as a team, or they can kick each other.

In the last decade, managers in business and industry have discovered that the secret to improving the bottom line rests in the top three inches of our anatomy. Collaboration brings out the best in people by acknowledging their importance to the group. To get the most from others in group situations, emphasize each person's strengths and talents. Everyone knows something that you don't know and can do something better than you; tap that resource by creating a win-win alliance. We are standing on a time line and whether we keep arguing or working, time keeps moving on. So we might as well think about how we get from here to there, together. Write down any groups or individuals that face danger like jackasses on the

Groups or individuals using jackass methods:

Teamwork forces people of different races, religions, genders, and cultures to trust each other enough to work together. Ideally, this should not be a problem. For years we have heard that America is a melting pot where religions, races, and cultures merged into each other. Actually, other races, religions, and cultures had to blend into a primarily WASP country. The result was sort of like Velveeta cheese, according to 3M Vice-President Richard Lidstad.

Recently, social and political forces have turned the melting pot into a salad bowl. Although the ingredients remain separate, the dressing binds everything together; the diverse ingredients enhance and enrich each other. While working toward a common goal, each person keeps an individual identity and unique attributes. Diversity in a team requires respect for others' backgrounds and points of view. Just tolerating those who are not like yourself won't cut it; each team member must trust the others and embrace different points of view to see how these contribute to the team.[13]

World Trade Center Teams.

On February 26, 1993, a team of terrorists detonated a bomb in the garage of New York City's World Trade Center (WTC) at 12:18 P.M. Six people died in the blast and more than 1,000 were injured. Considering that 50,000 people worked in the twin towers, and 40,000 visited each day, casualties could have been much greater. Later, insurance adjusters said any other building would have been destroyed; fortunately, in the twin towers' the structural supports run along the outer walls.

On March 18, Governor Mario Cuomo moved back into his WTC office; most of the other 400 displaced tenants returned by mid-April; the last were in by the end of that month. The WTC's quick comeback is a story of teamwork by its owners, the Port Authority of New York and New Jersey, and many others:

- Less than six hours after the blast, The Restoration Company had personnel on the scene to hire and train employees and to direct its 16-day cleanup of 8.8 million square feet. Around the clock—and during the winter storm of the century—2,700 workers cleaned 550,000 square feet a day. Also hard at work were marble cleaners, exterminators, and 200 union supervisors.

- The Real Estate Board of New York helped tenants find temporary office space nearby and encouraged landlords to rent at their cost.

- Despite its lack of a formal crisis management plan, the Port Authority coordinated hundreds of jobs at the same time, bringing in public utility workers, tradespersons, and craftspersons to remove all traces of the bomb's damage. It's not easy to make $510 million worth of damage just go away.

Staff members escorted tenants who needed to reenter the WTC to get keys, files, and vital documents. Employees who usually worked at the airports, bridges, and tunnels run by the Port Authority worked around the clock to get the WTC back in operation.

From their makeshift offices, staff members tracked down all of the tenants and called them almost daily at first. Later they messengered a twice-weekly newsletter advising tenants about trauma counseling, small business loans, new safety procedures, and anticipated dates of reopening.

Work Teams

Companies have discovered that teams work as well in business as in athletics. Autonomous, self-directed teams can be empowered to make decisions and to adapt quickly to market trends; once teams own a mission, they are free to innovate, experiment, and compete. Teamwork requires problem solving, risk taking, innovation, decisive action, and working smart. In the summer of 1996 the Gallup Organization surveyed American workers' attitudes about their employers for the Marlin Company, a business materials publishing company. Gallup found:

- 25 percent of workers feel somewhat or extremely angry.

- 27 percent of workers are anxious about losing their jobs within six months.

- 93 percent of workers feel some loyalty to their employers; 60 percent feel very loyal.

The reasons employees gave for their anger include the actions of a supervisor or manager, tight deadlines, a lack of others' productivity, and the actions of co-workers. We believe that attitudes of trust and teamwork could solve most of these problems.[14]

W. Edwards Deming taught teaming to the Japanese after World War II; it has taken the rest of the world a little longer to catch up. For example, Ford Motor Company saved $73 million on its 1996 Taurus production line by nickel and dime teamwork. At brainstorming sessions, line workers and engineers talked about changing parts or using different parts to save money. These small savings per car—$1.50 here, $5.00 there—added up to millions. More important, line workers are aware that now someone will listen to their suggestion that a less-expensive straight

hose will work just as well as an expensive custom-designed hose.[15]
    Work teams have an important place in manufacturing today; they
enable companies to cut costs and deliver value to customers. The following
companies are just two of many successfully using work teams:

- Hallmark Cards, Inc., has found that work teams better utilize the
  talents of specialized technicians and creative workers. To shorten
  the manufacturing time for each of the 40,000 cards and related
  items the company produces annually, Hallmark assembled teams
  for various holidays and occasions. The Thanksgiving team, for
  example, has merchandisers, accountants, artists, writers,
  designers, and lithographers. At its head office in Kansas City,
  Hallmark has relocated team members so they can work closely as
  a unit. Now each card moves through production faster; this saves
  money and time as well as allowing the company to be more
  responsive to changing trends.[16]

- Malcolm Grear Designers (MGD) was one of about 500 firms that
  applied to provide design work at the 1996 Olympic Games in
  Atlanta. MGD in Providence, Rhode Island, was one of six firms
  chosen; the firm designed the handheld torch, the medals, and the
  pictograms representing various sports. From the beginning, Grear
  involved his entire staff, family, and friends in the project. Late-
  night brainstorming sessions had only one rule: Don't try to be
  sophisticated—if you have an idea, put it down—there are no
  limits.
      Key ingredients in MGD's success have been the group
  process and collaborative management. Malcolm Grear says, "I
  don't like when people give me credit for all the work that goes on.
  My name is just on the door, and I'm the end art director, and I'm
  involved in every project, but everybody contributes." He continues,
  "When vanity intrudes is when design suffers. You include whoever
  and whatever you have to get the job done right, so no one can say 'I
  did this.'"[17]

Why Work Teams Work. According to Francis Fukuyama, "If
people who have to work together in an enterprise trust one another because
they are all operating according to a common set of ethical norms, doing
business costs less. Such a society will be better able to innovate
organizationally, since the high degree of trust will permit a wide variety
of social relationships to emerge."[18]
    He cites the U.S. Defense Department's contracting system as an
example of an organization showing an absence of trust. This department

assumes not only that contractors will cheat taxpayers but also that government officials given any discretion in dealing with contractors will abuse this freedom. Costs must be justified through extensive documentation that is audited regularly. That's why we paid $800 for toilet seats and $300 for hammers in the 1980s.[19] The bottom line: Even while factoring in possible errors in judgment, trust not only works better than red tape, it's cheaper.

Give your employer a teamwork grade from 1 (little) to 10 (lots) :

```
┌──────────────────────────────────────────────────┐
│                                                    │
└──────────────────────────────────────────────────┘
```

Self-Managed Teams

About one-quarter of all businesses use self-managed teams; by the end of the century, experts expect fully half of all businesses to do so. Companies that use teams include General Foods, General Motors, Hewlett-Packard, Prudential, Motorola, Goodyear, and General Mills. These companies make groups of workers responsible for a specific process from beginning to end. Workers decide on work assignments, select team members, and evaluate each other's performance.

Saturn Corporation uses teams in its state-of-the-art plant in Spring Hill, Tennessee. Each of the plant's almost 200 teams has budgetary and hiring responsibilities; members even can choose their own parts suppliers. Training includes instruction in awareness, conflict management techniques, consensus-decision making, and group dynamics.

Volvo also uses self-managed teams in its Uddevalla assembly plants. Seven- to ten-worker teams handle scheduling, quality control, work assignments, and hiring; they choose a team spokesperson who reports to the plant manager. Each team assembles four complete cars during a shift. The Swedish carmaker has been pleased with the speed and high quality of these plants.[20]

Family Teams

All families are teams; encourage yours to think and work together. Parents are automatically team leaders because they have empowered themselves to set boundaries for their children; this teaches young team members how to be competent in a secure setting. As a leader, focus on getting results—no wallowing, waffling, or wimping out—especially during times of change. You don't need to have all the answers; you do need to listen and show care, concern, and respect for other team members. Admit your mistakes. Understanding and appreciating the color of each family member's personality is an excellent tool for teamwork at every level.

Be sure everyone in your family understands exactly what your team's goals are. Build trust by being trustworthy. Nail down each member's responsibilities with clarity, precision, and attention to detail, yet allow some slack for individual differences. Create a supportive home environment; when one member is involved in a project, it's nice if other family members are there, too. Enter ways your family acts as a team, and ways it could act as a team here:

Family acts as a team:	Family could act as a team:

Community Teamwork

During each election year we have a national debate about values. One would think that as a nation we could not figure out that values come mainly from parents, and later from teachers, peers, and the community. Despite the values debate and campaign promises every four years, values cannot be legislated. Values can, however, be nurtured with a little teamwork.

Albuquerque, New Mexico, has taken on values as a community project by adopting Character Counts. The program reminds people that no matter their education, faith, or income level they can agree on six desirable character traits: respect, trustworthiness, responsibility, fairness, caring, and citizenship. Developed by the Josephson Institute of Ethics in California, Character Counts has been adopted by at least 200 cities in 29 states. Los Angeles millionaire Michael Josephson left a lucrative career to found this nonprofit program; he did this to make his children proud.

Albuquerue is the largest city to implement Character Counts in its schools. Beginning in 1993, one city school emphasized one character trait each month; an immediate result was a drop from 60 to 20 discipline citations per month. In 1994 the mayor made these six words the keystone of his campaign to stop youth violence. In 1995, all 118 Albuquerque schools received state funding to implement the program. Meanwhile, the Police Athletic Association, the Hispano Chamber of Commerce, the Boy Scouts, and churches signed on.

Although the jury is still out on the program's lasting effect, team members on the Character Counts leadership council are giving it everything they've got. Bank president Ed O'Leary put the six traits on billboards. AT&T executive Rick Johnson initiated an information saturation campaign. He wants adults to see the character traits everywhere—on utility bills, city buses, and kids' homework papers. Johnson believes that increasing adults' consciousness of the traits will make them treat each other differently. Ultimately he sees them not thinking about the traits, just living them; he's counting on everyone's innate desire to do right.

Twenty years ago Albuquerque's middle schools dropped athletics; when community leaders identified sports as a way to fight gangs and teach Character Counts, businesses ponied up $115,000 to put basketball in 23 schools for 1995-96. They have pledged more for the following year.[21]

Albuquerque's Character Counts program highlights the importance of community teamwork. Each community has programs to improve that corner of the world. Join a team to improve your community.

CYA Journaling Exercise: Discuss a community problem that you and your neighbors could team up to solve.

Friendly Teams

Working on a team gives all of us a chance to improve our people skills and develop empathy for others' feelings. Just the way someone says thank you can make you feel genuinely appreciated, patronized, or dismissed. Realizing this can help you send the right signals while working on a team. For instance, when psychologists studied engineers and scientists from Carnegie-Mellon University and Bell Labs, they found these workers had a wide range of people skills resulting in an equally wide range of attitudes toward them. Some of the people studied had established wide-ranging networks and received help immediately whenever they needed it; those lacking such networks had trouble even getting their calls returned.[22] Teamwork demands collaboration; by bringing out the best in people, everyone succeeds. If you are a fast tracker who can't get help from others or share success, take a hard look at your overpowering ego and CYA.

Of course, teamwork is a hallmark of Boy Scouts. During a hike through the woods, a troop discovered an abandoned section of railroad track that might as well have had a sign saying, CLIMB ME. One by one they climbed the rails; one by one they lost their balance and fell, hurting only their pride. Meanwhile, two boys stood off to the side watching; as the others rubbed their bruises, they bet them that they could walk the whole track without falling.

Derision met their offer; the bet was on. The first boy stepped on the left rail and the second on the right rail. After extending their hands to steady each other, they walked the section both ways without falling. There's nothing like a helping hand when you aren't sure of your stick-to-it-iveness. If you want to begin an exercise program, find a friend to exercise with. If you want to take a class, find a friend to join you; you'll have more fun and hold each other to the bargain. Be sure to agree on specific actions, goals, and rewards for yourselves.

THINK

Make time today and every day to exercise your brain. In this era of downsizing, staff reductions, and total corporate reorganization, it is just common sense to increase your knowledge base and skills training so you can adapt rapidly to new market demands. But who hasn't put off taking time to think because of the need to react to more immediate, urgent things such as watching the World Series? As the German poet Goethe stated, "Things which matter most should never be at the mercy of things that matter least." Some things, such as an overflowing sink, do have a certain sense of urgency. Other things, such as keeping current on the events at Buckingham Palace, don't. Abraham Zaleznik, Matsushita Professor of Leadership at Harvard Business School, observed that "Life is a combination of action and reflection"; he goes on to say that those who only act are cheating themselves.[23] We'll come back to making time for reflection in chapter 7.

Future Trends

Major companies such as Coca-Cola, Owens Corning, Signet Bank, and Avon have hired a thinker, Edie Weiner, to help them determine future trends in marketing. Weiner's approach to forecasting is to have clients look at new ideas and think about them. Other futurists use market surveys and financial forecasts; however, thinking is what Weiner does best. To determine emerging trends, she reads books, magazines, newspapers, and reports constantly and reflects on the readings. Her clients receive summaries of articles and meet every three months to discuss the readings and apply them to the business world.

Kerley LeBoeuf, president of the National Association of Convenience Stores, describes Weiner: "Edie gets you to reach outside the norm in your thinking and somewhere down the road you can apply that to your business." In this age of computers with RAMs measured in gigabytes, there is something reassuring about Edie Weiner getting people to think.24

A Brain Tune-up

Remember when you came home from school and your parents asked, "So, what did you learn today?" That question is still relevant because learning is important to the health of your brain. Learning does not keep you from getting Alzheimer's disease, but it does keep your brain alive and helps you stave off senility. New knowledge causes your body to make new connections between your brain cells. This process of arborization occurs when neurons actually grow microscopic filaments to connect to each other. When you learn something new, neurons secrete growth hormones that stimulate their own growth and that of their neighbors. Thoughts happen when the branches of brain cells connect; that's why you need to keep feeding your brain knowledge. Make learning a lifetime habit by becoming an habitual thinker.25

According to Arnold A. Lazarus of Rutgers University, you learn best when you spend a short time learning every day or every other day. Pulling an all-nighter as you did in college is counterproductive. If you are easily distracted, use self-talk to bring yourself back to the task. When you are learning something difficult, switch off and do something that comes naturally to you; then, return to the difficult subject. Succeeding at the easier things helps you achieve more with the harder ones.26 Choose something you want to learn more about and write it here:

```
I want to learn more about
```

Reality Checks

To break the habit of operating on automatic with your brain half engaged, use these three steps to think more effectively about what you are doing throughout the day:

- Pause five or six times a day to think about how your day is going and to see if you are moving toward your goals. These frequent mental check-ins help you lose less time to nonproductive activities.

- Stop what you are doing if you are not heading for success and figure out what caused your self-defeating mind-set. Think about why you feel angry, depressed, or like a failure.

- Pinpoint defective thoughts and replace them with effective thoughts. For instance, if you feel angry, determine what is making you feel powerless and create a powerful replacement thought.[27]

Effective Thinking

If you think your problems are too big to be solved, consider the villagers in Colombo, Sri Lanka. For centuries, these villagers lived in harmony with elephants; then a British company turned the elephants' forest land into a sugar plantation. Lacking a large enough area to find food, the beasts destroyed the sugar cane crop.

When the owners put up an electrified fence, that did not stop the hungry elephants. Armed with automatic weapons, an Elephant Control Unit shot more than fifty elephants. Still hungry and undoubtedly ticked off, the elephants raided the homesteads in nearby villages, going so far as to enter homes to look for rice and salt. Villagers were afraid to leave their homes at night; in twelve years the elephants killed seventy-five people. Villagers retaliated with shotguns, poison, or nails along elephant paths; seventy-five more elephants died.

The Department of Wildlife Conservation finally decided that the herd should be taken to Yala National Park, fifteen miles away. The problem was how: Elephants refused to be driven at gunpoint; they did not travel in the open sun and all the shade trees on the route had been cut down to grow sugar cane. Deputy Director General Nandana Atapattu solved the twelve-year-old problem with persuasion. He knew elephants were intelligent and wanted to be where food was plentiful and danger minimal. Atapattu devised a route through the cane linking a series of water holes. Villagers shouted encouragement and used flares to point the animals in the right direction. Whenever the elephants smelled water, they moved forward in a gigantic column; and so it went from one water hole to the next.

A week later the herd was home at Yala, with 3,000 times more space to roam. Not a single villager or animal was harmed during the elephant walk. A deep trench now separates the plantation and forest.

CYA Journaling Exercise: Describe a problem you solved in a creative manner.

When thinking about problems, we need to use creative thinking as Nandana Atapattu did. Broadly defined, creative thinking is coming up with something new. It is a process during which we gather ideas and mental images that transform the elements of reality into something new. Three ways to think creatively are by considering

- **Structure** (contrasts, differences, and distinctions). No two things are exactly the same when examined in great detail. *Example:* If you can't sell a hot dog for a dime, change the structure and sell half-dogs for a nickel each.

- **Relation** (similarities, connections, and affiliations). In spite of differences, we observe and respond to similarities. *Example:* Data are similar enough to be recorded by holes in punched cards.

- **Order** (change in time and space). Everything is changing at varying rates of speed. *Example:* A balloon full of hot air rises and stays aloft until the air cools.

The preceding elements can be combined by either level or point of view:

- **Level**—the more views we have of something, the more we become aware of our surroundings. You are someone's child, an adult, sibling, relative, employee, lover, and so on. *Example:* Fruits and vegetables can be preserved by changing their texture and environment.

- **Point of view**—finding other ways of looking at something expands the alternatives. People at a party may see a different person than your children see before the party. *Example:* A child views a toy differently than the adult who invented it.[28]

CYA Journaling Exercise: Describe a problem you want to solve.   How can thinking about the structure, relation, order, level, or point of view help you solve the problem?

Effective Thinkers

The following thinkers used the preceding elements creatively; they are a random sample loosely linked by the attitudes they share. Some were educated; others were not. Some became wealthy; others died in poverty. Some are dead; others are very much alive. They share these attitudes: the ability to think, a desire for success, and the courage to take a risk.

- When Herman Hollerith graduated from Columbia University in 1879, he began working at the U.S. Census Office where he saw the need for a mechanical way to tabulate statistics. Eventually he invented punched cards and machines to read and record data for the 1890 census. Hollerith kept finding more applications for punched card data processing and improved his system; by 1896 he opened the Tabulating Machine Company in New York City. Eventually that company became IBM Corporation.

- One evening Teressa Belissimo frantically surveyed the Anchor Bar and Restaurant's kitchen, looking for a late-night snack for her kids' friends who were due momentarily. When she saw chicken wings destined to become chicken soup, she thought why not? In a Buffalo minute, she deep-fried them; once they were crispy, she added red sauce. The Anchor now sells Buffalo wings plain, mild, medium, hot, or suicidal. A little desperation plus some thought equaled a new snack.

- While Nicholas Francois Appert was a cook in Paris, he often thought about preserving food. Appert devised a method of heating food and sealing it in glass bottles; we now call his process canning. In 1809 Napoleon gave Appert 12,000 francs because the French navy used his products on its ships. Appert later wrote a book, *The Art of Preserving All Kinds of Animal and Vegetable Substances for Several Years.* Unable to preserve his own fortune when his business was destroyed during political riots, Appert died penniless.

- Joseph and Jacques Montgolfier were French papermakers who observed that once the smoke from a fire was directed into a silk bag it became buoyant. This observation meant they discovered the first balloon. In June of 1783 their silk balloon rose 6,000 feet above the town of Annonay and stayed up for ten minutes. Later that year, after sending a sheep, duck, and rooster aloft, they sent a human up in a tethered balloon.

- During the Great Depression, Tony Packo opened a cafe in Toledo's factory district. Packo's dime hot dog was too expensive for the times; after some thought he cut his dogs lengthwise and sold them for a nickel. When times got better, Packo realized that he had a signature food and kept selling his half-dogs topped with mustard, diced onion, and chili sauce. Today Tony Jr. still sells his dad's half-dogs and chili and his mom's stuffed cabbage. (While playing Klinger on "M.A.S.H.," native Toledoan Jamie Farr made Tony Packo's internationally famous.)

- Earle E. Dickson's wife Josephine was accident prone; she frequently cut herself while working in the kitchen. Each time, Dickson wrapped her wounds in yards of gauze and tape. Thinking there had to be a better way, he put a small piece of gauze on a strip of medical tape. In 1921, his employer, Johnson & Johnson began selling Band-Aids in long strips; sales jumped, however, when they began selling precut Band-Aids in 1924.

- Mary Rodas thought her way into a job when she was only four. With a keen eye for detail, she told a man laying a new kitchen floor that he was not matching up his tiles. He just happened to be Donald Spector, the president of Catco, a toy company. Spector figured this was a bright kid, hired Rodas as a paid consultant to try out toys, and followed her suggestions. At age thirteen, Rodas became Catco's vice president of marketing. She has developed the neon-colored, fabric-covered Balzac Balloon Ball and a candy line called Balzac Glop. In addition to working, Rodas attends college even though she is a millionaire; at twenty she recognizes the value of thinking.

CYA Journaling Exercise: Describe someone you know who solved a problem with effective thinking.

Goose Sense

One of our favorite winged creatures is the Canada goose. Whether headed north or south, these geese always fly in a V formation. Scientists have discovered that they fly in formation because by flapping its wings, the bird in front creates an updraft for the bird behind. This allows the V-shaped flock to increase its distance potential by 71 percent. When the lead goose gets tired, it falls back and another goose takes the lead; to encourage the new leader, the geese behind honk.

When one of the geese is injured, sick, or shot, two of them fall with that goose and stay until it is either able to fly again or dies. And then they fly up to join another V formation and gradually make their way to their own flock. We need to get people to fly in formation because that increases our potential for achievement. We need to share difficult responsibilities and jobs. We need goose sense. In the next chapter, we continue talking about goose sense, or developing the right attitudes in your 360-degree life.

ENDNOTES

1. "Eye Injury Forces Puckett to Retire," *Columbus Dispatch*, July 13, 1996, p. 1B.
2. Haskell M. Block, ed., *Candide and Other Writings by Voltaire* (New York: Random House, 1956), p. 67.
3. Lydia Saad, "Children, Hard Work Taking Their Toll on Baby Boomers," *The Gallup Poll Monthly*, April 1995, pp. 22–23.
4. Ira Chaleff, "Overload Can Be Overcome," *Industry Week*, June 7, 1993, pp. 44–48.
5. Tina Lassen, "Sold on Risk Taking," *World Traveler*, March 1996, p. 48.
6. David Macpherson, "The Advantages of I, Incorporated," *DFMC Newsletter*, Spring 1996, pp. 12–13.
7. Robert D. Putnam, "Bowling Alone," *Journal of Democracy* 6 (1995), p. 73.
8. J. A. Byrne, "Gross Compensation?" *Business Week*, March 18, 1996, pp. 32—33; and W. Zellner, E. Schine, and G. Smith, "Trickle-Down Is Trickling Down at Work," *Business Week*, March 18, 1996, p. 34.
9. Walter R. Mears, "Credibility Gap Is Nothing New," June 22, 1997, ©Associated Press.
10. Francis Fukuyama, *Trust, the Social Virtues and the Creation of Prosperity* (New York: Free Press, 1995), pp. 270–73.
11. Fukuyama, *Trust*, p. 26.
12. Michael Jordan, *I Can't Accept Not Trying* (San Francisco: Harper, 1994), p. 24.
13 Richard Lidstad, "The Qualities of Success: Leadership, Diversity, Community Service, and Career Development," *Vital Speeches of the Day* 61, July 1, 1995, pp. 559–61.
14. "Most in U.S. Contented with Work," *Columbus Dispatch*, September 3, 1996, p. 1C.
15. "ABC World News Tonight with Peter Jennings," September 18, 1996.
16. John M. Ivancevich and Michael T. Matteson, *Organizational Behavior and Management* (Burr Ridge, IL: Richard D. Irwin, 1996), p. 601.
17. Shelley Roth, "Olympic Designs," *Self-Employed Professional*, July–August, 1996, pp. 55–59.
18. Fukuyama, *Trust*, p. 27.
19. Fukuyama, p. 153.
20. John M. Ivancevich and Michael T. Matteson, *Organizational Behavior and Management* (Burr Ridge, IL: Richard D. Irwin, 1996), pp. 254–55.
21. Patricia Edmonds, "Six Words Stirring a City," *USA Today*, August 8, 1996; and "ABC World News Tonight with Peter Jennings," July 31, 1997.
22. Daniel Goleman, "What's Your Emotional IQ?" *Reader's Digest*, January 1996, p. 52.
23. Robert K. Cooper, *The Performance Edge* (Boston: Houghton Mifflin Co., 1991), p. 57.
24. "Futurist Doesn't Need Crystal Ball to Identify Latest Business Trends," *Toledo Blade*, August 19, 1996.
25. Martin Groder, "Use It . . . or Lose It," *Bottom Line Personal*, September 15, 1996, p. 13.
26. Mark Bricklin et al., "Learn for Your Life," *Positive Thinking for Positive Living* (Emmaus, PA: Rodale Press, 1990), pp. 2–7.
27 Gerald Kushel, "All About Thinking and Very Effective Thinking," *Bottom Line*, September 15, 1996, p. 2.
28. Adapted from Gerald I. Nierenberg, *The Art of Creative Thinking* (New York: Barnes & Noble, 1996).

7

Celebrating Your Balanced 360-Degree Life

If you are what you do, what are you when you don't? TOM BAY

To begin our final chapter, we discuss my (TB) favorite topic—how right attitudes lead to a balanced, 360-degree life. We review seven steps to a balanced life to help you sketch out your own balanced life; then comes the hard part—living it. When you persist, you'll enjoy living a 360-degree life so much that you'll continually find ways to keep your life balanced. I (TB) have found all the juggling I have to do to keep my life in balance is totally worthwhile.

To tie the themes in *CYA—Change Your Attitude* together, later in this chapter we review the fifteen attitudes discussed earlier and look at how right attitudes create success and/or happiness. Happiness and success are not twins—they're not even fifth cousins twice removed. People who appear successful to others may be unhappy; meanwhile a person who does not appear successful in anyone else's estimation, may be happy. Eighty percent of Americans claim that they are happy with their personal lives. For the 20 percent who are not happy—or the rest of us who suspect that we could be happier—we discuss four characteristics of happy people. One thing that makes people happy is having control; the trick is recognizing exactly how much we can control in our lives.

The pursuit of success is a continuous do-it-yourself project. Our targets change as our lives change; the richer our lives become, the more often we readjust our definition of personal success. Wrong attitudes affect both happiness and success; we present some ways to avoid common wrong attitudes toward work: hating the job, workaholism, burnout, and toxic work syndrome.

YOU MAY HAVE A WRONG ATTITUDE IF . . .

- You are tired of pizza delivery guys complaining that you drive too fast.
- You eavesdrop on phone conversations and scream that co-workers should tell the #@?*! off.
- You and your ex have revived the cold war; your kids are MIAs.
- You crunch ice cubes all day despite hissed death threats from adjoining cubicles.
- Your smile is broken and its warranty expired years ago.
- Your dirty lunch dishes are someone else's problem.
- You moved to New Orleans and then discovered that they canceled Mardi Gras when they heard you were coming.

A BALANCED 360-DEGREE LIFE

If you are what you do, what are you when you don't? I (TB) love to ask people this question becaused it stops them in their tracks. Have you ever noticed how when people meet for the first time, one of the questions they ask is, "What do you do?" People habitually identify themselves by their occupations, without mentioning the other interesting parts of their lives. So, we have to ask, if your identity is based on what you do for a living, what are you when you are not working? Or, when you are laid off? Or when your job moves out of town?

The problem we all face is how to create a 360-degree life with room for something besides work; human beings require time for family, friends, recreation, and good deeds. When a person is a workaholic (see figure 4) that person's whole identity is tied to work. Losing that job means losing the identity. You may tell yourself that the company will miss you, but try this experiment: Take a bucket of water and try to put a hole in it

Figure 4   A Workaholic's Life

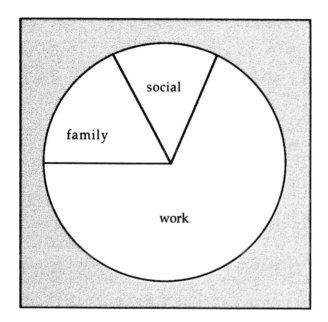

with your fist. As soon as you remove your fist, the hole disappears; that's how much your company will miss you.

I (TB) have noticed how we become so wrapped up in the necessary minutia of life we forget about being aware of daily life, really living it rather than just hanging in there until the undertaker comes. Architect Frank Lloyd Wright wrote to his daughter: "everyday life is the important thing, not tomorrow or yesterday but today. You won't reach anything better than the right now, if you take it as you ought."[1] Enjoy each day of your life instead of enduring it. Enjoy each role you play in your 360-degree life.

Simplify

To bring your life into balance, start out by simplifying all phases of your life. These first two suggestions are quick and easy: *First, do those little things you habitually put off.* As soon as you think I'll get to that tomorrow, stop and remind yourself to do it now. Take a moment to tighten the loose screw on the cabinet door or to reattach a button to your jacket.

Second, toss out things you are not using. Go through your house collecting things you are saving but not using such as the tight jeans you'll be able to wear just as soon as you lose ten pounds. We know, it's all good stuff—that's why you'll want to give it away to people who need it. Do this at least once a year, every year. List specific actions you want to take:

To simplify my life today, I can
Tomorrow, I can
Next month, I can

Balance

The next steps involve balancing your career with various other commitments: *Third, review your personal time commitment.* Do you allocate any time for yourself? If that question left you laughing hysterically, remember: We all need time to nurture ourselves by reading, listening to music, pursuing hobbies, or relaxing in a warm tub. We need time now to relax and renew ourselves; we can't wait for that day in the distant future when we have time or when we retire or when our lives are perfect.

Follow Donna Guthrie's example and make your own personal time just as important as your career commitments. Guthrie, a children's book author from Colorado, walked five miles in each of the fifty states in 1996 to *celebrate* turning fifty. In each state she bought a black T-shirt with the state's name, motto, flower, or mascot. Guthrie plans to have the T-shirts made into a quilt "and someday take it to the nursing home. . . . Late at night . . . my friends and I will pull our rockers into one big circle. I'll spread out my T-shirt quilt so it covers everyone's lap. Quietly, we'll take turns telling each other the stories of our lives."[2] On the next page, list things that you need personal time to do:

```
┌─────────────────────────────────────────────────────────────┐
│ I need personal time to:                                      │
│                                                               │
│                                                               │
│                                                               │
│                                                               │
│                                                               │
└─────────────────────────────────────────────────────────────┘
```

Fourth, review your community commitments. Are you really interested in all of your activities? If not, resign. On the other hand, if you would like to give something back to your community, look for ways you and your family can do this together. Try out various activities sponsored by civic or church groups until you find something that you can all do and enjoy.

In Washington, D.C., Lyn McLain started a youth orchestra in 1961; here hundreds of children have learned to play musical instruments on Saturday. Each child must be at least five years old, want to play, and pay a $25 fee. Even though these kids are not the best and brightest, McLain holds them to the standards of a conservatory. Some have become professional musicians. Although most do not become professionals, they learn the concentration and discipline they need to succeed. They also learn how to work with others and how to interact with adults. Every couple of years, McLain's musicians learn about the world when he takes the orchestra on tour.[3]

List three community activities you plan to investigate:

```
┌─────────────────────────────────────────────────────────────┐
│ I am interested in these community projects:                  │
│                                                               │
│                                                               │
│                                                               │
└─────────────────────────────────────────────────────────────┘
```

Fifth, review your social commitments. Must you bowl five nights a week? If not, drop out; if you must, ask yourself what you are avoiding by being so busy. On the other hand, can you respond spontaneously to your friends, or are you blocked by disabling attacks of the shoulds? When the shoulds are weighing in heavily, ask yourself if friendship is more important than being ultraprepared for an upcoming meeting.

While you are thinking about your friends, consider if each of your friends would pass the I-wouldn't-mind-being-shipwrecked-with-this-person-for-a-few-days test. If a friend is a putdown artist or you have grown apart, ease out of an outworn relationship. As motivational speaker Patricia Fripp suggests, we need to keep the sand out of our pastry:

Imagine someone baking a chocolate cake. In addition to flour, sugar, and salt, he adds a small spoonful of gritty sand to the recipe. The cake batter is stirred, carefully baked, frosted, decorated with nuts, cherries, and whipped cream. It looks perfect. At dinner, when you see that cake, what would you do? I would probably cut the biggest slice possible—without looking too greedy—and take a mouthful. My first reaction would be "Ummmmm." Then I would notice the sand, push my plate away, and say, "Thanks, it's a beautiful cake—except for the sand."

Fripp suggests telling chronically negative people who matter to you this story. Then, when they are negative, remind them they are putting sand in your cake.[4]

Comedian Robin Williams demonstrated how friends can be there for each other when actor Christopher Reeve was hospitalized after his horseback riding accident. Williams flew to the hospital and borrowed a pair of scrubs. Striding into the room he announced in a heavy accent that he was a proctologist there to examine Reeve. Some friends certainly go to extremes. Write down the social commitments you value most:

I value these social commitments most:

Sixth, review your career commitments. Think about where you want to be five or ten years from now. Take a tip from Patricia Fripp and plan your career with the same care you plan a vacation.[5] Decide what goals you have for your career and how much time, money, and energy they will take. Prioritize them and develop minigoals, as we discussed in chapter 4. I've (TB) found this really works.

If you work overtime and weekends, free up something and review the "Workaholism" section. If you have no energy for your family after work each day, reread the "Burnout" section. Researchers have documented that stress at home affects your job performance; that's why these parts of your life need to be in balance. Ask yourself this gut-check question: If I experienced a devastating accident or medical crisis, what would I wish I had done differently?

I wish I would have

Major companies have begun helping employees with their family responsibilities by allowing them to work flextime hours, by sponsoring seminars on family-related topics, and by providing day care for children and seniors.

Seventh, review your family time. Are you taking care of your parents as well as your children? Do you spend enough time with your family, or do you rely on material things to take your place? Researchers have documented that job stress affects your home life; one solution is spending more time with your family.[6] Gather your family around a calendar and block out specific times for family activities a full year in advance.[7] Spending time with those you love is so important; I (TB) speak from experience and I'm taking special care not to repeat the mistakes I made in my first marriage.

If your kids are into sports, Dr. Darrell J. Burnett suggests you do more than just attend the games. He believes that parents who have the following twelve attitudes (that form the acronym Kids in Sports) can help their kids have fun, feel good, and develop skills.

1. Keep it positive.	7. Show excitement, enthusiasm
2. Instill laughter and humor	8. Praise specifics.
3. Develop team spirit.	9. Offer a good example.
4. Step into their shoes.	10. Remember to have fun.
5. Involve yourself.	11. Teach skills.
6. Notice any and all progress.	12. Set reasonable expectations.[8]

CYA Journal Exercise: Describe your favorite childhood memory with a parent.

If you are an employed mother, lose those guilt pangs before working on your 360-degree life. Although both parents may work outside the home, usually the woman is the only one who feels guilty, perhaps because no one asks a father how he could choose between his children and his job. According to social psychologist Faye Crosby in *Juggling,* women no longer need to feel guilty. Research has proven that the advantages of having an employed mother outweigh the deficits:

- Children see more of their fathers and other family members.
- Kids learn more about the world of work.
- They meet children and adults outside of the family at child-care centers.
- Children are more open to new ideas and attitudes.
- Kids have more self-regard and initiative.
- They benefit financially, especially in single parent homes.

In addition to their children's increased well-being, Crosby found that the husbands of employed women enjoy psychological and economic advantages.

As an employed mom herself, Crosby believes the problem isn't the stress of juggling home and work, as much as sex discrimination at work, gender expectations at home, and the outworn tradition that each family should be self-sufficient.[9] Jot down three reasons why families similar to yours should or should not be self-sufficient:

After you have worked through these seven steps, draw in the various sections of your 360-degree life as they are now and label them on the first circle in figure 5. Then draw the balanced life you are working toward in the second circle.

Tim Russert, the anchor of NBC's "Meet the Press," and his wife appear to have achieved a 360-degree life. One tremendous influence was his father who Russert saw only at supper; his dad worked two jobs to support his family in Buffalo, New York. "I knew he was working. It wasn't like he had gone off to the race track or the golf course. But it was an invaluable lesson for me when I became a father. I realized how much just being there means."

Russert takes advantage of the flexibility his job allows to maintain a daily routine with his son, Luke. After they breakfast together, he drives the ten-year-old to school. Russert picks up his son after school and spends time with him before returning to work. When he was offered a promotion that involved a move to New York, Russert and his wife, writer Maureen Orth, knew it would be a good move for them. They decided, however, that their daily routine in Washington was worth staying put. The Russerts have their career and family priorities in balance.[10]

Another successful person who is working hard to balance her life is Rosie Donnell, who made a switch from standup comedian/film actor to television host because of her son. As Donnell explains it, "When I had my son, and I wanted to have a life that would be more stable for him, where he would be able to sleep in his own bed every night, I thought this would keep me home." As the executive producer of her show, the host, and the star, Donnell has to be an expert juggler.

When Robert Reich became our nation's labor secretary, his wife took a two-year leave from teaching law in Boston and moved to Washington. After she and their teen-age boys moved back, Reich

Figure 5 Your Life

Possible labels

Personal
Family
Social
Community
Career
Spiritual

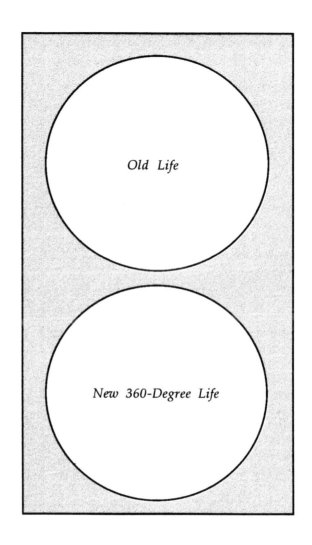

Old Life

New 360-Degree Life

struggled to balance work and family. He found the demands of his job continued during his weekends in Boston. After Bill Clinton was reelected president, Reich had to make a difficult choice: to continue in the best job he ever had or to see more of his sons. He commented: "I had to make a choice because I simply couldn't do more of the job I love and at the same time have more of the family I love." He decided, "There will be ample opportunity for me to sink myself 200 percent into another job, but there will never be another opportunity to be a father to a twelve-year-old and a fifteen-year-old."

In talking about how she balanced life in the House with life at home, former Rep. Susan Molinary of New York commented, "I don't feel like I do it very well. . . . There's a total feeling of exhaustion complicated by a total feeling of guilt." Molinari mentioned holding her daughter on her lap at meetings and bringing more work home. She would like to see the country offer more support to working mothers and do more to foster family time. "We need to redefine success," she said. "Are you successful if you work 80 hours a week, or should we revere families that spend more time together?"[11]

CYA Journaling Exercise: Explain which area of your life is most out of balance and how you will bring it into balance.

HAPPINESS

In the spring of 1995, eight out of ten Americans were satisfied with their personal lives according to the Gallup Organization. Six out of ten were happy with the way democracy works in the United States.[12] So, what is making all these people happy; why do they choose satisfaction over dissatisfaction? We all like to think other people can make us happy but they can't; the only person who can make you happy is the person occupying your skin.

One Valentine's Day when I (DM) was away from home, I sent the requisite eighty-four cards and my wife called to say, "No, I don't. It's not my responsibility, I don't accept it. By the way, how are you?" She was responding to one of the cards I sent her; it said, "You make me happy."

CYA Journaling Exercise: Write about three happy times in your life, explaining why you were happy.

Research indicates that happiness shows no favorites with regard to sex; race; culture; or changes in marital status, job, or residence. Of course, money is a different story; adults believe that 25 percent more income would make them happier because that translates into paid bills and more stuff purchased. But having more money won't do the trick because riches enlarge desires rather than satisfy them. One survey of the *Forbes* list of the wealthiest Americans reported they were only slightly happier than other Americans. And maybe more important, 37 percent were less happy than average Americans. So, happiness apparently lies in not only getting

Fifteen Right Attitudes

- **Require 100 percent personal *responsibility* and accept the *reality* of *risk*.**

When you get into a tight place and everything goes against you till it seems as if you can't hold on a minute longer, never give up then, for that's the time and the place that the tide will turn.   Author Harriet Beecher Stowe

When you get to the end of your rope, tie a knot and hang on.
          President Franklin D. Roosevelt

- **Ignite your *imagination*, initiate *innovation*, and enjoy *integrity*.**

To live is so startling it leaves little time for anything else. Poet Emily Dickinson

Does one's integrity ever lie in what he is not able to do? I think usually it does, for free will does not mean one will, but many wills conflicting in one man.   Author Flannery O'Connor

- **Give *graciously* of your time and money. Reach for *greatness* even if it exceeds your grasp. Pursue your *goals* tenaciously.**

Genius is 1 percent inspiration and 99 percent perspiration.
          Inventor Thomas Edison

It is for us to pray not for tasks equal to our powers, but for powers equal to our tasks, to go forward with a great desire forever beating at the door of our hearts as we travel toward our distant goal.   Author and lecturer Helen Keller

- **Hustle only *habits* that maintain physical, mental, and spiritual *health* and a sense of *humor*.**

Everything comes to him who hustles—while he waits.   Thomas Edison

Some people succeed because they are destined to, but most succeed because they are determined to.   Anonymous

- **Take loving care of *time* and use some each day to *think; trust* others.**

A part of control is learning to correct your weaknesses. The person doesn't live who was born with everything.   Swat king George (Babe) Ruth

Life consists in what a man is thinking all day.   Ralph Waldo Emerson

what you want but also liking what you get. List some times when you have gotten what you wanted and show if you ended up liking or disliking what you got:

Things You Wanted	Liked	Disliked

A 1996 survey by NFO Research, Inc., found that happiness was what 28 percent of 938 teens wanted most from life. Eric Arsenault of Chesterfield, Michigan, said, "My goal is definitely happiness. What would give me that? I don't know yet. But a lot of people in the 1980s made money and weren't very happy. I want more. My main reason for seeking further education is self-enrichment. I set goals and when I reach them, I think: What can I reach for now? I couldn't be fulfilled if I wasn't trying something new, learning something I didn't know before."

Stephanie Shields commented, "Happiness is my goal. Right now, I think that the best way of achieving that is through education and a career. But even though I can't see myself being happy by marrying Mr. Right and having children, I could change my mind."[13]

According to author David G. Myers, happiness depends on certain personality traits and on matching your skills to your work, having close relationships, and having an active religious faith. Happy people have these four characteristics:

- First, *happy people like themselves*. Dr. Myers found that high self-esteem is more likely to create personal happiness than a good family life, friendships, or high income. A University of Michigan study indicates that people who like and accept themselves feel good about life in general. Myers points out that healthy people use positive illusions about themselves to ward off anxiety and depression. Feeling inferior at some time or other is part of life; therefore, we need to look at ourselves through rose-colored glasses tempered with positive realism. And, we need to use self-talk, such as I like myself! when feelings of inferiority reign, or even knock.

  From the moment they are born, Red and Yellow personalities appear to have healthy self-esteem; actually, those in all four categories require self-analysis and effort to build their self-esteem.

- Second, *happy people are optimists*. They are healthier and have fewer common illnesses; they are less bothered by weather changes and even recover better when illness strikes. Researchers found that Harvard graduates classified as pessimistic in 1946 were the least healthy when restudied in 1980. Realistic optimists have a greater chance for success because they look at setbacks as part of the success cycle, part of life's journey. Using the scientific research approach, they list mistakes as they occur for reference and study, and remain confident that they are moving ahead.

  Optimists don't whine. They say yes to life more than no, and also realize that a realistic mix of both responses is necessary for real success. An optimist allows for limits—the top is too narrow for everyone to be there. In every two-person race, one is a loser; and the mortality rate for humans is still 100 percent. Inspite of all that reality, life is worth living. Myers recommends this recipe for well-being: "simple optimism to provide hope, a dash of pessimism to prevent complacency, and enough realism to discriminate those things we can control from those we cannot control."[14]

  Persons with Blue personalities are natural whiners who must work harder than the Reds, Whites, and Yellows to be more optimistic.

- Third, *happy people are social and outgoing*. Extroverted folks are happier because they expect others to like them; after all, what's not to like? Outgoing people experience more fulfilling and positive events—right away. Because they have a large circle of friends, extroverts receive more affection and greater social support.

  Through planning, extroverts fill and manage time more efficiently than unhappy people, who have unfilled, open, uncommitted time. To increase your sense of personal control, set deadlines for yourself; when you meet them, you'll feel wonderfully in control of your own destiny.

  As you might suspect, persons with Yellow personalities are most likely to be extroverts. Those with Red personalities also are more outgoing than their Blue and White friends. This does not mean that Blues and Whites are neither social nor outgoing—they just need to make more of an effort.

- Fourth, *happy people are in control*. Control is a real factor in guiding personal success. For more than seven years both of us have presented seminars on time management all over the country to tens of thousands of people. Our message is always the same: Greater control of the important things in life leads to greater success and happiness.

Researcher Angus Campbell summarized a nationwide survey by the University of Michigan: "Having a strong sense of controlling one's life is a more dependable predictor of positive feelings of well-being than any of the objective conditions of life we have considered."[15]

Naturally those with Red personalities relish being in control; Blues can handle control, too; Whites and Yellows can learn to take control of their lives.

Check off your personal levels of the characteristics of a happy person:

	Low	Fifty/fifty	High
Self-esteem			
Realistic optimism			
Social, outgoing			
Control of life			

Being in Control

For five years I (DM) worked at a nursing home in northern Kentucky. We had two groups of retired guests—those who controlled their lives and those who had no control. Those in control were involved in more of the social and religious activities provided by the excellent staff at Madonna Manor Nursing Home. Those in control displayed a higher morale and enjoyed better health; they were living proof that we are what we think we are. Those who had abdicated control just existed.

Can you really change your basic temperament—that bundle of attitudes and values you have carried around since your late teens? Not if you continue to use failed methods of the past, you can't. Once you realize you are the only architect of your future, start acting as if. That's right, fake self-esteem, pretend you are an optimist, act outgoing. Despite the phoniness you feel at first, you'll get over it as your motions put your emotions in gear (see chapter 1).

Bob Wieland is a person in control of his life. In the late 1970s and early 1980s, Wieland held the Amateur Athletic Union (AAU) world record in the bench press. His personal best was 507 pounds—that's about what a refrigerator weighs. When his AAU records were nullified later because he did not take part in other contests that the AAU required, Wieland changed course. On September 30, 1995, he began a 6,200-mile bicycle trip across the country and back, returning to Jacksonville, Florida, on January 28, 1996.

Bob Wieland used a 21-gear, hand-powered bicycle for that trip because he left his legs in Vietnam. A combat medic, Wieland was running to help ambushed buddies when he stepped on a mine. His body flew in one direction, his legs in another. After a five-day coma, Wieland awoke to find that he weighed less than half of the 205 pounds he weighed the week before.

While in the hospital, a doctor handed Wieland a five-pound weight. Even though he couldn't sit up in bed, he knew that someday he would lift that weight. Eight years later he was competing with the strongest men in the country in the bench press. He went on to be a strength trainer for the Green Bay Packers. Today he can still bench-press more than 400 pounds. At fifty, Wieland is a spokesman for the Congressional Medal of Honor Society's youth program, Beating the Odds. He often starts his talks with "I'm here today to tell you, don't ever let somebody else goof up your dreams." Wieland also works for a company that sells fitness and health products. In his spare time, he's working on a movie about his life.[16]

Bob Wieland's story reminds us that we control only part of our lives. There are some events in our lives we believe we can control—such as weather, traffic, the time of day, or other people starting wars—but we cannot. There are some events in our lives we believe we cannot control—such as our driving, what we wear, or what we eat—but we can. Because we have the ability to adapt, we must take responsibility for controlling these things. Teens are notorious for thinking they have everything under control: Just give them the keys and get out of the way. They expect to live forever; in reality, of all kids age sixteen to nineteen who die, 40 percent die in traffic accidents. Sometimes being confused about how much control we exert over our lives involves a life or death situation. Fortunately, at other times it is downright funny.

I (TB) was at the airport at 6:00 A.M., standing in line with a bunch of other suits who had no luggage. I stepped up to the counter and got my ticket validated; to be courteous, I stepped aside while I put my ticket back in my Day Planner. The next suit stepped up and asked for a flight to Chicago. The young lady didn't accept the ticket and politely said, "Sir, I'm so sorry, that flight was just canceled," while pointing up to the monitor, which was flashing CANCELED next to his flight number.

"Canceled? Every time I fly this damn airline . . ." and the suit's fist started slamming the top of the counter. "Food's no good and your uniform really sucks." He covered everything and kept slamming away, slamming away. She couldn't get a word in. I watched my Day Planner jump as he banged away.

Finally I said, "Sir, I'm so sorry for interrupting, but I've thought of something that might help you. Banging on the ticket counter hasn't helped, the monitor still says canceled. Possibly, kicking the counter might work." Wrong answer. He looked at me, verbally flipped me off, and left the counter. The young lady said, "That was so funny, to talk to a customer that way was great." I answered, "Boy, he didn't have a sense of humor, did he?"

The next suit in line stepped up and asked for a flight to Chicago. The young agent said, "Sir, I'm sorry, that flight has been canceled."

"Canceled," he said slowly shaking his head. "That's the way this trip has been going. Well, do I have to go over to another airline, or can you make arrangements? Oh, do you know what, I've got to call my client and let her know I've got a problem. And my baggage—I already checked my baggage, can you help me get it back?" Note the difference between the two suits. The first crashed; he thought he had control over a canceled flight, but had none. The second recognized he had no control over a canceled flight and focused on what he could do to make the best of the situation.

CYA Journaling Exercise: If you could exercise complete control, describe how your life would be.

Twenty-Eight Secrets to Happiness

- Live beneath your means and within your seams.
- Return everything you borrow.
- Donate blood.
- Stop blaming other people.
- Admit it when you make a mistake.
- Give any clothes you haven't worn in the last three years to charity.
- Every day do something nice and try not to get caught.
- Listen more; talk less.
- Every day take a 30-minute walk in your neighborhood.
- Skip two meals a week and give the money to the homeless.
- Strive for excellence, not perfection.
- Be on time.
- Don't make excuses.
- Don't argue.
- Get organized.
- Be kind to kind people.
- Be even kinder to unkind people.
- Let someone cut ahead of you in line.
- Take time to be alone.

- Reread a favorite book.
- Cultivate good manners.
- Be humble.
- Understand and accept that life isn't always fair.
- Know when to say something.
- Know when to keep your mouth shut.
- Don't criticize anyone for twenty-four hours.
- Learn from the past, plan for the future, and live in the present.
- Don't sweat the small stuff.[17]

Add your personal secret to happiness here:

My personal secret to happiness is

RIGHT ATTITUDES CREATE SUCCESS

The granddaddy of all motivational speakers, Earl Nightingale, said, "Attitude will always affect your success, and you'll know it affected your success when you take credit for your success—that's the good side—or you blame somebody—that's the bad side."

John Maxwell tells this story about taking responsibility for attitude. After seeing how-to-improve-your-attitude books in his father's briefcase during a vacation, Maxwell said, "Dad, you're seventy years old. You've always had a great attitude. Are you still reading that stuff?"

Melvin Maxwell looked his son in the eye and answered, "I have to keep working on my thought life. I am responsible to have a great attitude and to maintain it. My attitude does not run on automatic."[18] So, we not only choose our attitudes but they are also a continuing choice. "20/20" anchor Hugh Downs defined a happy person not as someone with a certain set of circumstances, but with a certain set of attitudes.[19]

Attitude also has a lot to do with aging gracefully. Gene D. Cohen of the National Institute on Aging stated that attitude determines whether people use preventive health practices such as maintaining a good diet, not smoking, and taking action on the early warning signs of problems. A positive outlook also benefits health, especially in dealing with a major illness or the death of a spouse.

Attitudes, not aptitude, initiate and sustain success; your individual success is a personal achievement. Success begins when you follow your heart to do what you should and avoid fulfilling the shoulds of others. The yardsticks you use to measure your success cannot measure anyone else's success; nor can you use another's yardstick to measure your own. Your solutions to problems and responses to opportunities are driven by your attitudes; they are the sum of your life. Ideally, success is ongoing, not a trophy for some wonderful month in 1984. By discovering your greatest strengths, you can be successful in most aspects of your life, as long as you are totally involved—mind, body, and spirit.

CYA Journaling Exercise: Define success. Are you successful, why or why not?

The right attitudes we discuss can help you live a successful life—but only if you internalize them before you put *CYA* on your self-help book shelf. No one can make you responsible or help you deal with reality or take risks, any more than someone else can make you happy or sad. Our emotions don't happen to us, we choose them. As Dr. Bernie Siegel points out, our thoughts, emotions, and actions are the only things we really do control. It all boils down to deciding if you want to be successful and how you define success. While one person helps abused children, another increases his stock portfolio, and someone else helps adults study for their GED exams. Success has many faces.

According to motivational speaker Joel Weldon, "Mental attitude is the better part of success. It calls for serenity, poise, faith, patience, humility, tolerance, honesty, confidence, courage, initiative, imagination, optimism, cheerfulness, enthusiasm, joy, and love."

SUCCESS

As we move through life, we learn that success is a moving target. Success at age 2 is different from success at 20, which is different from success at 102. Dr. Gilbert Brim wrote about the changes in his father as he grew older: At sixty his dad retired from teaching college and moved to Connecticut where he and his wife remodeled an abandoned farmhouse. For years he thinned the trees on the hillsides; gradually he became tired earlier in the day and sometimes hired help. Then, his efforts centered on the land and trees around his house. Next, he stopped planting the gardens and he concentrated on border flowers and window boxes. When even that had to be given up, the 101-year-old man turned to listening to talking books.[20] What a story of change; what a parable of successes.

The A to Z of CYA

Allow time for yourself.
Benefit others from your successes.
Climb the highest pinnacle of success.
Divide your day and conquer.
Endow yourself and others with wisdom.
Forgive, forget, and move forward.
Go in the direction of win-win.
Help others win.
Initiate some change each day.
Jump at the chance to improve your life.
Know kindness is a necessity on our planet.
Live today as today, not as a rehearsal for tomorrow.
Master the highest levels of capacity and control so they
     come naturally.
Nourish others with praise.
Oscillate between work and rest every day.
Play the hand you are dealt.
Question your motives when dealing with others.
Risk intimacy.
Smile often.
Tally your successes each day.
Utilize all your talent.
Visualize your success.
Work with the stress in your life.
Xplore all avenues of successful service to others.
Yield to the best way to change.
Zip through boring work at the beginning of the day.

Opportunities for growth and mastery allow us to achieve; we are not content with what we already know and can do; we want action and growth whenever we believe we can be successful. Just like the sixty-five-year-old who enjoyed thinning trees, we choose perplexing challenges that test our abilities but are not tough enough to cause us to fail badly or often. When we are successful, we immediately increase the difficulty; winning raises our hopes, losing lowers them. Once a child can stand successfully, she attempts walking.

As adults, we are most strongly motivated to take a stab at success when our chances are fifty-fifty. We set different risk levels for various situations because risk makes achievement much more rewarding. List five of your personal successes:

Successes:

Failures or Teachers?

"Success is never final; failure is never fatal," according to Penn State football coach Joe Paterno. The coach is right on both counts because change affects both success and failure. Whether we make a mistake and call ourselves failures or we learn something from a mistake and continue pursuing a goal depends on how we perceive ourselves and our success. If there is no question about our success, we never fail, but learn an awful lot.

Take for example, Steve Jobs who, along with Steve Wozniak, started Apple Computer in his parents' garage on April 1, 1976. In an age when business computers were roomsize, both Steves saw the need for desktop, easy-to-use personal computers. A decade later, Jobs left Apple because he did not like the company's direction and started NeXT Inc., where he planned to build personal computers. The firm languished; finally Jobs shut down manufacturing. Did he think he failed? No, maybe he stumbled, but Jobs seems to have been learning because meanwhile, he spent $10 million to buy Pixar, a computer graphics firm. Jobs foresaw the importance of computer graphics; after adding another $50 million, his company produced *Toy Story*, and went public. Jobs is a billionaire today and has returned as a consultant to Apple, which bought NeXT to develop its new system software. Jobs learned lessons in a difficult business situation and did not consider failure.[21]

One way to keep your head on straight when you are in a learning mode is to remember successfully reaching goals in the past and to keep moving forward past failure, past momentary loss, to success ahead. List two times when you failed and learned:

Failures:	Lessons:

Fear of Success

We would like to have just $1 for each person who feared success and allowed that fear to keep her from making a major change. Why would someone stay in a job he does not like? Why would a student drop a course of study she loves? The reasons are as varied as the fearful people; they generally boil down to four categories:

- If I succeed, something awful could happen. If I succeed in getting a raise, I may make more money than my husband; he'll feel just awful.

- If I succeed now, I could just mess up later. I may ace the aptitude test, but fail to do the job.

- If I succeed now, I could be stuck later. I may succeed at a new job and then find it is boring.

- If I succeed now, I could outdo my old man. If I become a mine manager, he'll hate me because he was a miner all his life.

Fortunately, fear of success is not fatal; people shoot themselves in the foot like this every day and live to tell about it. If you identified with any of the preceding fears, you have already begun step one, overcoming that fear. The second step is to recognize what you are doing and to figure out why. What are you really afraid of? Most of the time, you can talk to someone about your fear. For instance, find out just how much variety is in a job you are considering by talking to someone doing that job. The third step is to determine what's the worst thing that can happen and then figure out if that is what you actually fear.[22]

CYA Journaling Exercise: Describe a time when you felt afraid to succeed.

Success Is

- **Living a long, active life with no regrets.** Jeanne Calmet celebrated her 122nd birthday in February of 1997. Blind and nearly deaf, this French woman used a wheelchair; her mind and wit were just fine, thank you. Calmet was the oldest person in the world according to *The Guinness Book of World Records*, but young at heart. She had recounted her memories on a CD with a rap background, the proceeds of which went to buy a minibus to take Calmet and other rest home residents on seaside outings.

At the 1996 party her hometown, Arles, threw for her, Calmet commented that she was not afraid to die. "One day, I'll surely meet the good Lord. In the meantime, life will last as long as it lasts. Like everyone, I've known sad times, but life has smiled at me. I hope to die laughing. At any rate, I'll go without regrets. I've made the most of it." Jeanne Calmet died on August 4, 1997.

- **Continuing a tradition.** At Wulf's Fish Market on Harvard Street in Brookline, Massachusetts, success is providing fresh fish. Since Samuel Wulf opened his door in 1926, this market has featured fresh, cut-to-order fish. His son, Alan, is proud that they specialize in fish not carried by supermarkets and serve third- and fourth-generation customers. Visiting kindergarten classes learn that not all fish come in plastic wrap and may see a shark's head if they time it right.

- **Defining success.** To laugh often and much; to win the respect of intelligent people and the affection of children; to earn the appreciation of honest critics and endure the betrayal of false friends; to appreciate beauty, to find the best in others; to leave the world a bit better, whether by a healthy child, a garden patch, or a redeemed social condition; to know even one life has breathed easier because you have lived. This is to have succeeded. RALPH WALDO EMERSON

- **Finishing a marathon.** Fifty-nine-year-old Harvey Mackay ran in the Boston Marathon knowing that he would not bring home any prize money. For 26 miles and 385 yards he was not competing against 38,000 runners; Mackay was running against himself, against the interior voice that kept yelling "Stop." So why run? Because then you know there is nothing you can't do. Mackay says successful people have the determination, will, focus, and drive to complete tough jobs. They do those things unsuccessful people don't like to do, such as finishing a marathon.[23]

- **Joining the Women's Hall of Fame.** Mary Halloran enrolled in the first Army officer candidate school for women shortly after Pearl Harbor was bombed. During World War II Halloran commanded the first Women's Army Corps (WAC) battalion in England and later served in France and Germany. After the war, as the third director of the WACs, her initial assignment was to get legislation passed to allow women to enlist in the regular army.

After retiring in 1960, she became the director of Women in Community Service—a national organization she helped start—that finds training and jobs for impoverished women. She retired for a second time in 1978. In the fall of 1996, at eighty-nine, Mary Halloran of Arlington, Virginia, was inducted into the Women's Hall of Fame in Seneca Falls, New York.

• **Serving the community.** To find out why Robert Kraft bought the New England Patriots football franchise for $161 million in 1994, you have to go back to his childhood. "When I was 11," he says, "the Braves picked up and left town, went to Milwaukee. Part of me died that day. I've never forgotten it." Although Kraft's day job is being CEO of Rand-Whitney Group, which makes paperboard and packaging materials, he is better known as the man who kept the Patriots in Boston. Some fans walk up and shake his hand, others hug him. Kraft says that his father always told him, "The best thing you can do is earn a good name." About purchasing the Pats, he says, "It's a good business in terms of an asset. But I'm also doing what I love. And if I do a good job, I'm doing a service to my community as well."[24]

• **Getting back up.** Now Tweezerman is a successful entrepreneur, but he's certainly paid his dues. In 1969, armed with an MBA from Harvard, Dal LaMagna (rhymes with lasagna) had dreams of turning drive-in movie theaters into discotheques. Didn't work. Then he sold lasagna pans and produced a coming-of-age movie. Struck out again. In 1982 LaMagna was almost broke and discouraged; so much so that he moved back home and took a job at an electronics firm for $6 an hour.

At work he looked at the needle-nose tweezers used to pick up tiny electronic parts and thought about removing splinters. After repackaging some industrial tweezers, he sold them to lumberyards for splinter removal. Today, he markets 60 grooming products and expected to sell 2 million tweezers with lifetime guarantees in 1996.[25]

• **Saving a college.** Sister Bernadette Madore, S.S.A., took immediate action when faced with closing Anna Maria College (AMC), which was losing $1 million a year. This college president made some drastic changes: the Paxton, Massachusetts, college became co-ed; the new board had lots of business savvy and raised funds to build a library, performing arts center, activities center, and to renovate the chapel; 550 students increased to almost 2,000; twenty undergraduate and graduate satellite programs began in central and eastern Massachusetts.

Elaine Walter, a 1959 AMC graduate who is the dean of music at Catholic University of America, commented: "In essence Anna Maria College should have closed; . . . why is Anna Maria still there? Sister Bernadette Madore and [her mentor] Sister Irene Socquet . . . shared the dedication and the plain good sense to accept the responsibility to create an institution over all because they had vision. Now it is flourishing."

- **Doing What You Gotta Do.** I (DM) met Charlie Hauck about forty years ago on Turkeyfoot Lake near Akron, Ohio, while working at a camp. Hauck was sixteen at the time and entertained us with his rather sophisticated sense of humor. Early on he sensed that humor was the talent he had to develop.

    Hauck went to school, got married, and started to work. While living in Pittsburgh, Hauck announced to his wife and four small children that there was something he had to do. He was going to Hollywood to be a writer. He promised to send for them as soon as he had steady work, even if that meant being a full-time waiter. At least they could enjoy the warm Southern California weather.

    Because of Hauck's attitude and talent, as well as his family's patience, he landed a job: Norman Lear hired him to write for the sitcom, "Maude." Hauck's been writing and producing sitcoms ever since. He has written two books and is the executive producer of "Home Improvement." I knew he had talent when he was sixteen. So did Charlie.

List five characteristics of successful people:

WRONG ATTITUDES CREATE FAILURE

Failure is a necessary part of success. In his autobiography, Lee Iacocca, former head of Chrysler Corporation commented: "Mistakes are part of life; you can't avoid them. All you can hope is they won't be too expensive and that you don't make the same mistake twice." Most of the time we learn more from our mistakes than our successes, mainly because we are too busy patting ourselves on the back to recognize any lessons we learned. The failures we talk about in this section are common wrong attitudes toward work: hating the job, workaholism, burnout, and toxic work syndrome.

Take This Job . . .

Today's workplace demands greater productivity from employees at the same time co-workers are competing for jobs. Mergers, acquisitions, and downsizing, as well as corporate and government restructuring, make for lean and mean organizations. Employees who believe their employers are either dishonest or do not have their best interests in mind have more stress and dissatisfaction; they sometimes use theft to equal the playing field. Thus, employers with dishonest corporate cultures need an ethics makeover to remain competitive. We suggest they CYA and empower employees by developing empathetic attitudes of honesty, fairness, trust, and caring to create a safe, secure workplace.

During these changing times, maintaining a positive attitude is more important than ever; your career success depends on your attitude. How can anyone having only minimal control cope with a job, let alone maintain a positive attitude when work is repetitive and boring? By taking a new look at that job and by using a more positive attitude:

1. Accentuate the positive. Make a list of what you like about your job (good pay, excellent benefits, compatible co-workers) and what you do not (difficult boss, work overload, disagreeable clients, dicey job security). Think about the things you like, talk about them, and act like a professional worker. Don't think of working as the opposite of pleasure. Your job is not causing your unhappiness or negativity—your attitude is.

2. Face facts—you must work to earn money to live. Look forward to going to work; make your workplace somewhere you want visit because of those positive things on your list of positives. Look forward to Mondays as much as Fridays.

3. Make time to have fun on the job. Instead of considering work an endurance test, think of ways it can make you feel good about yourself. Keep focusing on the positives.

4. Consider your co-workers as a team; be friendly and upbeat. Develop a feeling of belonging or achieving a common victory.

Don't listen to negative co-workers who can make even upbeat people negative.

5.   Put yourself in position for future career moves if your company has a stable employment situation. Select a job that you want to be promoted into, and then line up another promotion after that. Give yourself something to aim for, a job goal.[26]

6.   Take out attitude insurance. If your job could be eliminated or you dislike everything about your job (even after doing the first five steps), update your resume, take classes in your specialty, and start networking.[27] If you have no particular special skills, visit a career counselor for guidance. Write one step you can take to improve your attitude toward your job here:

```




```

Job Burnout

Job burnout is like driving on an uncrowded highway and suddenly finding yourself off on the berm with your car up on cement blocks. What happened? you ask yourself. You were happy with your job one day and by the next afternoon you have lost interest and become dissatisfied. Feeling burned out can seriously affect your attitude about your job; some of the causes of burnout are

- Attempting to do too much. You want to coach little league, work a fifty-hour week, take care of your aged inlaws, and manage your church's fund-raising—all in this lifetime.

- Feeling unappreciated. The harder you work, the more your boss expects. As this mind-numbing circle continues, you're doing as much as you physically can but your boss continues to demand more.

- Being bored and unchallenged. You've learned everything there is to learn about your job.

Burnout affects your body, mind, and emotions. Your body is always tired and, therefore, more susceptible to sickness. Your emotions are frayed;

you hate going to work and feel cynical, trapped, and bored. Your mind turns forgetful; you are panicky, confused, negative, and helpless.

At this point, we suggest a nice Caribbean cruise. If that's not possible, then you need to take six steps:

First, figure out why you feel burned out.

Second, rearrange your life to create balance and eliminate overtime.

Third, make time to exercise and relax; start taking care of yourself.

Fourth, take a vacation or leave of absence.

Fifth, talk to your boss about the source of your burnout.

Sixth, talk to a friend, spouse, or counselor about burnout.[28]

List two actions you can take to avoid burnout:

1
2

Workaholism

Another work stress is workaholism. Those of you who don't have this problem probably are wondering why would anyone in his right mind would want to work all the time. Three of the chief reasons are

- You may be tired of taking care of others. For instance, those in the sandwich generation may be taking care of both their children and parents.

- You are trying to avoid remembering something negative in the past. Examples might include a messy divorce, the death of loved ones, or childhood trauma.

- You desire approval and acceptance from superiors.

If one of these reasons sounds like you, keep reading the symptoms of workaholism:

- You go on vacation and can't relax—or you bring along a little work.

- You are depressed.

- Your stress affects your relationship with your family.

- Your responsibilities at home have been taken over by your family.

- Your friends have given up trying to contact you.

- Your children cry when you leave and won't let you alone when you are home because you spend so little time with them.

If you have many of the preceding symptoms, start by figuring out something that will have a bigger payoff than the reason you became a workaholic. Note how lopsided a workaholic's life can become in figure 4. Perhaps, closeness with your family would have a bigger payoff; if so, gradually integrate the reason with a bigger payoff to replace the reason for workaholism. Don't try to stop working long hours cold turkey; neither you nor your employer would be comfortable. Meanwhile, plan things that you like to do to fill the newly freed-up hours. Enjoy![29]

Toxic Work Syndrome

Career counselor Barbara Bailey Reinhold, Ed.D., uses the term *toxic work syndrome* (TWS) to describe a "condition of emotional or physical pain or illness that happens to people when they allow their lives to get out of balance, when things seem to collapse in on them, when they lose their resiliency." If you are an employer, you'll want to know the prescription for curing TWS: Employers need to trust and value their people, who for the most part, "want to do a good job, want to believe in and belong to an organization." To keep their employees healthy, bosses can "create strong teams where people are valued and encouraged to work hard and achieve."

If you are an employee feeling job stress, take Reinhold's quiz in figure 6 to see how stressed you are. Those who have been doing the same jobs for some time need to realize how the stages in a job can affect their work life:

Stage 1 is getting started. Your energy is high, you make some mistakes.

Stage 2 means things are getting better. You are more focused and confident and make fewer mistakes.

Stage 3 is your peak performance. You could do this job forever!

Stage 4 is the feeling that something is missing. You have less energy and feel frustrated, bored, and disappointed.

Figure 6   Work Stress Quiz

For each item, write your response on the line at the left. Rate each item from 1 (almost never) to 4 (almost always):

———————   I'm worried I won't find another job if I lose this one.

———————   I wake up worrying about work.

———————   I'm upset about the increased demands at work.

———————   I find myself getting irritable or angry.

———————   I speed impatiently from one task to another.

———————   I don't have enough control over how I do my work.

———————   I don't feel trusted and appreciated at work.

———————   I'm worrying about whether I can keep up at work.

———————   I wonder whether I'm really doing a good enough job.

———————   It seems that nobody wants to know what I'm feeling.

———————   I have trouble knowing what I'm really feeling.

———————   I hold in my feelings until they finally erupt in some way.

———————   It's hard to make enough time for friends and family.

———————   People close to me complain that I'm not available enough.

———————   I'm too worn out to give much time to my relationships.

If your score is

       less than 25, you're managing stress well.
       25–34, expect some physical or emotional discomfort.
       35–44, talk with others at work about reducing stress.
       over 45, you are probably under a doctor's care and should talk to a
          career counselor.

Source: Barbara Bailey Reinhold, *Toxic Work: How to Overcome Stress, Overload and Burnout and Revitalize Your Career* (New York: Dutton, 1996), pp. 37–40. Reprinted by permission of the publisher.

Stage 5 means you're in trouble. Your self-esteem is nosediving, you are stressed and have physical ailments.[30]

Reinhold suggests that people in Stage 4 can revitalize their attitudes toward work, rather than finding a new jobs, by making changes in their jobs or other areas to balance their lives. She found that strong ties to families and communities help people overcome work stress.

CYA Journaling Exercise: Discuss how your wrong attitudes, or those of someone you know, caused failure in a work situation.

RULES FOR BEING HUMAN

1.   You will receive a body. You may like it or hate it, but it will be yours for the entire period this time around.
2.   You will learn lessons. You are enrolled in a full-time informal school called Life. Each day in this school you will have the opportunity to learn lessons. You may like the lessons or think them irrelevant and stupid.
3.   There are no mistakes, only lessons. Growth is a process of trial and error; experimentation. The failed experiments are as much a part of the process as the experiment that ultimately works.
4.   A lesson is repeated until learned. A lesson will be presented to you in various forms until you have learned it. When you have learned it, you can then go on to the next lesson.
5.   Learning lessons does not end. There is no part of life that does not contain its lessons. If you are alive, there are lessons to be learned.
6.   There is no better than here. When your there has become here, you will simply obtain another there that will again look better than here.
7.   Others are merely mirrors of you. You cannot love or hate something about another person unless it reflects something you love or hate about yourself.
8.   What you make of your life is up to you. You have all the tools and resources you need. What you do with them is up to you. The choice is yours.
9.   Your answers lie inside you. The answers to life's questions lie inside you. All you need to do is look, listen, and trust.
10.   You will forget all this.

ENDNOTES

1. Jo Coudert, "Living for the Moment," *Women's Day*, June 4, 1996, pp. 54, 57.

2. Kirsten Chapman, "Strangers Indulge in Sights, Smells along Five Miles in Columbus," *Columbus Dispatch*, May 16, 1996, p. 5B.

3 Merrow Report on PBS, "Searching for Heroes," August 2, 1996.

4. Patricia Fripp, *Get What You Want* (Mansfield, OH: Bookcrafters, 1996), p. 161.

5. Ibid., p. 170.

6. Adapted from Elwood Chapman, *Attitude, Your Most Priceless Possession* (Los Altos, CA: Crisp Publications, 1990), p. 41–43; and Jo Coudert, "Living for the Moment," *Woman's Day*, June 4, 1996, pp. 54, 57.

7. Robert Cooper, *The Performance Edge* (Boston: Houghton Mifflin Co., 1991), p. 57.

8. Darrell J. Burnett, *A Guide for Parents: Youth, Sports, and Self-Esteem* (Indianapolis, IN: Master Press, 1993), p. 16.

9. Faye Crosby, *Juggling* (New York: Free Press, 1991), pp. 140–45.

10. Randy Rieland, "No. l Job for Fathers: Being There," *Columbus Dispatch*, June 16, 1996.

11. Maggie Jackson, "Fame Doesn't Ease Life's Juggling Game," *Columbus Dispatch*, December 27, 1996, p. 4C.

12. David W. Moore and Frank Newport, "People Throughout the World Largely Satisfied with Personal Lives," *Gallup Poll Monthly*, June 1995, p. 1.

13. Dianne Hales, "How Teenagers See Things," *Parade*, August 18, 1996, pp. 4–5.

14. David G. Myers, "The Secrets of Happiness," *Psychology Today* 25, July–August 1992, p. 38.

15. Ibid., p. 42.

16. Robert Albrecht, "Legless Vet's Story Lifts Students' Spirits," *Columbus Dispatch*, March 5, 1996, p. 6B.

17. "28 Secrets to Happiness," *Total Fitness*, February 1992, p. 1.

18. John Maxwell, *Developing the Leader Within You* (Nashville, TN: Thomas Nelson Publishers, 1993), pp. 102–3.

19. Ibid., p. 104.

20. Gilbert Brim, "How to Manage Success and Failure Throughout Our Lives," *Psychology Today*, September–October 1992, pp. 48–51.

21. Michael Warshaw, ed., "Never Say Die," *Success*, July–August 1996, p. 38.

22. Adapted from Marian Thomas, *A New Attitude* (Shawnee Mission, KS: National Press Publications, 1991), pp. 48–49.

23. Harvey Mackay, "Don't Listen to the Voice That Says Life's Too Much," *Detroit Free Press*, May 6, 1996, p. 10F.

24. Tina Lassen, "Patriot Games,"*World Traveler*, October 1995, pp. 45–46.

25. Jane Applegate, "Tweezer Success Gives Entrepreneur the Time, Money to Run for Office," *Columbus Dispatch*, September 2, 1996, p. 13.

26. Adapted from Elwood N. Chapman, *Life Is an Attitude: Staying Positive When the World Seems Against You* (Menlo Park, CA: Crisp Publications, 1992), pp. 55–65.

27. Chapman, *Life Is an Attitude*, pp. 97–99.

28. Adapted from Marian Thomas, *A New Attitude*, pp. 70–72.

29 Adapted from Marian Thomas, *A New Attitude: Achieve Personal and Professional Success by Keeping a Positive Mental Outlook* (Shawnee Mission, KS: National Press Publications, 1995), p. 79.

30. Barbara Bailey Reinhold, *Toxic Work: How to Overcome Sress, Overload, and Burnout and Revitalize Your Career* (New York: Dutton, 1996), p. 134.

Index

Time
    definition, 144-145
    lack of, 144–45
Time-conscious goals, 92
Toffler, Alvin, 8
Toxic work syndrome, 200–202
Tracy, Brian, 20
Trela, Rose DiMaggio, 36–37
Trust, 148–66
Tschohl, John, 19
Turf Nazi, 5
Tuskegee Airmen, 106–107

U.S. Olympic teams, 61, 131–32,
    161
Vidmar, Peter, 61, 93
Virtual reality, 59
Vision, 69–77
Visionary companies, 73
Visualization and sports, 59
Visualizing, 18, 59–62
Voltaire, 144
Volunteering, 99
Volvo, 163

Waitley, Denis, 86, 89, 129
Walesa, Lech, 108
Walking meditation, 133
Walton, Sam, 72
Weiner, Edie, 166–67
Weldon, Joel H., 65, 98, 190
Wells, Tony, 73
White personalities, 154–55

Whitestone, Heather, 11, 51
Wieland, Bob, 186–87
Williams, Redford, 120
Williams, Robin, 178
Williams, Ruth, 29
Wolf, Stewart, 131
Women Airforce Service Pilots, 106
Work and humor, 139-40
Work stress quiz, 201
Work teams, 161–63
Workaholism, 174, 199–200
Workers' feelings about jobs, 160
Working mothers, 179–80
World Trade Center teams, 160–61
Worriers, 3
Wright, Bishop Milton, 57
Wright, Frank Lloyd, 175
Wright, H. Norman, 159
Wright, Orville and Wilbur, 26,
    43, 57
Wrong attitudes, 3–7, 196–97
Wulf's Fish Market, 194

Yellow personalities, 155–56
Zadig, 144
Zaleznik, Abraham, 64, 72, 165
Zoe's Place, 76, 94
Zyman, Sergio, 45